G000150793

To Dear Freddie
With love on your
74th birthday.
Joy. 17.8.93.

GUBBINS AND SOE

Also by Joan Bright Astley:

History of the Northumberland Hussars Yeomanry, 1929-1949
(Mawson, Swan & Morgan, 1949)

The Ninth Queen's Royal Lancers 1936-1945 (Gale & Polden, 1951)

The Inner Circle: a view of war at the top (Hutchinson, 1971)

GUBBINS AND SOE

by
Peter Wilkinson
and
Joan Bright Astley

LEO COOPER

LONDON

First published in Great Britain in 1993 by
LEO COOPER
190 Shaftesbury Avenue, London, WC2H 8JL
an imprint of Pen & Sword Books Ltd.,
47 Church Street, Barnsley, South Yorks, S70 2AS

A CIP catalogue record for this book is available from the British Library

ISBN 0 85052 002 9

Typeset by Yorkshire Web, Barnsley, South Yorkshire in Plantin 10 point
Printed by Redwood Books,
Trowbridge, Wiltshire

To Jo

(Major-General J.C.F. Holland, CB, DFC)

CONTENTS

ACKNOWLEDGEMENTS

This book has no academic pretensions. Wherever possible references and attributions have been checked. However, a narrative of this nature depends greatly on "personal knowledge, private information". Some readers may find that scant attention, or none, has been paid to events in which they personally took part, or to which they attached special importance; but this is not a history of SOE but the story of Colin Gubbins.

An inestimable debt is owed to Professor Michael Foot and Professor David Stafford who blazed their separate trails through the tanglewood of European Resistance. Special thanks are also owed to Christopher Woods, until recently the Foreign Office Adviser on SOE. At the time of writing the authors had no access to SOE's secret papers; and it was only thanks to Mr Woods' tireless research that it proved possible to recreate events which happened half a century ago.

The authors wish to thank Lady Gubbins for allowing them to see Sir Colin's papers, and members of his family who supplied information about his early years. Their thanks are also due to John Andrews, Librarian, Ministry of Defence, the late Jack Beevor and to Mary, his wife, who volunteered to transcribe the first draft of the present book; and to Colonel Andrew Croft, Sir William Deakin, Professor David Dilks, Sir Douglas Dodds-Parker, General Sir David Fraser for access to his father's account of the Norwegian Campaign, Dr Jòsef Garliński, Professor Ben Pimlott, Sir Brooks Richards and many others who contributed their knowledge. Above all our thanks to Vera Long, a founder member of SOE, whose help in preparing the book has been of the greatest value.

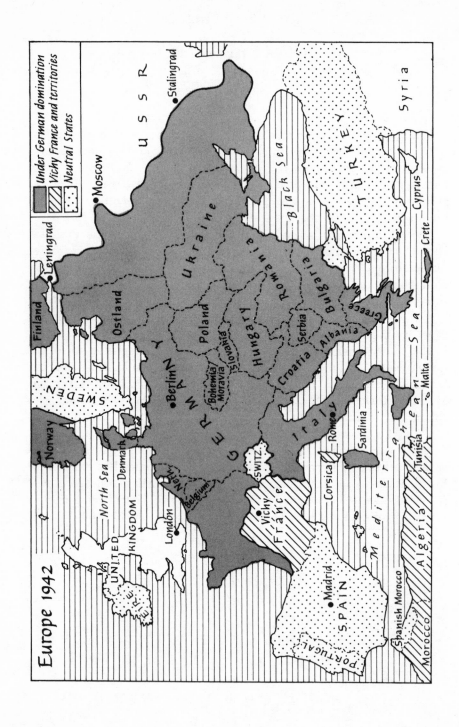

Europe 1942

Legend:
- Under German domination
- Vichy France and territories
- Neutral States

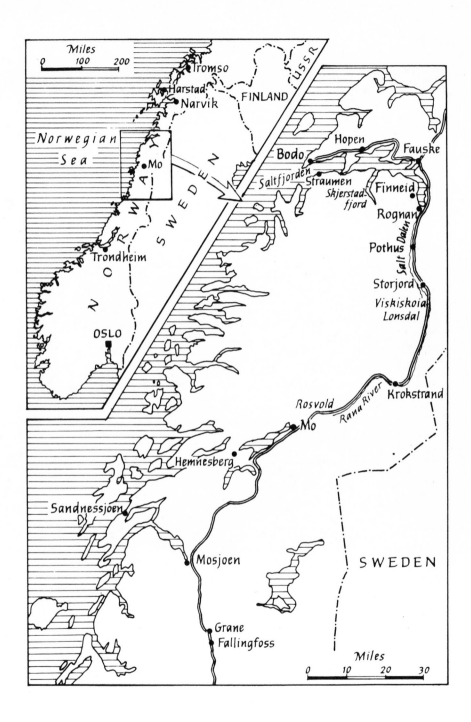

INTRODUCTION

There is little doubt that in the Second World War SOE's influence was considerable both in exacerbating the 'tension, battle and unrest' endemic in most of the Occupied countries, but also, some would say, in eroding the limits of warfare still generally respected in 1939. However, there exists no satisfactory assessment of the contribution made by the Resistance to the Allied victory. Subjective estimates are numerous and vary considerably; moreover, in retrospect, things are apt to appear more orderly than they seemed at the time. However, most agree that in purely military terms resistance was of secondary importance and in no sense decisive. Nevertheless, it was not negligible: at one time the Balkan guerrillas contained more Axis divisions than the Allied armies in Italy, while guerrilla operations in North West Europe and South East Asia unquestionably facilitated the advance of the Allied armies which led ultimately to the enemy's surrender. Nor is there agreement on the importance of the part played by SOE. Clearly, once the defeat of the Axis powers seemed certain and merely a matter of time, widespread insurgency in the Occupied countries was likely to develop. But to Gubbins it seemed no less certain that without outside coordination this valuable potential would be dissipated in clandestine activities of merely local significance. This view was shared by SHAEF and, in a report to the Combined Chiefs of Staff dated 18 July, 1945, General Eisenhower's deputies, Generals Morgan and Bedell Smith, gave it as their considered judgment that 'without the organization, communications, training and leadership which SOE supplied … resistance would have been of no military value.' It is no coincidence that the features singled out were those to which Gubbins had given his personal attention. Indeed, it is at least arguable that without Gubbins' professional guidance SOE might have gone the way of Section D.

Dr Dalton cherished the idea of a 'Fourth Arm' which would bring the enemy to its knees through subversion and propaganda, followed by a general rising of the working classes. Gubbins, on the other hand, was sceptical about what SOE and its agents could achieve on their own; he envisaged rather a paramilitary effort by indigenous resistance nourished and coordinated by SOE, acting not independently but under the operational direction of a theatre commander. It was a conception which involved transforming Baker Street from a civilian organization, geared primarily for sabotage, into a paramilitary headquarters with procedures compatible with those of regular troops. Nor was that all. In the early days SOE's country sections had been responsible for enlisting their own agents; these were mainly volunteers with dual nationality or foreign expatriates living in the United Kingdom who, after individual training, were sent in to the field where they operated directly under the country sections' orders. By mid-1941 the supply of these persons was dwindling, and was in any case inadequate for the large-scale operations which Gubbins had in mind. Nor was he convinced that their minor acts of sabotage, unless very carefully targeted, justified in military terms the appalling civilian reprisals which they occasioned. More and more Gubbins became convinced that, generally speaking, resistance to be effective needed to be on a scale which could only be achieved in cooperation with the Allied governments and representative committees now established in London, several of whom were in contact with, if not in control of, patriot elements in their respective countries. If they would provide the men, SOE would train them, arrange for their despatch to the field and handle their radio communications thereafter. Such an arrangement was clearly of mutual benefit, but Gubbins displayed considerable diplomatic skill in establishing the confidence required to bring it about. The Poles were no problem, for he already had many Polish friends including General Sikorski; and he soon established almost equally close relations with the Norwegians and the Dutch. Even the dour Czechs came to refer to him as 'our Englishman'. The facilities which SOE had to offer, and the practical advice which he was able to give these Allied leaders, both formally and more often informally, gave Gubbins a unique standing in Allied circles which in turn aroused jealousy and criticism in Whitehall. Yet, looking back, Gubbins' unpopularity in some military circles seems inexplicable. However, it was recognized by Lord Selborne in the following letter dated 17 October, 1945, which he wrote privately to the Secretary of State for War, recommending that Gubbins, when he relinquished his appointment as CD, should be made a substantive instead of merely a temporary major-general:

"I am aware that Gubbins is not universally popular in other departments, and I believe he has his critics in some parts of the War Office. About this I would only say that no Minister was served more loyally than I was by him, and that when a strong man is fighting to create a new organization which had to be carved out of the three services and other departments, it is not unnatural that he sometimes trod rather badly on people's toes."

From the moment they met in 1942 Selborne had trusted Gubbins absolutely, and there is ample evidence of his dependence on him, as indeed there is of the affection and respect which Gubbins had for Selborne. But Gubbins was loyal to his ministers as a matter of course, and he had been no less correct and, indeed, cordial with Dalton, who shared Selborne's high regard for him.

On the whole Gubbins seems to have got on with ministers better than he got on with generals. The exception was Anthony Eden to whom he took a dislike on account of his condescending manner and his ruthless hostility to SOE; however, though he identified him with SOE, which he was determined to abolish, there is no reason to think that Eden disliked Gubbins personally; on the contrary, he respected his ability. Churchill, more tolerant than Eden of SOE, always had a good opinion of Gubbins who had caught his eye during the Norwegian campaign.* In the summer of 1940 he had shown a personal interest in Auxiliary Units, had approved of Gubbins' subsequent secondment to SOE and, at Selborne's instigation, intervened with the War Office on at least two occasions to prevent him being removed from Baker Street.

Gubbins' most useful friend at court was General Ismay. Having frequently to deal with recalcitrant foreigners himself, Ismay realized what Gubbins was up against and also appreciated the valuable work that SOE was doing. Consequently he invariably found time to brief Gubbins regularly about strategic developments affecting SOE, and did his best to mitigate the frequent unhelpfulness of Whitehall departments which seemed to derive a special satisfaction from keeping SOE out in the cold. Only SOE's protracted death throes in the summer and autumn of 1945 seemed to try the inexhaustible patience of this great man for whom Gubbins had the highest regard and whose support he particularly valued.

The attitude of General Brooke, the CIGS, was more equivocal than Ismay's. Gubbins, who greatly respected him, had not only served under Brooke when the latter was Director of Military Training, but had briefly acted as his personal staff officer when Brooke was reorganizing the anti-aircraft defences immediately before the outbreak of war. They were members of the same regiment and knew each other well. Brooke was GOC Southern Command when Gubbins had returned from Norway hoping, if not for an active command, at least for a good training appointment. Although Brooke had not offered him either, he had shown considerable interest in Auxiliary Units and had as C-in-C Home Forces certainly opposed his transfer to SOE, possibly for Gubbins' own good. Like most professional soldiers he disapproved of paramilitary organizations divorced from the

* "An enterprising officer, Colonel Gubbins..." *The Second World War*, Vol 1, p.510.

Army.* When CIGS he showed little appreciation of SOE as an organization, though he was interested in individual members of the resistance groups, particularly Frenchmen, whom Gubbins arranged for him to see. At meetings of the Chiefs of Staff he was apt to show impatience with SOE's affairs, and in 1946, when Gubbins' appointment came to an end, Brooke seems to have made little effort to find him further employment.

Charles Hambro recognized that Gubbins was indispensable and immediately made him joint deputy with Hanbury-Williams, while continuing to treat him as an outstandingly competent general manager. Admittedly there were times when Gubbins would have endorsed Gladwyn Jebb's opinion that "Hambro lived by bluff and charm" but they worked well together and remained good friends. There is no truth whatever in the rumour, fairly widespread at the time, that Gubbins used his influence with Selborne to secure Hambro's dismissal; disloyalty of this sort was simply not in Gubbins' nature.

When Gubbins succeeded Hambro as CD, his position in SOE was unchallenged, indeed it was unassailable. Although there remained a few conservative heads of section who genuinely deplored the paramilitary road which SOE had taken, their personal loyalty was beyond question. Resistance was a vocation for the young, not only in the field but also at headquarters, and to the younger members of his staff, both men and women, Gubbins was an authentic hero, possessing what E.M. Forster called the three heroic virtues: courage, generosity and compassion. Moreover, he was not only a natural leader of the young, but he shared with the great Duke of Marlborough "the power of commanding affection, while communicating energy", enabling others to make use of abilities they had always possessed but had previously failed to recognize. With these exceptional powers of leadership Gubbins might, in other circumstances, have emerged from the war as a popular hero, but owing to the secrecy imposed on SOE and its activities he was, in his lifetime, virtually unknown in his own country. Abroad it was otherwise and he received high honours from many foreign governments.

However, wartime security was not the only reason why Gubbins received more acclaim abroad than at home. Britain was spared the shame and misery of enemy occupation; without this experience it is difficult to appreciate the part played by clandestine resistance both in restoring national self-respect and in permitting courageous individuals to escape from the ignominy of their situation. This spirit of resistance, which in many eyes Gubbins personified, is elusive in a mainly factual account of his achievements. However, it is not merely as the protagonist of a novel and controversial

* See Brooke's comments on Commandos in *The Turn of the Tide*, p.245.

mode of warfare that he deserves to be remembered. It was as a resistance leader that he came to fashion SOE, and to write his own page in the history of almost every country occupied by the enemy in the Second World War.

1

THE FAMILY 1649-1902

If asked, Colin Gubbins would say he was half Scottish and half English, his mother a McVean, his father born in India and raised and educated in England. But he could also claim Irish stock through an ancestor, Joseph (or George) Gubbins, a Captain of Dragoons who campaigned for Oliver Cromwell in Ireland, and decided in 1649 to acquire land and settle in County Limerick. The family prospered, married judiciously and became a county family of substance. There were no more soldiers in the family until 1775 when Colin's great-grandfather, Joseph, was born; then there were no more soldiers until 1896 when Colin was born. As chance had it, the two of them were to share in a similar experience. In 1802 Joseph returned from service abroad and spent three years fortifying the southern counties of England against a threatened French invasion; in 1940, one hundred and thirty-eight years later, his great-grandson did much the same in command of a force raised to combat an invasion threat from Nazi Germany.

Joseph (1775-1832) married Charlotte Bathoe of Bath; he served in Santo Domingo with the South Hampshire Regiment, in Holland, Malta and Egypt with the 2nd Somersetshires and finally in 1810 he went to Nova Scotia as Inspecting Field Officer of Militia with the North American Force in New Brunswick. From Government House, Fredericton, the Governor's wife, Lady Hunter, wrote on 2 October that:

> "an addition of fourteen to our family... Colonel Gubbins, his wife, three children and nine servants ... arrived here after being three months on board ship, and with not a place to put their heads on. Of course, we took them all in .... They have taken a house ten miles down the river, which will hold them all when put in repair, but that will be a work of time. Conceive fine, dashing characters, Bath people, quite the *haut-ton*, arriving knowing nothing of the country, with fine carriages, fine furniture etc. and where they are to be set down you could not drive a carriage fifty yards in any direction."

However, on 14 December, she was writing that:

"our river is frozen fast, and become a post-road. The Gubbins ... are quite new-fangled, and delighted with it, and come flying up here — ten miles — even to pay a morning visit, with a strong north-west wind and the glass below zero. Mrs Gubbins says she never saw anything so beautiful as the roads and the prospect of everything."[1]

In 1816, aged forty, Joseph returned to England and retirement. His wife Charlotte died in 1824, and he, by now a major-general, died in 1832.

Their third son, Martin Richard (1812-1863), Colin's grandfather, joined the Bengal Civil Service and later married Harriet Louisa, granddaughter of Sir Evan Nepean, Governor of Bombay. In 1856, a year before the outbreak of the Indian Mutiny, Martin was Financial Commissioner for Oudh Province. A man of decided views and independent thought, a thorn in the flesh of orthodox bureaucrats, he was zealous in his concern for the natives, mixing freely with them as he toured the area on horseback, often alone. He chose to be known as the "Intimate Adviser and Confidant of Sir Henry Lawrence, Chief Commissioner", a choice not shared by Sir Henry who, in 1857, under siege in Lucknow, wrote that he was "fretted into exhaustion by the activities of Martin Gubbins, whose gallant spirit was, unfortunately, uncontrolled by discretion.... He is the one malcontent in the garrison ... a gallant, energetic, clever fellow, but sees only through his own vista, and is therefore sometimes troublesome."[2] In his unfinished memoirs Colin Gubbins wrote that:

"Martin was a first class rifle shot, his house was on the perimeter of the defence overlooking the mutineers' trenches .... A man of irascible temper he was put in charge of the commissariat and made himself very unpopular with the military command by insisting that the food supplies could be made to last longer than calculated because no account had been taken of casualties ... not only from fighting but from disease and appalling heat, specially among women and children. He advised strongly against requests sent to the Commander-in-Chief by messenger for early relief as he felt that such forces as could be mustered for this though possibly strong enough to fight their way into the Residency would be quite unable to fight their way out again taking the garrison and all the human impedimenta with it through a countryside infested with mutineers and a hostile population; he felt such a move would only add to the difficulties of defence. He was overruled. General Havelock's relief force fought its way in with great bravery — and was shut in!"

When Sir Henry Lawrence was fatally wounded on 4 July, his place should have been taken by the Financial Commissioner, who was next in seniority, but, a month before, Lawrence had recommended to the Governor-General that in such an event Gubbins should not be put in charge; his advice was taken, and all that Gubbins could do was to write furious protests to the authorities.

When his *Account of the Mutinies in Oudh and of the Siege of Lucknow Residency* was published in 1858, Martin Gubbins was a Judge of the Supreme Court in Agra. But there had been an inquiry into his conduct during the siege and his justifications for it were not accepted. He returned to England in January, 1863, a sick man; four months later, in a fit of mental depression, he committed suicide at his brother's house in Leamington Spa.

"My grandmother had the unenviable task of bringing up five sons (another had died very young in India) and a daughter; somehow she managed to put all the boys through public school, my father going to Harrow .... Small in height, just five feet, she had the heart of a lion."

Colin's father, John Harington Gubbins (1852-1929), the youngest of Harriet's five sons, was eleven years old when his father died. In his boyhood, his family life must have been influenced by the stifled shame of a father's suicide, and by the self-containment of a mother determined to do her best by her sons within a code of behaviour which held little in it for laughter and fun. From Harrow, if his mother had been able to afford it, he would have gone to Cambridge. Instead, he answered an advertisement for interpreters in Japan and China, took the Japanese exam and passed into the Consular Service. At the age of nineteen he went to the British Legation in Tokyo as Student Interpreter for the Japanese Language and for the next eighteen years continued upwards through the grades until, in 1889, he became Japanese Secretary, a rank in those days just behind that of a consul and before a vice-consul. His preoccupation was in the making of a personal dictionary, a necessity for interpreters who had to cope with the difficulties of pinning down the multiplicity of words in the Japanese language. It was a task which he found intellectually absorbing.

Mrs Hugh Fraser, the Minister's wife, wrote:[3]

"The Japanese Secretary (that is to say the Englishman who superintends the Japanese side of the chancery) shakes his head and tells me that, though he has been working at it for seventeen years, though he has translated three dictionaries and is now publishing one of his own, though he is examiner-in-chief for the Consular Service, he feels that he is but at the beginning still and that many life-times would not put him absolutely in possession of the whole language as it is used by the learned Japanese today."

During his thirty years in Japan as the member of Chancery who, speaking Japanese, was the expert on local customs and history, Jack Gubbins served seven Secretaries of State and five Ministers of Legation. He published three volumes of a *Dictionary of Chinese-Japanese Words in the Japanese Language*, two of a *Translation of Civil Code of Japan with introduction of Japanese Family System*, one of *The Progress of Japan 1853-1871*, two others − a *Japanese Handbook for the Foreign Office* and a *Report on Taxation and Tenure* in the Parliamentary Papers series − and, finally, a book dedicated 'To the Memory of my Wife', *The Making of Modern Japan (1922)*.

Jack Gubbins was a serious young man, old for his age, his stiff demeanour softened by a low and attractive speaking voice. He met his future in-laws when he first arrived in Japan. Colin Alexander McVean (1838-1912) was a civil engineer, a surveyor-in-chief to the Japanese government. With his wife, Mary Wood Cowan, he lived in an old temple at Chogi, near Tokyo, the house standing at the top of a flight of stone steps lined with trees and leading from a courtyard in which stood an ancient statue of the Diabotz Buddha. Here, on 23 March, 1869, Mary McVean gave birth to their first child, Helen Brodie. Six more children were born until, in 1877, the McVeans retired to the Isle of Mull where they rented Killiemore House, Kilfinichen, and had three more children. Over a period of sixteen years they invited Jack Gubbins to visit them during his home leaves. He watched Helen grow from babyhood to teens and, as time went by, his feelings changed from brotherly affection to an overpowering love and longing for possession. The band which later clasped them in marriage was forged not only by his need for something young and warm to cherish but also by his concentrated desire to become a member of a family who for him possessed all the attributes of grace and favour which had been lacking in his own life. They became engaged and when he arrived in England in December, 1892, he wrote to Helen in not perhaps the most selfless or passionate vein that:

> "I want to have a long rest, sweet − and it is for you to turn it over in your head, love − as to whether I shall take the absolute rest I need before we are married or afterwards. I have so much overstrained myself that when I am badgered by the Foreign Office I feel that every time I write takes something out of me — and more especially, love, the writing I do for them .... I want your love to cheer me up when I am fagged out."

On 10 March, 1893, a note says he will be in Mull in a few days' time and asks Helen to "meet me if you can outside the house, near the last gate, and we will walk up to the dear old house together". Three weeks later, from Aunt Jane Watson's house in Edinburgh, they were married. He was forty-one, she twenty-four.

A year passed and almost to the day, at her mother-in-law's house in Wimbledon, Nonie (the name Helen was always known by) produced her firstborn, Hugh Power Nepean. During that year, 1894, Jack had been retained in London to work on the negotiations which led to a Treaty with Japan. By now he was earning a salary of £840 a year, plus £150 house allowance, which enabled them on their return to Tokyo to live in a half-European, half-Japanese suburban house in Shiba with a staff of seven including a gardener, and a groom for the brougham and one horse.

In July, 1895, a former colleague and predecessor of Jack's, Ernest Satow, returned to Tokyo as British Minister, to fill at short notice the vacancy caused by the sudden death of Hugh Fraser. There grew a warm friendship between the two men, based on intellectual equality and mutual respect, which lasted until Sir Ernest died in 1929. (Satow in 1898 was instrumental in getting John Gubbins an award of Companion of St Michael and St George. Jack's mother, Harriet Louisa, would have been proud; she had died in 1895, the lady with the 'heart of a lion' to whom her children owed so much.)

In June, 1895, Nonie produced a second child, Una Maclean, and a year later, on 2 July, 1896, a son, Colin McVean. His birth sign was Cancer: whether or not astrological readings are taken seriously, the characteristics of this one, picked at random from a book, have much in common with the man Colin was to become:

> "Enthusiastic, quiet driving force, as thinks so becomes, thinking out first then applying action; says what means and holds to beliefs; keen sense of justice, steadfast and loyal; insight into others' characters; reserved, disciplined, with logic and integrity; orderly mind; deep rooted compassion; fond of home and children; immaculate in appearance; a shy character."

Mrs Gubbins was a social asset to John: she was gay, quick-witted, with wide interests, musical, poetic and quite unselfconscious. She introduced into her home the tough kindliness and warm hospitality of Killiemore House, and the language students and consular officers were devoted to her.

For Jack, the bridge between past and present was more difficult to cross. He was a man who liked lines of behaviour to be firmly drawn; within these he had before enjoyed his position as a seasoned bachelor and as a Japanese expert to whom people turned for counsel. Now, here he was, back in the same place but with a young and gregarious wife and a houseful of babies. He wanted the pattern to continue on his terms, and for his wife to adorn a place beside him (yet he kept her short of money and she never had the right clothes). He was incapable of relaxed fatherhood, would not brook disturbance when he worked at home and regarded it as his right to shout for silence or service. His inborn irascibility was aggravated by tri-geminal neuralgia (a sporadic and acute pain down one side of the face) and recurring rheumatic pains which were the result of rheumatic fever in his youth.

Nonie was a Highlander, with a full measure of Scottish reserve, who could not communicate her inner feelings, and found it difficult to stand up to her dark, volatile and loving husband. She recognized that he was formed in a mould in which he would remain throughout a life made hard for him by his intolerance and, where his home life was concerned, by his inability to come to terms with his children, who remained in fear of him throughout their youth and into maturity. Hugh suffered the most from his father's behaviour, and because his firstborn was not a strong-fibred boy but "a poor thing", the proud ambitions of John Harington Gubbins became increasingly centred on Colin, small, dark, energetic Colin. A contemporary photograph shows Una, Hugh and Colin at Karuizawa, Hugh fair, slight, light-eyed, Una and Colin's eyes deep-set and dark under dark eyebrows.

That year, 1898, Nonie's second daughter, Marjorie Mary, was born and life continued as before until, in 1900, just as they were preparing to go on home leave, Jack Gubbins was posted as acting Chargé d'Affaires to Seoul in Korea. Nonie was again pregnant and did not go with him; instead, she went to Scotland, had another daughter, Helen Ruth Martin, in September, and then took her children to her parents' home in Mull where Jack joined her early in 1902.

2

THE SCHOOLS 1902-1913

At the end of Jack's leave early in 1903, he and Nonie returned to Japan, where he was promoted to the local rank of Secretary of Legation in the Diplomatic Service and given a house in the Legation compound. With their parents went the three girls, Una, Mary (Mouse) and Helen. Hugh was already at school and living with his grandparents in Mull; Colin, seven years old, would now do the same.

There was no shock of separation: accounts of Killiemore House — the most hospitable in the district, with "piles of lovely scones, home-made jam and cream" — and of the family that lived there, had been part of their upbringing. Hughie and Colin could be companions without fear of criticism for the one, or of favouritism for the other. They did not see their parents again for over five years and when they did, and far into the future, their own home could never take the place of the house at Kilfinichen, nor could their parents usurp the role of the McVeans: their grandparents, Colin and Mary, and five daughters and three sons aged at that time between thirty-two and twenty-one — Susie, Mary, Flora, Betsy, Iona, Donald with Helen his wife (Aunt Elsie), Alick and George. With open doors and open arms, with laughter and song, pettings and scoldings, five lively girls added Colin to their charge of Hugh. Colin, small and wary, his dark eyes observant, had learned in his short life that it was wise to keep quiet; he would not let himself be fooled by all these aunts who called him 'Cockie' and vied with each other to engage his attention. Aunt Betsy adored him and he became particularly fond of her; Aunt Flora was artistic, temperamental, a gifted photographer; to Aunt Iona, Colin was prime favourite and she kept a photograph of him near her all her life. Aunt Elsie, tall and strict, who rarely let a child sit down "because it encourages indolence", found him a "sensitive small boy, the sight of a bull or cows in a field and a small hand crept into (hers)". Colin was too imaginative not to remain aware of fear during all his life but he mastered it to the extent of being physically and morally brave. Perhaps he had a skin too few because he could be easily and deeply hurt, something he was frightened of being but which he was able to disguise from most people, and he genuinely disliked hurting another's feelings.

In the memoirs he began to write not long before he died, Colin spelled out what the years in Mull meant to him:

"In turn we passed through all their hands as they got married or took up careers − rare for women in those days. Susie went to the Boer War as nurse, Mary to be a speech therapist for the deaf. Two brothers, Donald and George, were in the Indian Army and the third, Alick, in Canada with Hudson's Bay Company. When they were at home they were always willing to take us on the hills or rivers with them. Alick whose interests were almost entirely in the life of the wild was in some far outpost where the mails penetrated rarely, so a blank book was kept in the hall at Kilfinichen in which we all wrote letters and pasted photographs until the book was full and despatched to him. He joined up as a private in the Canadian Army in 1914 when well over forty years old, refusing a commission or even non-commissioned rank for which he felt himself too old, and was severely wounded in March 1918 but survived. Once during the war when we were alongside his Canadian division, I rode over on my horse and managed to find him − a happy and unexpected meeting.

"Mull offered my brother and me everything that healthy and active young boys could possibly wish for, the sea ... at our door, the mountains behind rising over three thousand feet to their peak in Ben More, small burns for brown trout, a river where the sea-trout ran, and game on the hills when we were old enough to shoot, grouse, snipe, and woodcock and blue hares... there it all was − a physical paradise.

"But Mull gave me also other things of lasting value and pleasure ... especially a deep preoccupation with and interest in the wildlife around me, the birds from the golden eagle to the golden-crested wrens, the mammals from seal and otter to the weasel and stoat, the butterflies and even the adders ....

"My grandfather was a fine-looking man, tall and fair, unlike my father's family who were short and dark, dressed always in his kilt .... He was an ornithologist of some repute, an original subscriber to the publication *A History of the Birds of Europe* by H. E. Dresser whose volumes were kept under lock and key in his study. I read them in the long winter evenings lying on the carpet at his feet ....

"From my years in Mull too came a very special attachment and faith in all things Scottish and particularly Highlanders being superior to anything the rest of the world could show! This was carried to the point of irrationality but persisted for many years in certain aspects. I can say only that this somewhat dangerous dogmatism was imbibed from those around me — an unassuming pride in being Highland ran through all my elders in Kilfinichen, never openly expressed unless challenged by some visitor, never thrust on anyone outside the family, but nevertheless it could be felt — and respected. To me it came in more direct form from my aunts and uncles whenever I failed their somewhat rigid standards as to how young boys should grow up and behave, a rebuke to the effect that Highland boys never did things like that though Sassenachs might: that Scottish boys were hardier than English and should never admit to being hungry or cold: 'Run round the house twice if you are cold' was the cure for that!"

Schooling for Colin started at the age of six when he was sent to join Hugh at Normanton Grammar School in Yorkshire. Founded in 1592, the School had been given a facelift in 1897 with a new building, and a new charter which provided "an ample course of studies for boys residing with their parents, guardians and near relations".

"It was day boys only .... It seems an odd choice and it certainly was. A connection of ours, a Dr William Scobie Mackenzie, was an elderly doctor of high local standing in Normanton, a governor of the School and friend of the headmaster, Mr Corbett W. Atkinson: the easy way was taken, without I feel much consideration, and my brother had gone off to Normanton to live with Dr. Mackenzie and attend the School. I followed him but was boarded with the headmaster, thus the only boarder in the School and so an object of some ridicule among the other boys generally who were all of them considerably older and more experienced in the ways of the world than I was."

It was a hard period during which the wariness which Colin's earlier life had made instinct in him developed into something tougher: he learned to conserve his temper, to keep himself to himself, to stand his ground and to fight back.

"It lasted some two years, when Mr Atkinson moved on to be headmaster of Ilkley Grammar School, a much superior and bigger establishment where at least there were five or six other boarders .... We moved with him. The change from what was virtually a small coal-mining town, gloomy and smoky, to a relatively high-class residential area with heather-clad hills round it was much more to my taste. Mr Atkinson himself was a brilliant, if domineering teacher, no sparer of the cane."

Atkinson was a Cambridge mathematics graduate, a man of energy and enterprise who, at the age of thirty-four, was chosen out of two hundred applicants to bring Ilkley Grammar School into modern times.

Hugh went to Loretto School near Edinburgh in 1907. Two years later, the Ilkley School magazine offered its heartiest congratulations to Colin Gubbins for getting an Honourable Mention in Form VIB, and for winning an Exhibition of £30 a year to Cheltenham College. He left at the end of the summer term, the return journey to Mull giving "joy all the way".

"The summer holidays were of course the longest and best and we were allowed to run pretty wild provided we were home by evening. Our house, Killiemore House, was not large by Scottish standards at that time .... The land was at most forty acres of arable all down or near the sea but with a vast out-run for the sheep and cattle up and over the hills behind, heather and deer grass culminating in their peaks in shale and rock with rough shooting galore but only one river holding sea-trout but no salmon, and several brown trout burns. Rabbits were in their hundreds in the hills ....

"Our river, as I have said, was not very good .... But it did have some magnificent pools and runs .... My brother and I went exploring it once, some three or four miles from its estuary where it ran up into the steep hills far above the big falls which sea-trout could not pass, water which had not been fished in living memory, if ever. It was a pouring wet day and as usual we were in our kilts and blue jerseys ... but we had seventeen trout in the first pool, and nothing else mattered. We staggered home − too late we knew − with a bag of eighty-two, to meet an aunt sent out to find us. Retribution was as heavy as the bags, but we were allowed to go again next day.

"Our house stood only two hundred yards from the sea, another source of infinite delight in summer, our only regret being that we were not allowed to go out by ourselves.... In the later summer evenings it was pollock and mackerel fishing, and in the early morning, if the half-dozen lobster pots were out, depending on the weather, one of the aunts would take us out to lift them .... Oysters were to be had here too.... There was a very occasional trip in our sailing boat to Iona where many of my grandfather's Maclean ancestors are buried ....

"My grandfather was bi-lingual in Gaelic and English, and spoke always in Gaelic to the farm hands and his working manager.... In the local church only one service a month was held in English, much to my private relief; instead there was usually a short service in our drawing-room, a few hymns and a reading by Grandpapa from a book of sermons ....

"One grand religious event however I did enjoy — my Aunt Iona's wedding from the house. She was marrying a Captain Houston of the Indian Army, a friend of my Uncle Donald. Three pipers arrived the night before and at eight o'clock next morning two started playing in front of the house, marching up and down. The bride's procession started off on foot to the church, about a mile away, led by the two pipers, and half way there we picked up the bridegroom and his best man and the third piper and there was a joint procession to the church ....

"After the ceremony we all returned to the house for a wedding lunch .... It was an open invitation too for all the crofters of the area and their friends and relations and they sat in the big hayfield (fortunately already cut) in front of the house and had a tremendous *ceilidh*, singing and dancing, with the three pipers playing in turn, and food and drink being circulated. In the evening was a more formal affair held in the big hay barn with the byre underneath and the dancing went on until daylight, the hay not yet in from the fields but still stacked. The moment I enjoyed most was when, dancing a foursome reel with the bonny and enthusiastic wife of our shepherd Hector MacLean, she put her foot right through the floor. I was convulsed. The cattle were still on the hill so no harm was done."

The cattle would stay on the hill for years to come but for Hugh and Colin, by the time of Iona's marriage, the pattern had changed. The year before, in 1908, their parents, Una (aged 13), Mouse (10) and Helen (8), people they hardly knew, had come back to England for good, their return ending the right to regard Killiemore House as home. Jack Gubbins was fifty-six, his wife thirty-nine. His official retirement dated from 10 September, 1909, and carried with it a pension of £777.15s.7d. a year. At the instance of Lord Curzon, at that time chancellor of Oxford University who knew of Jack's work in the cause of Anglo-Japanese relations, Gubbins was given an Honorary Master's degree and made Lecturer on Far Eastern Affairs at Balliol College. During the next three years the numbers of interested students fell away and the authorities decided to end the appointment. It was bad luck on Jack; the academic life had been most congenial and the emoluments a welcome financial contribution. Because he was happy and fulfilled, life had been tolerable for Nonie and the children, and there had been variety in their vacations.

In 1910, they went to Mull for Easter, and to Ireland to a rented house at Baltimore, in County Cork where there was good sea fishing. The rector had two daughters with whom their cousin, Norah Warren, came to stay in 1911. Colin was fifteen and she was sixteen. He fell in love with her and swore he would marry none other. Norah Creina Somerville Warren was slim and lively, with a long face and gentle ways, who, like Colin, had been separated at an early age from her parents, her mother having died when she was seven and her father three years later. He was a retired Royal Navy doctor who ran a home for psychiatric patients at Headcorn in Kent. Norah (or Nonie), born on 19 September, 1895, was his second surviving child, five having died in infancy, and there was an elder sister, Madeleine, a younger, Harriet (Kit or Kitty), and two brothers, Patrick and Desmond. On the death of Dr Warren, the children were dispersed to relatives: Kitty, Pat and Madeleine went to two aunts of great personality in Harrold, Bedfordshire, Desmond elsewhere, and Nonie to an aunt in Ireland.

The secret heart into which Nonie fitted so easily was for Colin a shield against the exclusive maleness of school and the loneliness inherent in having a mother he scarcely knew, whose prime preoccupation was to stand guard between his father's fierce tempers and the vulnerability of her children. At the time he met Nonie, he had been at Cheltenham College for two years and in his own quiet way had achieved a reasonable reputation as a games player and, as a scholar, one good enough to win a Jex-Blake Award of £20 a year, tenable for three years for boys going into the army. It was his second distinction. His first had come on entry when he wore 'velvet' round his mortarboard, the sign of a scholar, in his case one who had sat for a Mathematics and won a Classical Scholarship.

Founded in 1841 and built on the edge of Cheltenham Spa, the College had a high reputation for passing boys into the top places at the Royal Military Academy at Woolwich. It had three departments – Classical/ Modern, Military and Junior. In the Military, to which Colin was assigned, except for Greek, boys studied the same subjects as in the Classical but with emphasis on Mathematics, Engineering and Chemistry. In 1909 the head of the Military side was William Martin ('Scabs') Baker, an outstanding mathematician whose teaching had brought the College's entry into Woolwich and into the Royal Military Academy at Sandhurst from an average of six boys a year to fifteen; it was judged a bad record if the College did not get most of the top places on the list and beat their nearest rivals, Wellington and Clifton. The headmaster, Reginald Waterfield, an old Wykehamist, good in sense and in manners, was thirty-two years old when he was appointed in 1899. His Australian wife "created a sense of fun wherever she was ... entertained everyone; new boys to breakfast, prefects to dinner, grown-ups at all times. She was irresistible." For the first two or three years, boys shared rooms in which they did their work and enjoyed a measure of autonomy under their own leaders; then they went into studies known as 'shacks'. The House – Colin's was Boyne's – was the main focus for loyalty, its place in the games pecking order being keenly contested. The routine was as dull and unvarying as in any other boarding school: up with the bell, tottering and leaping to the cold showers, breakfast, chapel, classes, break — when boys were able to buy buns from trays set out on tables in the quadrangle at the College's centre. Colin's father never gave him enough pocket-money so for him the bun was not a routine affair. In the afternoon and evening, games, work, high tea, prep, and before lock-up the final dissipation — an issue of milk and biscuits or bread and cheese.

His years at school represented for Colin a period of little enjoyment and, in later years, he rarely spoke of them. "English boarding schools like mine were somewhat dull and daunting places; four or five hundred boys herded together at the beginning of each term and not allowed out of school grounds — except for two hours on Sundays when all the shops were shut. I felt all the time that I was in prison." Nevertheless, he had been lucky to have had two such masters as Corbett Atkinson and 'Scabs' Baker. "He was," says a contemporary, "a very quiet pleasant boy built on the small side"; outwardly yes, but caught inside him was an inner reserve and watchfulness which responded to the strength and tenacity of purpose of these two men; it became his armour against the narrow restrictions of school and the insecurities of home, and made of him a private and self-reliant person. At the same time, he developed family characteristics: from his father a meticulously observant eye, a good memory and a huge capacity for hard work; from his mother stoutness of heart and a gaiety which was never far below the surface; and from his upbringing in Mull a constant love of nature, a strict sense of duty and a sort of piety which owed less to the worship of an Almighty God than to the demands of a responsive conscience.

3

THE SHOP AND THE GREAT WAR
1913-1918

Cheltenham College did for Colin Gubbins what it was intended to do: it got him into the Royal Military Academy at Woolwich. His Personal File (War Office No. P/14618) dated 13 September, 1913, showed that Gentleman Cadet Colin McVean Gubbins was aged seventeen, stood sixty-five inches high, weighed one hundred and sixteen pounds, and that he had a chest measurement of thirty-three to thirty-five inches. His military career had begun.

The R.M.A. (generally known as 'The Shop'), which was situated on Woolwich Common in rather a beautiful and elegant seventeenth-century building, comprised a two-year training course for Engineer, Artillery and Signals cadets, during which time they studied mathematics and science, artillery and engineering work, riding, infantry drill and military history. At the end of the first year, the cadets would have a basic knowledge of drill on the square and of minor tactics, a working experience of the eighteen-pounder and the 4.5 howitzer, some confidence to command a company, and as high a standard of horsemanship as could be reached (in this last Colin Gubbins excelled). For the trainees of 1913-1914, however, the course was destined to end half way, at the end of the summer term. As they packed their bags and dispersed for the summer vacation, these young men did not know that the split-second timing of their tough first year's training would shortly become the drum beat of their mobilization for war.

Colin was graded fifty-sixth out of seventy cadets, a position which caused him no pain because

"I was heading, I hoped, after a further year, for a commission in the Royal Field Artillery. Having by then showed no great aptitude for higher mathematics, but a certain inherited predilection for foreign languages, it occurred to my father that it might give me a leg-up if I learnt German .... When therefore 'The Shop' closed for the summer recess, I was bundled off on about 20 July, 1914, to a German family in Heidelberg .... There was no thought in my head as I left of any possible trouble on the Continent, nor among my colleagues and instructors at 'The Shop'; no serious reference in the press .... It does seem strange that my father should have allowed this trip .... He must, however, have consulted his friends in the Foreign Office as that department issued me with a special kind of *laissez-passer* describing my status as a military cadet."

In Heidelberg Colin lodged with a widow and her spinster daughter, and started his tuition, but not for long. On 1 August, strolling in the town, he saw men in uniform and notices stuck on lamp-posts from which he learned that Germany and Russia were at war.

"That was enough for me! I hurried back to my lodgings; my teacher confirmed with tears in her eyes that it really was war and that Austria and Serbia were already fighting .... I packed my large trunk and suitcase as she got together some food for me to take ... and pressed a ten-mark piece into my hand."

Colin went first to the British Consulate, which was closed, and then to the railway station where he dumped his large trunk and found the right platform for trains to Cologne. It was then about 2.30 pm; that night he scrambled aboard a packed train and in Cologne went to the British Consulate, which was closed. Returning to the station he sought help from "a tall and particularly well dressed man who seemed quite unperturbed by all the excitement going on around and looked just like the proverbial Englishman of those days". He was English and, on hearing of Colin's predicament, lent him a golden sovereign which, with the ten-mark piece, purchased a third class ticket to London. On the journey to Brussels, Colin escaped a document inspection by sitting "motionless looking at some paper and trying to look innocent; the three women in our compartment they did not question; myself after one glance they completely ignored .... I do not know why I was not questioned even as to my nationality but think it must have been because I looked too young and boyish and under-developed and insignificant to be of any use in war to any country at all." Colin landed at Dover on 3 August, the day before the British declaration of war, and reported back to Woolwich the next day. Three other cadets who had gone to Germany at the same time as he had were not so lucky; they were arrested and spent the war in a prison camp.

"My escape from being imprisoned in Germany was due entirely to the

15

kindness of the Englishman, a complete stranger, who lent me £1 on Cologne platform. This was of course sent back to his address as soon as possible, and I was delighted to hear from him that he too had avoided arrest ....

"There was a further, delightful and unexpected epilogue to my odyssey .... Some three months later, when I was already in France with my battery, my father wrote that my trunk ... had just been delivered intact to his London flat by the well known agents Dean & Dawson of Piccadilly, that there had been one shilling and sixpence to pay and that on the lid was painted in large white letters 'American Citizen's Luggage'."

Three months later, almost to the day, Second-Lieutenant Gubbins was reporting for duty with 126th Battery, XXIX Brigade, 4th Division, III Corps at a spot on the map of France somewhere near Armentières; the Battery had come out of the First Battle of Ypres and was moving to rest up in three farmhouses on the rolling plains of Artois.

XXIX Brigade was equipped with 18-pounders, each of its three batteries having a complement of some 160 men and 120 horses. 126th Battery spent the first long winter in and out of action in the Ploegsteert area south of Ypres, "a very lively spot" some three hundred yards from the German lines; over Christmas it had even been "fairly comfortable and ... lots to eat, large numbers of parcels having arrived containing warm clothing, cigarettes and plum puddings".[1]

The Germans were caught up in their Russian offensive and did no more than contain the line on the Western Front. When spring came they would use gas, which in the rain-soaked and muggy conditions of the Ypres salient they believed would effectively drive the Allies from their positions. On the evening of 22 April, 1915, therefore, they opened the Second Battle of Ypres (to 25 May) with an intense artillery barrage, at the same time releasing an ugly slow-moving yellow-green cloud of chlorine gas across the northern sector of the Allied line, which was held by French African and Territorial Reservist troops. A gap opened as troops fled, choking, but the Canadians on the flank of the breach held firm until the arrival of English and Indian reinforcements. The three batteries of XXIX Brigade were near the village of Brielen by the Comines Canal, all guns firing in conjunction with the French who held the left of the semi-circle round Ypres. On 15 May the Germans abandoned their position on the west bank of the Canal and, ten days later, the battle ended.

On 9 June, 1915, Colin Gubbins was promoted Lieutenant. In July, after four days rest, XXIX Brigade returned to the front line at Colincamps, ten miles south-west of Arras, where they endured cold, misty, miserable weather "being shelled right through Christmas Day when there was no attempt at peace-making from either side. The Germans left their trenches at safe points to walk across the open – and were fired on. The men had an excellent dinner of soup, pork, roast beef and plum pudding; a bottle of Bass for each man and a bottle of port between four."[2]

After some months out of the line for training and rest, XXIX Brigade returned to the Colincamps area in preparation for the Battle of the Somme (1 July-15 October, 1916). The build-up of artillery for this battle was the British Army's biggest of the war so far: along the whole line from the British front north of the Somme, through the French front to the south, the preliminary bombardment, which began on 24 June, was of such intensity that it blasted the air making men dizzy. ("Near us a yellowhammer nested and reared its brood between the sandbags of the emplacement of one of our big guns; no matter how much the gun fired, it never moved although only six feet away from the muzzle.")[3] At 7.30 am on 1 July, a bright, dry day, "all guns lifted on to objectives as laid down". The batteries of XXIX Brigade on the Beaumont-Hamel front were blasting away with all they had when, for the first time in their battle experience, one received a direct hit – 126th Battery – and suffered the loss of three men and one gun. For showing conspicuous gallantry in action, Colin Gubbins was awarded the Military Cross: "When one of his guns and its detachment were blown up by a heavy shell, he organized a rescue party and personally helped to dig out the wounded while shells were falling all round."[4]

The first phase of the battle failed along most of the front; the British infantry had advanced in dense and rigid formation, aiming to swarm into the enemy trenches when the guns lifted, but the enemy had stayed put, their machine-gunners crouching in the dugouts and shell holes. When the barrage stopped, they came out and let fly a deadly hail of machine-gun fire.

"Streams of wounded were coming down the road ... practically all with bullets from machine-guns. One man came along early in the morning with only one arm, as cheery as possible and saying in a laughing voice 'Souvenir!' By about nine pm we were back in our old front line – a terrible disaster with enormous losses. In our 29 Brigade, the casualties were about fifty, of whom twenty were killed."[5]

In late July XXIX Brigade moved back to the comparative quiet of the Ypres sector where it relieved other units and where, on 16 August, Gubbins was promoted to Acting Captain and served briefly on the staff of GOC Fourth Army. At the end of September he rejoined the Brigade on its return to the Somme, to a position on the front line between Morval and Le Sars where tanks had been in action for the first time. At Morval on 7 October,

Colin was wounded by a gunshot in the neck, admitted to 20 General Hospital and discharged eleven days later. A fellow officer, Edward Beddington-Behrens, wrote to an uncle: "One of the officers in the battery got wounded yesterday. Gubbins, a ripping little fellow, a regular, who has been out here nearly two years and who got the Military Cross about a month ago. He was ADC to the GOC Fourth Army when we were at rest but he refused to stay at GHQ when the battery came into action."

Once more, both sides dug in for the winter. The autumn rains had come early and combined with the effects of bombardment to turn the earth into a sea of mud through which men, horses and transport could scarcely struggle. It was beastly, a frozen nightmare of hardship and gloom, during which Gubbins was lucky enough to have three home leaves. In December his father wrote to Sir Ernest Satow that, "Our gunner boy — now a captain (temporary) at twenty — came last week and returns to the front tomorrow," and again, on 25 February, 1917:

"Colin is at home again for a fortnight to go through an extra gunnery course at Shoeburyness and a Battery Commander's course at Larkhill. As he is only an acting captain (he was in command in January for a month while his major was on leave), this is a feather in his cap, I think. He is really a good lad and has found, I hope, his *metier*. In the Army Order ordering him on leave for this purpose was a paragraph saying only captains *especially chosen to command* batteries were selected for this purpose."

The winter of home leaves and courses in England — one at Arras on 'Cooperation with Aircraft' — ended on 14 March, when he went to Buckingham Palace to receive his Military Cross from HM The King. Next day he was back in France.

March, 1917, came and went.

"Over the land freckled with snow half-thawed
The speculating rooks at their nests cawed
And saw from elm-tops, delicate as flowers of grass,
What we below could not see, Winter pass."[6]

The Germans had taken advantage of the winter and carried out, in great secrecy, a systematic withdrawal designed to shorten and strengthen their lines of defence, while at the same time pushing through a reorganization of their manpower and supply programmes. It was some time before front line troops realized that the trenches opposite them were empty; the first mention in XXIX Brigade's war diary is on 25 February when it quotes messages coming in "reporting evacuation of trenches by Germans". The retreat was thorough: felled trees, mined roads and railways, towns and villages razed to the ground.

Thus was the stage set for the Battle of Arras (9 April-4 May, 1917). On 5 April the weather was fine: "a beautiful pale hazy moonlight and the sag and flap of air." On 6 April "artillery makes air flap all night long". On 7 April "a cold bright day of continuous shelling". On 8 April "a bright warm, Easter day".[7]

At 0530 on 9 April, the battle began, with a showpiece of spectacular gunnery:

"the most impressive I have ever witnessed, with a bombardment that was a symphony in our ears, for it was all coming from our side. Our preparations and counter-battery work has been so thorough and effective that every German gun was silenced, and not a shot was heard from the other side for hours."[8]

The initial advance was indeed rapid − six thousand yards on the first day which included the capture by the Canadians of the long-coveted Vimy Ridge − but the momentum was not sustained, and the French, facing the vacuum of a German tactical retreat, lost their power of punch.

Gubbins, for the first but not the last time in his life, met Carton de Wiart:

"He had taken over command of an infantry brigade in Fourth Division, in which I was serving as junior gunnery captain. By May of that year (1917) when our Arras offensive was slowly grinding to a halt, our guns were to support his brigade in a further limited attack. I was sent to his headquarters as liaison officer and joined him in the dug-out. He was already a legendary figure with his Victoria Cross, his black eye patch, his stump of an arm and his formidable bearing. When the divisional orders for next day's attack reached him − long and voluminous − he read these through twice, questioned me on one or two gunner matters, then deliberately tore up the orders and sent for his battalion commanders; a ten-minute conference; a few clear verbal orders from him; and it was all over. He could not abide what he called 'bumph war'. He was wounded again soon after, so we lost him in 4 Division."

On 14 September XXIX Brigade left Arras and returned to its old fighting ground near the Comines Canal to prepare battery positions along the River Steenbeck. The Commanding Officer noted that conditions during October were particularly trying and severe, demanding great endurance and fortitude from all ranks, the ground waterlogged, the weather atrocious; enemy shell fire was continuous; on most nights there were heavy concentrations of gas shells which meant long periods of wearing gas helmets. Gubbins was in temporary command of 125th Battery and, for a period with rank of major, of two of the other batteries, three majors having needed replacement within three weeks. His father wrote of "the fortunes of war" telling Ernest Satow that "our gunner boy has been very busy in the firing line ... in command of his battery again, his major having been attached to the staff for six weeks. We met one of his friends lately ... who ... said nice things of Colin."

In November Jack Gubbins reported that Colin had been on home leave "gassed but fortunately not badly .... We are trying to get a room for our gunner boy in Jermyn Street ... to store things in when he is at the front and our flat is not large enough! He has moved ... further south."

The gassing had come from mustard gas, and the move south was to Ronville near Arras where, on 9 November, the batteries of XXIX Brigade took over positions on either side of the Cambrai road ready for action in support of the Battle of Cambrai (20 November, 1917).

From this battle, from the British sector opposite Cambrai, there came two surprises: predicted shooting, which put an end to the practice of prior artillery bombardments which had so often defeated their own ends by rendering impassable the ground over which the advance was planned to follow; and the appearance of some four hundred tanks in a brilliant attack which achieved complete surprise but which, through lack of reserves, faded away, allowing the Germans to recover and counter-attack. By December both sides had settled back into the familiar routine of minimal advance and retreat. The fourth Christmas passed. XXIX Brigade was in Corps reserve enjoying a peaceful period, with its headquarters in Arras where the billets were comfortable and there was a good officers' club. On 12 February Gubbins was promoted captain, commanding 126th Battery. On 15 March the Brigade polished its boots and buttons and took part in a Divisional Commander's inspection on the racecourse, with full march past, advance in review order and an address by the General.

Meanwhile, on the other side, stealthy preparations on a huge scale were being carried out for the first phase of an offensive on the Somme by which the German High Command hoped to gain a military decision before the threat of social and economic collapse in Germany and the arrival of the Americans in strength could become reality. The aim of the Battle of St Quentin (21 March-4 April) was an investment of Arras in a two-pronged attack designed to drive a wedge between British and French forces.

The battle opened with a synchronized bombardment consisting of all types of artillery, high explosive and gas shells. It was so devastating that it overwhelmed all means of retaliation and communication and forced the Allies into retreat. Ignorant as yet of the horrors to come, at midnight on 20 March, after dinner at the club, cheerful and full of good wine, officers of XXIX Brigade returned to their billets, intending next day a leisurely preparation to take over a position north of the River Scarpe. Their ease was short-lived however; the pre-battle bombardment began at 3 am and it was not until ten o'clock next morning that word reached them of the major battle which had opened to the south of Arras. That afternoon XXIX Brigade reached its position north of the Scarpe, on the right flank of the German offensive, where its batteries were in full view. On 27 March 126th Battery moved forward to continue harassing fire; on the 28th, at three am, there was heavy shelling and a strong smell of gas round Headquarters and Battery positions, 126th Battery doing great execution with Behrens at Observation Post. By 7 am all telephone wires were cut

"and we were out of touch with everybody except three of the Batteries. We had no idea what was happening .... From eight am we got some messages through from the Batteries, who were intact but being heavily shelled. 126 had had one gun destroyed; also the officers' mess had been blown up with all their kit, but luckily there had been no casualties .... At ten-fifteen we were still out of touch with Division ... and at eleven-thirty we got one line through to Brigade OP who reported that about six Boche batteries had just advanced and were coming into action on the old no-man's-land. No doubt he was working on a programme and expected to be near our HQ by noon, in which case these batteries would have been all right and our observers unlikely to see them. As it was, we looked on them from a range of about two thousand yards. 126 got on to them at once and soon obtained two direct hits on their limbers, blowing up ammunition, horses and drivers. The Germans dropped their guns into action and then left them, running as fast as they could to dug-outs in their old front line."[9]

All day the battle raged; the Allied line bent but did not break. "I have a vivid memory," wrote Brigadier Mockler-Ferryman years later, "of Colin bringing up ammunition wagons through the heavy shelling."[10] By 4 April the Germans had won back the ground they had lost two years previously and with it large quantities of men and material. But they had not achieved their objective and victory was short-lived; the end of the war was not far off.

For Colin Gubbins it ended on 17 April when an attack of trench fever so weakened him that he was shipped home on sick leave. In his fourth and last battle, which had been severe and vital, he had handled his battery with skill and authority, proving not for the first time that he was a good soldier.

That he enjoyed an easy relationship with his fellows can be seen by this pencilled note which he received during the battle:

"Dear Gub, Corporal Jones wrote and told me he is very shorthanded .... Our line has advanced a bit on the right of the river last night. The Infantry reported Boche massing in their trenches — we fired umpteen rounds and repelled them trying to bomb up our *tranchées*. The Inf sent thanks to Brig for our support! Bow Wow! nothing new. Cheerio! Bertie."

4

THE SERVICE OVERSEAS: ARCHANGEL, IRELAND, INDIA 1918-1930

"Colin is home ... very run down and suffering from overstrain and trench fever," wrote Jack Gubbins to Sir Ernest Satow on 17 April, 1918, and a week later that he was "in a very grand hospital on Denmark Hill under a civilian doctor who had reported that ... considering the time the boy had been in France it was not surprising that he was suffering from overstrain".

The war had not changed the pattern of Colin's home, which continued to be the centre of uncertain paternal behaviour. Often, when Colin had returned on leave from France, all his father had done was to glance up from his censorship of Japanese correspondence for the Foreign Office, ask, "What are you doing here?" and return to his work. It was small wonder that the son found it difficult to communicate with the father. With his mother he had never had a close relationship, but throughout the war she had found time to write to him every day in spite of her full-time work for the VAD (Voluntary Aid Detachment); this had grown into his heart and when she died in December, 1922, he felt it deeply. His brother Hugh had always loved his mother but he now lived in Canada and in the years ahead he and Colin did not see much of each other. They had shared their childhood in Mull, but, with time, they grew increasingly apart and had little in common.

"I hope he won't marry too soon," said Jack Gubbins in 1917. He was referring to Colin's attachment to Nonie Warren and her family, and his constancy in wishing to marry her. She was a VAD nurse in England and in France ("a very good one"; men asked for "the girl with the gentle hands"). She lived with her aunts at Harrold in Bedfordshire, where Colin stayed frequently and where he felt at home because this was a house as warmly hospitable as had been Killiemore House in Mull. The two aunts were unique ladies: Aunts Mill and Matey had married two Irish doctor brothers, one of whom ran the house as a nursing home for the mentally ill. Aunt Matey supervised the establishment from her bed, never rising before midday; Aunt Mill was the practical one, wore a dark skirt with high-necked white blouse and smoked a pipe. The household was Irish and eccentric where all were welcome, the uncles and aunts generous to a fault but carefree and careless, cheques sometimes not being cashed.

In September, 1918, Gubbins was passed fit for active service and sent as an instructor to No. 3 R.A. Cadet College at Weedon; he also attended courses at the Schools of Education at Oxford and of Instructors at Bockhampstead. On Armistice Night, 11 November, he danced the night away at the Savoy and, with a fellow officer, climbed a pillar in the restaurant. He took his twenty-year old sister Mouse to revues and to dance at Ciro's, and he rode to hounds with the Quorn or Pytchley, mounted on good horses lent to him by his brother officer, Edward Beddington-Behrens, who was a wealthy man and devoted to Colin.

This period ended with his appointment as ADC to General Ironside, GOC Archangel Expeditionary Force in North Russia, and his departure for Murmansk on 22 March, 1919.

Allied intervention had begun early in 1918 when at Brest-Litovsk the Bolshevik government, dominated by Lenin and Trotsky, had made a separate peace with Germany. By the autumn there were about 15,000 British and American troops occupying an area in Northern Russia, their objectives the continued denial to Germany of the ports of Murmansk and Archangel, the protection of the Northern supply route to Russia and the support of White Russian, anti-Bolshevik forces fighting under the command of Admiral Kolchak. Ironside had occupied Archangel and had advanced along the railway line to Petrograd; a force, supported by a flotilla which included river steamers fitted out as gunboats and mostly manned by British crews, had reached Troitsa, some 250 miles from Archangel, but had had to withdraw when the River Dvina froze for the winter. It was a strange campaign: at first the Germans had been the enemy; then, after the defeat of Germany, the Bolsheviks became the enemy; but neither could compete with the worst enemy of all — the climate. While the Armistice was being celebrated in Europe (and Colin was climbing the pillar at the Savoy Hotel), the White Sea was frozen and the troops trapped without hope of relief for six months. It was hard and bitter, a grim and isolated war which, by the time Colin Gubbins disembarked at Murmansk, was all but over. What in 1918 had been a straightforward attempt to maintain the Eastern front against the Germans after Russia's withdrawal from the war had become a twisted and untidy offensive against Bolshevism. Resistance to the Allied intervention was overt from White Russian soldiers in the field and covert from the Bolshevik Underground. There was mutiny among the White Russians and British officers were shot; as the Bolshevik forces increased and strengthened, so did desertions to their ranks. Kolchak's efforts were failing and there was nothing further that the Allies could do but to evacuate. However, when Colin Gubbins, with an ADC's red band round his cap and ribbons of the Military Cross and campaign medals across his chest, arrived in Murmansk on 13 April, he only knew that his new boss was physically a mighty man, six foot four inches tall, with shoulders in proportion, and that he was a natural linguist with a forceful personality and an unconventional outlook which made him an ideal commander of a mixed and, where the White Russians were concerned, unruly army. A fellow officer in North Russia at the time writes as follows:

"In 1919, I met Gubbins for the first time when he was Ironside's ADC. At the time of the mutinies of the White Russians I and my company (I was then serving in a machine-gun battalion) were rushed down the River Dvina in a couple of days to Archangel; and then trained up the railway line to Oberskaya, supposedly to help quell a mutiny at the latter place. We were put on the C-in-C's private river steamer, and the only officer on board other than my own subalterns was Colin Gubbins. I remember we started by having something of a row, very naturally, as I wanted all the cooking facilities for my soldiers, and Colin as a good ADC was anxious about the state of the C-in-C's private ship! I remember him then as a very smart and dapper officer .... I had the World War I contempt of the young infantry regimental officer for young red-hatted staff officers in general and ADCs in particular. Further, in 1919 I was a temporary major and I think Gubby in North Russia was a captain."[1]

Preparations for evacuation began when the thaw came in May. It had been hoped to support Admiral Kolchak's troops advancing from Siberia, but the defeat of the Siberians put an end to that and there was no alternative but to disengage and hand over to the White Russian commanders. Contingents were embarked in turn, the British being the last to leave. In all, some 17,000 persons, soldiers and civilians, were transported in British ships at a time when shipping had been much reduced by German submarines. Withdrawal continued until 27 September when the last five thousand men, with the GOC and his ADC, were embarked, and the evacuation of Archangel was complete.

In the five months or so that he had spent in North Russia Gubbins acquired the Order of St Stanislav Class III of the North Russian Expedition, a smattering of the Russian language (which he was later to turn into an interpretership), and a deep hatred of Communism and all it stood for.

Her name a forlorn reminder of the crumbling empire they had left behind them, SS *Czaritza* disembarked General Ironside and Gubbins at Liverpool on 5 October, 1919. There was a railway strike, but a special train brought senior officers and their staffs to London. On 10 October Colin relinquished his appointment and went, with "some lovely furs" to join Nonie at her aunts' house in Harrold.

Twelve days later, on 22 October, Colin McVean Gubbins married Norah Creina Somerville Warren at Harrold Church, and General Ironside came to the wedding. Jack Gubbins had not been enthusiastic but he became fond of Nonie, in fact he remained on much better terms with her than with any of his daughters. She dressed well, was taller than Colin but she was not an extrovert like he was, did not have his energy nor share in his love of sport and the social life. She was above all a home-maker — a quality which was stretched to its limit when she married Colin: "we were in seventeen different rented houses in the first three years of our married life — a nightmare of house-hunting and moving ... how we hated it." The 'nightmare' and 'hate' could only have been felt at second-hand by Colin because, on 1 November, he was posted to Ireland.

On 2 December, 1919, Gubbins reported to 47th Battery, XLI Brigade, 5th Division RFA, Kildare, and spent the next three years in Ireland, returning to England on leave from time to time to one or other of the seventeen houses. John Michael McVean was born on 11 July, 1921, and in that same month Colin sat a French examination in London and gained a Second Class interpretership.

In Ireland the military situation was much the same as it had been when the Gubbins forbears had settled there two hundred and fifty or so years earlier. The English were still the enemy, the conditions for military action remained alien and uneasy. In France, Colin had known what it was like to fight on an extended front alongside men who, like him, had little choice in their actions and were often in ignorance of the battle objectives. In North Russia, from the edge of the people's resistance, he had seen the potential strength of the resister who was able to choose the terrain, the target and the moment to strike. Now, in Ireland, he was "being shot at from behind hedges by men in trilbys and mackintoshes and not allowed to shoot back!"; he had stepped from one kind of disarray to another, this disarray laced with the skein of a well-organized guerrilla resistance; the colour of it suited one who had all the instincts of a good 'I' officer; he settled in to learn all he could about clandestine warfare and the intelligence without which it could not function.

In 1920 a three-day course in Guerrilla Warfare was organized by HQ 5th Division, designed to give officers and men special training to deal with the type of irregular warfare at which fighters like Michael Collins excelled. Collins was the guerrilla fighter *par excellence* in the ranks of Sinn Fein. He had taken part in the Easter Rising of 1916 and was now a commander who controlled communications, operations, administration and intelligence (wherein he had a spy system second to none). With the truce of 1921 he emerged from the shadows and joined a delegation negotiating a treaty with Britain, but a general election in the following year made matters worse: the Republicans refused to submerge their rights as a minority in Parliament and the IRA took advantage of the situation to step up their acts of violence and arson. Dublin became the centre of bitter fighting. On 28 June, 1922, the Republicans, with their leading insurgent, Rory O'Connor, captured the Deputy Chief of Staff of the pro-Treaty Army and held him prisoner in the Four Courts which, with other buildings, they had turned into strong points. This was a challenge which Collins could not ignore and it was decided to proceed against the stronghold. Gubbins, who was Brigade Major RA with 5th Division at the time, took part in the attack. With a Sergeant, he was "mounting six 18-pounders on a lorry and watching the insurgent Rory O'Connor and his minions taking on the newly established Eire government at a hundred yards range (maximum) across the Liffey in the heart of Dublin. Eventually I had orders to hand over our 18-pounders to the Eire people ... and the fun was soon over and Rory O'Connor shot. What I did not like was having to provide a gun carriage and six black horses for the funeral of Michael Collins, assassinated shortly after."[*][2]

There is no open page relating to Gubbins' sojourn in Ireland; it had begun on 2 December, 1919, and had ended on 27 September, 1922. He had had two attachments as Brigade Major RA to HQ 5th Division at the Curragh in Dublin from 28 November, 1921, to 21 January, 1922, and from 28 March until his return to England in October, 1922.

Until March, 1923, Gubbins was held on the strength of HQ London District while attending a Russian Course at King's College which yielded him a Second Class Interpretership. He had no difficulty in learning a foreign language, in fact he related easily to other countries and nationalities. Nonie did not feel the same, but a posting to India was such a normal proceeding in the British Army that she was happy enough to pack her bags and set sail with Colin and Michael aboard SS *Malwa* on 2 March. At Port Said – to generations of British soldiers, India-bound, the dividing line between East and West – tropical uniform and cotton dresses replaced winter clothes, and life on board began to hum with fun: fancy dress dances, ship's concerts, deck sports, flirtations and bingo, ten days of recreation until the ship docked at Bombay and duty began.

Gubbins reported on 1 April to Lucknow where (shades of his grandfather,

---

[*] Ten days after the Four Courts attack, Collins was shot in an ambush by irregulars, a 'lost leader' at the age of thirty-two.

Martin), he remained until 22 February, 1924, when he went to Mhow for eight months as officiating GSO3 (Intelligence) Central Provinces District. Here he was able to indulge his passion for mounted sport. The successful man after pig was he who had the nerve to ride on a loose rein and let the pony have his head whatever the going: "Colin was one of this type," wrote a contemporary, Peter Colley, "he was completely fearless. There was a 'bobbery pack', a motley collection of mongrels, terriers, spaniels, greyhounds, airedales, anything in fact which would chase a jackal or fox. These dogs, many of which belonged to soldiers, were brought to the meet by their owners, and then moved off as a pack to scour the country, hunting almost entirely by sight .... Colin joined in with his usual fervour and here again when hounds were running there were no half measures; it was neck or nothing."

Nonie did her best to keep up with him, but she seldom accompanied him on mounted excursions, not being particularly fond of riding. Hers was a quiet and retiring disposition, no sort of match for that of her extrovert husband but she was a good story-teller, a witty conversationalist and she got on well with young people. Peter Colley remembered her as "tall and willowy" and "Gubby" as

"a slight, superbly built young man with dark hair, rather beetling eyebrows, penetrating eyes and a gravelly voice. He was Scots but not obtrusively so and there was something about him which made him somehow different − a wild devil-may-care streak. He had an infectious smile and abounding physical fitness .... He was certainly attractive, perhaps too small to be handsome, a great party man; not a lady's man; he liked women around but he was not a womanizer. There was a quality of sensitiveness about his features when in repose."[3]

During that summer Gubbins sat for the preliminary Urdu exam, which he passed. On 28 October, 1924, he rejoined 15th/XXVI Brigade at Jubbulpore, a city district of the Central Provinces which was situated in beautiful surroundings, wooded and fertile. After two months Colin was sent as Adjutant XXIII Field Brigade RA to Nowshera in the North-West Frontier Province. The Brigade was put into a heavy training programme, soldiering close to the Khyber Pass being taken very seriously in this Frontier area. Colin moved his family into a bungalow within a stone's throw of the polo ground − and became tied to his office chair! In March, his son Michael was very ill with dysentery and went home with Nonie, to Harrold and to Mull, where they saw Jack Gubbins, who wrote that the 'Mull air is doing her and the boy much good'. Colin, meanwhile, qualified in June at HQ Northern Command's Annual Intelligence Course, the Colonel's report saying that he had 'worked with the greatest keenness throughout the Class and was suited in every way for Intelligence work especially in the Far East'. It began to look as though what he most enjoyed about the Army — regimental soldiering — would be replaced by desk work, his experiences in Ireland and in North Russia and his three interpreterships making him an obvious candidate for Intelligence.

The next appointment, on 11 October, 1925, took Gubbins to AHQ Simla as Officiating GSO3 (gazetted "Appointed" on 21 April) in MO3 where he stayed until he entered the Staff College at Quetta on 16 February, 1928. During the two years he spent in Simla, he put his knowledge of Russian to good use by reading and translating secret intelligence to do with Soviet Government policy, many of whose communications were being successfully intercepted by the intelligence bureaux of the British raj in India. Few departments stayed up in the hills during the winter so the place was deserted and usually under snow. Deprived of the horse riding which he so enjoyed Colin found it boring, the only physical exercise available being to skate on flooded tennis courts, a sport which in summer he pursued on roller skates. Against the physical boredom, he could set the fact that he was advancing his military career in the work that he was doing, and on a friendship level he could produce two colleagues, both of them outstanding in the field of Signals communications: Bill (John Hessell) Tiltman, a master crypto-grapher, and Nick (Frederick William) Nicholls, GSO3 at AHQ who had succeeded in setting up direct wireless communication with the British Embassy in Kabul during the Afghan Rebellion and who, in the Second World War, served under Gubbins as a unique Director of Signals with the Special Operations Executive.

Nonie and Michael returned from England and life resumed its pleasant pattern in the beautiful surroundings of Simla. On 28 November, 1927, Rory Martin Somerville was born and the family was complete.

Gubbins passed 4th into the Staff College, Quetta, on 16 February, 1928, and was congratulated by his Commander-in-Chief, Field-Marshal Birdwood, for having done so well. "It was an excellent performance on your part," he wrote, "... and I am sure the whole family will be very happy at Quetta, and the small boy, I know, will be a real jockey by the time you leave there!"*4

The Staff College course was stimulating and instructive. For two years, free from all day-to-day responsibility, the students could study all aspects of the art of war: the intricacies of Staff Duties on all levels up to and including Army Corps; the higher direction of war, relating past battles to present conditions; the impact of air power; combined operations with the

* Michael had distinguished himself by winning first prize in a children's riding event.

Royal Navy; the uses of Signals intelligence and so on. Gubbins, who was in the Senior division, wrote to his cousin Helen on 16 May, 1929, that he was going through "the hardest years of work ... being watched the whole time, every scrap of work ... noted and marked against you .... The one ambition of all the students now is not to get a 1st class report but just to get thro' safely and get it over. I do hate working up to 2.30 or 3 o'clock in the morning." However, for a man who loved horses, it had its compensations: Colin hunted with the Quetta Hounds and played polo in the Staff College polo team (his handicap was 2).

John Harington Gubbins died in 1929. In the same letter to Helen, Colin wrote that he was glad Nonie had been there and sad "that he died when he did, after two or three years of being really frightfully lonely and depressed tho' he rarely mentioned it and then only to me. If he had lived he was to come and live with us as soon as I came home, and he knew we had planned that and it did make him happier. He was very good to us in his Will, as I'd never really expected anything, he'd always said that everything would have to be for the girls. Actually all four of us get £75 a year each ... and he also left £500 to Michael to pay for his public school. It was jolly decent of him. Don't think that I blame my sisters for not living with him, as I know that they simply couldn't do it; it was absolutely impossible." (Of Hugh, there was no mention; Jack Gubbins never did come to terms with him, but he left Nonie £100.)

During the last months in India, Colin's leanings were towards home and the future. He saw General Ironside who had come up to Quetta and found him "so nice ... the kindest-hearted man I know, and if only you work hard will do the best he can for you." "Work hard!" Colin said that the two years at the Staff College had been the hardest years of work he would ever have. He told Helen that he was fed up and was going to enjoy himself for a change. "I've spoilt all my life so far ... by always looking and working for the future and never just sitting still and enjoying the present. I've accepted jobs all over the place which I didn't want but which I thought might help me to get into the Staff College, and have given up leave, and money and everything to do it. I've only had five months leave in the last eight years!"

In the Staff College report of 18 December, 1929, the Military Secretary said that Gubbins was "strong-minded, good balance; thoroughness and quickness of mind".[5]

5

THE NINETEEN-THIRTIES

On the family's return to England in January, 1930, Colin, after a year with 5 Light Brigade at Ewshott, was sent to the War Office as GSO3 in MI3(c), the Soviet section of the Military Intelligence Directorate.

From her aunts' house at Harrold in Bedfordshire, Nonie rented a cottage at nearby Carlton. It had black beams and an orchard in which Colin built a tree house for his children. Here Nonie lived the sort of life she liked best; she was near her aunts, Michael was at his preparatory school, and three-year old Rory was at home. When Colin went to London, a place which had never appealed to her, she did not join him, but counted on seeing him for weekends.

The early 1930s was a fascinating period in which to follow the development of Stalinism in the USSR; however, the everyday work of the Soviet section was relatively dull. The one-time cypher pads adopted in 1927 for Soviet diplomatic and intelligence signals traffic continued to defeat Western cryptographers. Consequently there was virtually no high grade intelligence coming out of the Soviet Union and much of Gubbins' work as GSO3 consisted of reading the Russian press and other published material in an attempt to establish the Soviet order of battle and identify the leading personalities, industrial developments, communications and other items of military interest. It was a laborious task, but Gubbins enjoyed his first experience of working in the War Office; he found the urbane and somewhat cosmopolitan atmosphere of the MI Directorate a welcome interlude from regular soldiering.

This interlude came to an end on 8 April, 1933, when he was appointed Brigade Major RA to 4 Division, HQ East Anglian District at Colchester. He spent two years at Colchester, living in Army quarters with Nonie and the children. At 4 Division, he was responsible as a senior captain for recruiting and training the artillery component of the local Territorial Army. Equipment was in pitifully short supply, making realistic training virtually impossible; however, organizing the TA annual camps and field firing courses brought him into contact with a wide variety of enthusiastic part-time soldiers, often constructively critical of established military procedure. Gubbins, who got on better with civilians than did many of his army contemporaries, encouraged these exchanges of view.

He did well at East Anglian District and was promoted to Brevet Major in July, 1933; but it was not until 14 February, 1934, that he became a Substantive Major – at the age of thirty-eight. A year later, on 1 February, 1935, he returned to 4 Division as Brigade Major RA of 14 Field Brigade.

In professional terms this was considered a good appointment since 4 Division was one of the two infantry divisions earmarked for the 'notional' Expeditionary Force. Nevertheless, the Army's deplorable state of preparedness was such that even this notional expeditionary force was generally considered to be fit only for use in a colonial war. Moreover, it was widely held that to commit a force consisting of at most two infantry divisions to a Continental war would be to invite not only disaster but international ridicule. Throughout this period the Government concluded that Britain could make its most valuable contribution to 'collective security' by concentrating its limited resources on equipping the Royal Navy and the Royal Air Force. This policy of 'limited liability' was considered unrealistic and, indeed, barely acceptable by many middle-ranking Army officers. These, including Gubbins, considered it would be impossible to avoid sending an expeditionary force to the Continent if Germany attacked France and, rightly or wrongly, were openly critical of current policy which placed financial stability before rearmament. However, the frustrations of a Brigade Major RA were nothing compared with those which Gubbins was shortly to experience when, eight months later, October, 1935, he was once again posted to the War Office and appointed GSO2 in a new section of MT1, the policy-making branch of the Military Training Directorate.

On arrival in MT1, Gubbins' first task in addition to his other duties as head of the artillery section was to act as personal staff officer to Major-General A. F. Brooke. Before becoming Director of Military Training and while still Inspector of Artillery, the latter was carrying out a general review of Britain's anti-aircraft defences which, under the policy of 'limited liability' had been given high priority. For Gubbins it was a useful experience, since providing training for the six newly-formed anti-aircraft regiments when essential equipment, such as predictors, was often unobtainable, was to tax his patience and ingenuity to the utmost during the next three years. Meanwhile, his close association with General Brooke, soon to be his departmental head, was not only immediately advantageous but was to have unforeseen consequences for his subsequent career when Brooke became successively GOC Home Forces and CIGS.

So far as the Army in general was concerned, the three years that Gubbins served in MT1 was a revolutionary period. The mechanization of the cavalry, the employment of armoured units and the role of the Territorial Army were only three of the controversies confronting a General Staff hitherto not given to intense intellectual effort in peacetime. By its nature MT1 was in the thick of it; and not for nothing was it known in the nineteen-thirties as 'Whipsnade'.

Gubbins, who in July had attained the rank of Brevet Lieutenant-Colonel, was nearing the end of his MT1 assignment when he was selected as a member of the British Military Mission which, under the terms of the Munich Agreement, was to monitor the withdrawal of the Czech forces from Sudetenland. The Mission, headed by Brigadier P. de Fonblanque, left Croydon for Berlin on 3 October, 1938. Gubbins found the whole business distasteful. He disapproved of the Munich Agreement and admired the Czechs, later describing them as "a thoroughly decent democratic little nation" and their Sudeten Germans as better treated than any other minority in Europe. However, it was certainly an eye-opener for him to witness at first hand the brutal force of Nazi expansion. Apart from establishing an agreed demarcation line, there was little for the Mission to do and, as soon as the Czech forces had withdrawn, it returned to London. His experiences confirmed Gubbins in his conviction that Hitler was bent on war at the first opportunity, and for the rest of his life he felt a sense of shame that, owing to British and French unreadiness, the Czechs should have become the victims of this *coup de force*.

Despite Hitler's vacillations and the unremitting efforts of the Chamberlain Government to come to terms with the dictators, by the autumn of 1938 it was generally believed in the War Office that Hitler would invade Eastern Europe as a prelude to confronting the Western powers. In this event it seemed likely that insurrection and patriotic resistance would occur in the occupied territories which might be turned to good account by the Western powers.

Two years before this, in 1936, General Adam, Deputy Chief of the Imperial General Staff, had set up in the War Office a small section known as GS(R) (General Staff (Research)). Its object was to enable a Grade I staff officer, freed from departmental responsibilities, to spend a year studying a specific subject of current interest to the Army Council. This 'think tank' had already produced studies on Army Education and the Army Medical Service. In October, 1938, the officer appointed to GS(R) was Lt.-Colonel J. C. F. (Jo) Holland, DFC, RE.

Holland had been at the RMA a year after Colin. He was commissioned into the Royal Engineers and in 1916 attached to the Royal Flying Corps as an Observer. He served in the Balkans and took part in at least one raid on Sofia, a hazardous operation since owing to the range there could be no fighter escort. He was Mentioned in Despatches and awarded the Distinguished Flying Cross. He served for some months in Ireland during the 'troubles' but, if he and Gubbins met, there is no record that they discussed irregular warfare.

At this time the General Staff was still expressly forbidden to hypothesize that a British Expeditionary Force would be sent to the Continent. Consequently, Holland's formal brief in GS(R) was to study in depth the characteristics of guerrilla warfare with particular reference to recent operations in China and Spain and to consider the implications for colonial operations. At the same time, however, he was given most secret instructions by the DCIGS to report on the possibility of providing British support for insurgency in any country of Eastern Europe overrun by the German Army. In view of the extreme sensitivity of this subject, it was decided that Holland should carry out these studies under the umbrella of the recently formed Section D of the Secret Intelligence Service (SIS) which was already planning sabotage and subversive action against the Axis powers in neutral countries.

On the strength of his preliminary report, in January, 1939, Holland was authorized to expand GS(R) by the addition of two Grade II staff officers: an expert on demolitions and explosives and an officer to be in charge of organization, recruitment and training. For the first of these appointments Holland chose Millis Jefferis, a somewhat eccentric and extremely able sapper major. For the second, he decided to approach Colin Gubbins. Gubbins not only spoke French and Russian but he knew him to have had personal experience of the Bolshevik revolution and of the Sinn Fein rebellion in Ireland. Gubbins himself describes how he was sitting at his desk in the War Office when

"a cold hand took me literally by the back of the neck and a voice I knew said, 'What are you doing for lunch today?' I whipped round – it was Jo Holland – and I replied that I was going to my regimental races at Sandown; there, beside me, were my field-glasses. 'No, you are not,' he replied. 'You are to lunch with me; the CIGS says so.' We knew each other very well and I naturally agreed. In a private room at St. Ermin's Hotel I found that the real host, who was waiting for us there, was another sapper officer whom I also knew well. Over lunch he told us that he was the head of Section D and explained his charter .... "Holland, as well as being a far-seeing and imaginative man with a first class brain, was also a severely practical and down-to-earth man. He started me off on the preparation of secret pamphlets on guerrilla warfare which were entitled *The Art of Guerrilla Warfare*, *The Partisan Leader's Handbook*, and *How to Use High Explosives*, and which were intended for the actual fighting partisan, tactical and not strategic. My

34

difficulty was that, strangely enough, there was not a single book to be found in any library in any language which dealt with this subject."

Millis Jefferis had already been attached to Section D's technical branch where, in cooperation with Lt. Commander Langley, RN, he was producing the prototypes of sabotage devices. In the late spring Holland and Gubbins wrote papers on the theory and practice of guerrilla warfare, working in strictest secrecy in Section D's offices at 2, Caxton Street, Westminster, a stone's throw from SIS HQ in Broadway Buildings. Like Holland, Gubbins made fun of Section D's obsession with security, and of the eccentricities of its head, Laurence Grand, with his black homburg hat, dark glasses, tapered cigarette holder and all the paraphernalia of the 'spy master' of popular fiction. Nevertheless he enjoyed his time in Caxton Street, liked and admired Holland and found the revolutionary nature of their work exhilarating. About Section D itself his feelings were mixed: while often aghast at the amateurishness and sheer extravagance of some of its wilder projects, he enjoyed the company of enterprising young businessmen used to cutting corners and to taking risks. If their approach at times seemed unprofessional, it was also a welcome change from the ponderous hierarchy and financial stringency of the pre-war War Office.

Hitler's occupation of Prague in March, 1939, had lent fresh impetus to the work of GS(R) and, after Chamberlain's guarantee of Polish independence on 31 March, the DCIGS decided that the time had come to give formal support to Holland's recommendations and to re-integrate GS(R) in the General Staff. With Gubbins now established (since 4 April, 1939) as his assistant, Holland was authorized to expand his section and also to earmark suitable British personnel for special employment, to arrange for the latter to be given training in sabotage and the theory of guerrilla warfare and, where necessary, to be commissioned in the Officers' Emergency Reserve in advance of general mobilization. Finally, under the pretext of exploiting the potential intelligence value of patriot forces, it was decided that Holland's section, while remaining for the time being in Caxton Street, should come under the supervision of the Director of Military Intelligence, Major-General F. G. Beaumont-Nesbitt, and in future be known as Military Intelligence (Research) MI(R).

Holland was content with this arrangement. Apart from giving him access to secret information essential for MI(R) planning, it simplified the recruitment of personnel. The DMI was responsible for the deployment of all military intelligence resources including the appointment of military attachés and their staffs and, on mobilization, for the recruitment of civilians with special qualifications to supplement the linguists and other regular officers earmarked for intelligence duties on the outbreak of war. These personnel matters were the responsibility of a section headed by another of Holland's friends, Lieutenant-Colonel Gerald Templer, Royal Irish Fusiliers. On receiving his new instructions, Holland dropped all the other research functions and concentrated on producing various reports for the DMI dealing with irregular warfare. Gubbins meanwhile concentrated on recruiting polar explorers, British expatriate business men, oil executives and regular officers with special qualifications, and preparing a syllabus for three MI(R) training courses which it was proposed to hold during the second half of June. It was intended, in Holland's words, that "these gentlemen should accompany any military missions we might send to any other countries in order to form, as it were, the 'left wing' of their missions and to maintain contact with any elements that might be able to operate behind the Germans".

The activities of MI(R) during the first six months of 1939 are summarized in *GS(R) Report No. 8 'Investigation of the Possibilities of Guerrilla Activities'*, which enclosed Gubbins' training manuals with a note that "the translation of these manuals into various languages is being investigated, and a German translation is already in hand". Annexed to Holland's memorandum was a report on a flying visit made by Gubbins to Poland, Roumania and the Baltic States, a report by Jefferis on the state of production of sabotage devices and, thirdly, a section dealing with the progress of Recruitment and Training. This section noted that it was planned to hold three courses, perhaps sixty students in all. These training courses would provide an opportunity for choosing a few very carefully selected individuals who would be sent abroad, "their expenses being met from funds which have generously been made available for us from another organization". The section concluded prophetically, "even so, it must be remembered that we are still only dealing with likely Englishmen. There is much more to do in establishing contact with possible national leaders and movements. In fact, while we may be able to provide for the T. E. Lawrences, we have also to find the Feisals and provide them with opportunities."

In July Gubbins was officially notified that on mobilization he would be GSO1 and Chief of Staff of a British Military Mission to Poland to which it was proposed to attach a sizeable MI(R) element for whose activities, if overrun by the Germans, he would be personally responsible.

On receipt of these orders, he paid a second visit to Warsaw and made contact with Polish Intelligence. There is some evidence that he secretly visited Belgrade, the centre of Section D's Balkan operations. When he returned to London on 19 August, Intelligence suggested that the Germans would invade Poland before the end of the month. Accordingly Holland obtained the CIGS's permission to muster the MI(R) elements of missions for Poland and Roumania without waiting for general mobilization. The telegrams ordering them to report immediately to the War Office were despatched on 22 August. It was not a moment too soon: on the following day Joachim von Ribbentrop and Vyacheslav Molotov signed the German-Soviet Non-Aggression Pact in Moscow. The fate of Poland was now sealed and Gubbins' immediate task was to get the MI(R) element to Warsaw before the German invasion took place.

6

THE POLISH MISSION

The shock waves caused by the Ribbentrop-Molotov Pact were still reverberating around Whitehall when a small group of regular and reserve officers met in the War Office on 24 August, 1939. They were to form the MI(R) element of No. 4 Military Mission to Poland, and they had met for a briefing from Colonel Templer. The Head of the Mission was the redoubtable General (Sir) Adrian Carton de Wiart, a familiar figure in Poland between the wars and first known to Gubbins at Arras in 1917. The General was already in Warsaw, and with the Service attachés, the language officers and some locally recruited British residents he had formed the nucleus of the Military Mission. To complete the establishment, all that remained was for Gubbins to arrive with what Holland had described as the 'left wing' element.

Gubbins had not been the first choice as Carton de Wiart's chief of staff. However, when it was decided to include an MI(R) element, Holland recommended Gubbins as being the only officer who could combine the functions of GSO1 and future guerrilla leader. Gubbins had had the opportunity for what he described as 'a quick look round' during his second visit to Warsaw earlier in the month but he still had to brief himself on the latest strategic and political developments. That this briefing was far from satisfactory was not Gubbins' fault. In July, 1939, the Chiefs of Staff had warned the Committee of Imperial Defence that the fate of Poland must depend on the ultimate outcome of the war, and that would depend on the Allied ability to defeat Germany in the long run, not to relieve pressure on Poland at the outset. Moreover, although discussions with the French were proceeding, no agreement had been reached on the crucial question of whether targets in Germany should be bombed in reprisal for German air raids on Poland. This indecision was to prove a constant embarrassment to Carton de Wiart, Gubbins and members of the Mission in the days to come. Nor, it was agreed, were there any means of Britain being able to provide material support: aircraft which had been ordered and packed were in fact never to reach Poland at all. As late as 28 August, a number of Hurricanes were held up in Denmark because of a wrangle with HM Treasury over who should pay their onward carriage to Poland.

Despite all this, the War Office stressed the importance of inspiring confidence among the Poles; the irony was not lost on the members of No. 4 Military Mission.

At this late stage it was considered inadvisable for British officers to travel across Germany; and at a time when Mr Chamberlain was making his final bid to preserve the peace, it was feared that the arrival in Sweden of a British military mission bound for Warsaw might be taken by Hitler as an act of provocation. It was therefore arranged that the MI(R) party should travel to Egypt, as inconspicuously as possible, by the same means as a number of officers and senior officials who had been recalled to duty in India and the Middle East.

The journey across France took thirty-six hours; it was hot and uncomfortable and notable for the almost interminable halts while priority was given to French troop trains. In contrast to the peacetime calm still prevailing at Newhaven, French railway stations were thronged with reservists, which British officers with memories of 1914 took as a sign that the French meant business. At Marseilles, HMS *Shropshire*, a County class cruiser, was waiting with steam up and cast off as soon as the last man was aboard. Only the most senior officers were allotted cabins; the remainder slept on deck which was no hardship under the Mediterranean stars as *Shropshire* steamed at speed along the North African coast. The Polish Mission, however, enjoyed the privacy of an open ship's boat in which they kept their secret papers under officer guard. After a brief call at Malta, HMS *Shropshire* docked at Alexandria early on 31 August.

By now the German invasion of Poland was expected hourly and Gubbins was ordered to leave for Warsaw without delay. An Imperial Airways flying boat was chartered and the Royal Air Force, with some reluctance, provided two additional Short Sunderland flying boats. At first light on 1 September, the three aircraft took off for Athens. On landing at Piraeus, however, and learning that the Germans had crossed the Polish frontier, the three flying boats – as instructed – unloaded their cargo and returned forthwith to Egypt, leaving the MI(R) party stranded on the quayside at Piraeus surrounded by their personal kit and eighteen large packing-cases containing their signals equipment. In desperation Gubbins appealed to the Polish Minister, who promptly requisitioned two Lockheed Electra aircraft belonging to Lot, the Polish national airline, which were fortunately staging in Athens *en route* for Bucharest and Haifa respectively. Having arranged for the bulk of the radio equipment to follow on by sea to Roumania, Gubbins collected his party and drove out to Tatoi airport. Brushing aside the voluble protests of the Greek police, they drove straight on to the tarmac, helped the crew load the baggage and took off immediately, ignoring urgent radio signals from the airport authorities instructing them to return to complete formalities. After a refuelling stop at Salonika, the two aircraft landed at Bucharest where, at the Athenée Palace hotel, the members of the MI(R) party spent their first comfortable night since leaving England.

Bucharest was full of rumours but none reliable. However, stopping at Cernauti to refuel, it was confirmed that the German air force had bombed airfields near Warsaw and had left most of them out of action. It seemed prudent to continue the journey overland and, after a sumptuous luncheon provided by the Polish consul, a fleet of taxis conveyed the party to the Polish frontier. It was a glorious summer afternoon: the ox carts bringing in the harvest and the golden clusters of ripe maize hanging from the balconies of the Bessarabian farm houses giving an impression of timeless peace and prosperity. Yet, once across the River Dniester, the scene changed abruptly, the blacked-out windows and reservists waiting to rejoin the colours providing ample evidence that Poland was at war.

The arrival of the Mission at the frontier caused consternation. The passenger train to Lwow had already departed, and no other was due until the following day. However, an antiquated first-class coach, located in a distant siding, was coupled to a local goods train. In this ancient relic of the former Austro-Hungarian empire, its plush upholstery still faintly redolent of Central European cigar smoke, the Mission trundled through the night along the single track railway which, less than a fortnight later, was to become Poland's only rail link with the outside world.

Arriving early next morning at Lwow, the party were met by a liaison officer and a motor bus, were given breakfast and then taken on a brief visit to a hospital and a school which had been damaged by air raids the previous day. Gubbins was visibly embarrassed when asked what the British Government proposed to do about the wanton bombing of open cities. At Lublin, where they stopped for lunch, news was received that Britain had declared war on Germany. It was an enormous relief to every member of the party, and haste was made to change into uniform. Emerging amid cheers and showers of flowers, Hugh Curteis, a member of the Mission, in his tartan trews, attracted particular attention from the Lublin ladies and also from a stalwart black-bearded man who hugged him and kissed him warmly on both cheeks.

The outskirts of Warsaw were reached as dusk was falling. Isolated fires could be seen burning in the industrial suburbs, but the centre of the city did not appear to have been badly bombed. People thronged the streets and squares; cafés were crowded; there were long queues at the news-stands. From the nonchalance of the Poles it was hard to believe that their country was already almost beyond help; their air force virtually annihilated, their forward troops outflanked, their munition factories destroyed or overrun.

It was with a sense of modest achievement that Gubbins and the 'left wing' element of the Military Mission reported to General Carton de Wiart on 3 September, 1939, barely six hours after Chamberlain's announcement of Britain's declaration of war on Germany. Nevertheless, the speed of the German advance was dictating Gubbins' every move. An understandable sense of grievance among the Polish General Staff overshadowed the discussions which Gubbins attended with Carton de Wiart. To add insult to injury the BBC news bulletins gave more coverage to British football results than to events in Poland; which prompted a long and somewhat emotional personal signal from Gubbins to Holland which ended "and must football go on?"

As the Poles revealed the extent of the losses they had suffered during the first few days of the war and their formidable list of requirements, it was clear to both sides that there was no way in which these losses could be made good in time, and Gubbins decided to send Tommy Davies (formerly of MI(R)) back to London via the Baltic States to explain personally to the CIGS the desperate state in which the Poles now found themselves, a state which exceeded the War Office's most gloomy predictions. On a more practical level, it was clear that no time should be lost in making the Mission mobile since the speed of the German advance made it imperative that they should be ready to move at the shortest notice. Almost every spare car in Warsaw had been requisitioned. However, MI(R) had arranged for a fund of gold sovereigns to be available at the Embassy for the use of future resistance groups, and this enabled the Mission to purchase for cash two new American motor cars and a five-ton diesel truck.

On the morning of 5 September Gubbins and General Carton de Wiart met the Polish Deputy Chief of Staff and the Director of Military Intelligence "who", reported Gubbins, "could tell us very little indeed as the battle was so fluid and Polish communications were already out of action". Later that morning, however, Gubbins was informed that the Polish General Staff was leaving Warsaw and that accommodation had been arranged for the British Mission at Lukow, a small town about fifty miles south-east of Warsaw. Neither the Embassy nor the Mission had had a chance to rehearse its role and that afternoon the scene was chaotic. Inside the Embassy cases of the Ambassador's wine lay abandoned in the hall, his butler was in tears and the steps were littered with all sorts of personal kit, including an immaculate pair of polo boots belonging to an officer of the Life Guards who had been on attachment to the Polish cavalry. In the forecourt General Carton de Wiart had taken personal charge of the loading and during a lull in the anti-aircraft fire his voice was heard loud and clear, *"Mon Dieu, les ressorts,* where is that fellow Buggins?"

At Lukow, which was already filled with civilian refugees, the Mission was billeted in two small villas and a school. Here, the following afternoon, news came that the Polish General Staff was now established at Brzešz nad Bugiem. Accordingly, at first light on 7 September, Gubbins, accompanied by Wilkinson, set out to make contact. Marshal Smigly-Rydz, the Commander-in-Chief, and his Chief of Staff, General Stachiewicz, had remained for the time being in Warsaw; however, Gubbins called on General Malinowski, the Deputy Chief of Staff, and on the Directors of Operations and Intelligence. The news was bad. Polish troops were withdrawing all along the line and Warsaw was seriously threatened. Without air defence, without even her arms factories, Poland now depended entirely on her allies, the British and the French; from their attitude, they appeared clearly to understand that this was a forlorn hope.

Gubbins and Wilkinson returned to Lukow, which had been bombed; the wife of the Passport Control Officer had been killed, the first, and in the event the Mission's only casualty. They learned that General Carton de Wiart had decided to move his headquarters to Adampol near Wlodawa, an estate which belonged to his friend Count Zamoyski. Meanwhile, early next morning Gubbins and Wilkinson had set out again for Brzešz. In the darkness of the blackout Wilkinson narrowly missed running into a bomb crater but Gubbins remained imperturbable. There was little fresh news to be had and they reached Adampol early in the afternoon. The Zamoyskis were doing everything possible to make the Mission feel at home. They not only provided hot baths but invited the officers to tea, and it might well have been a week-end party at an English country house; children and dogs much in evidence and everybody too well-mannered to discuss the war.

Late that night Gubbins and Wilkinson went back to Brzešz where they were shown into a large hall in the centre of Brzešz fortress where the Operations Staff had set up their office. At one end of the long table were the remains of a meal; at the other, and just out of Gubbins' sight, were spread the maps giving the latest Polish dispositions for which the War Office was clamouring, but which the Poles, mistrustful of the security of British ciphers, were reluctant to communicate in detail. The Director of Operations had been talking for about ten minutes when there was a slight stir in the doorway. Everyone stood up as a group of officers entered, headed by Marshal Smigly-Rydz, the Commander-in-Chief, who had that evening arrived from Warsaw. He was a dapper, balding little man, who moved briskly and looked rather like a retired naval commander and not at all the swashbuckling figure portrayed in the press. Addressing the Polish officers and certainly unaware that there were foreigners present – Gubbins was in the far corner of the room – the Marshal made a very short speech. Despite the desperate efforts of the defenders, the German advance was continuing unchecked. He had therefore ten minutes ago ordered a general withdrawal to the line of the San, Vistula and Bug. At the same time he had given orders for the divisions covering Warsaw to stand and fight it out. He then turned on his heel and left the room. His departure was followed by a shocked silence. Gubbins and Wilkinson left as soon as they decently could to report to General Carton de Wiart and by signal to the War Office.

The Marshal's decision to withdraw his main forces meant the end of the Mission's comfortable stay at Adampol, and the departure of the Polish General Staff from Brzeŝz for yet another undisclosed destination posed a problem as to whether the Mission should move northwards or southwards in its withdrawal to the east. The General was all for going north-east towards his home in the Pripet Marshes, an area where, he was convinced, the Poles should be able to hold out almost indefinitely against the German armoured columns. Gubbins favoured withdrawal to the south-east, feeling that at this stage the first duty of the Polish General Staff would be to remain tied to the Stanislawow-Cernauti railway, their only source of supplies from the West. Carton de Wiart reluctantly agreed with him.

The Mission moved to Strusow, some ten miles south of Tarnopol. On 13 September Gubbins and the Air Attaché went to Lwow to make contact with General Sosnkowski, commanding the South, but the General was not there. Next day the British Embassy was located at Krzemeniec "in a fine state of flap", but the whereabouts of the Polish General Staff remained unknown for days until, driving through Miynow, Gubbins was lucky enough to catch sight of Colonel Smolenski, the Director of Intelligence.

Smolenski told Gubbins that the main Polish headquarters was already heading south towards the Roumanian frontier; the northern front had collapsed, the units in the centre were inextricable and there was now a serious threat to the southern flank. They were facing total defeat. This time Gubbins was told the new location of Polish headquarters: it was to be set up at Kolomija, the frontier station where less than a fortnight previously Gubbins and his party had entrained for Lwow *en route* for Warsaw.

When Gubbins returned to Strusow late that evening General Carton de Wiart had already ordered the Mission to move south the following day. At first light next morning Gubbins and Wilkinson left for Kolomija and had a short meeting with the Chief of Staff. Freely admitting that he had no knowledge of the battle, General Stachiewicz confirmed the Polish plan for withdrawal into a bridgehead on the Roumanian frontier, there to make a last stand against the German invaders. It was a gallant effort but, as Gubbins knew, doomed to failure.

When, on 16 September, General Carton de Wiart and Gubbins saw the Chief of Staff again, he insisted that, despite its obvious disadvantages, the line selected for holding, from the River Dniester to the River Stryj, was the most advanced possible until the arrival of reinforcements. He repeated his plea for action by the Royal Air Force. General Stachiewicz also mentioned that he had been unable to establish communication with General Dembinski's headquarters on the River Stryj for lack of radio equipment. Gubbins was quick to offer one of the mobile sets which he had brought out from England and for which he had so far found no use. While the equipment was unpacked and tested, Gubbins, accompanied by Curteis and Wilkinson, set out to visit the front line. General Dembinski appeared confident and relaxed; his sector was quiet and earlier that morning his troops had driven the Germans out of one of their forward positions. Moreover, news had just been received that General Sosnkowski had put in a successful counter-attack against one of the German armoured divisions surrounding Lwow, capturing over a hundred tanks. Gubbins asked to have a look at some of the forward positions. He did not get far; the main bridges had already been demolished, the oil wells set on fire and the railway bridge at Stryj destroyed. On the way back a sentry stopped the car and asked for identity papers. An elderly reserve major appeared and, in French, Gubbins asked him about his dispositions. The major told him that he was commanding an artillery battery. When Gubbins then asked where his guns were, he answered sadly that his unit had been mobilized when war began and that he believed the guns were still in England. But, he added, his officers had their pistols and there were a few rifles.

Back at Dembinski's headquarters, Gubbins was shown the latest situation reports and Dembinski mentioned, almost as an afterthought, that he had just heard that Soviet troops had crossed the Polish frontier at several points. Leaving Curteis, who spoke fluent French and Russian, to act as a liaison officer with Dembinski, Gubbins and Wilkinson returned to Kolomija. General Stachiewicz was alone, his office lit by a single candle. Obviously on the verge of total exhaustion, he listened to the news Gubbins brought from Dembinski's headquarters, and agreed that the Russians showed no signs of halting. He had given orders that they were not to be opposed, he said; but in a sudden bitter outburst he inveighed against Soviet treachery, seeing the Russian invasion as a stab in the back just when the German assault seemed to be running out of steam. *"Hier soir,"* he remarked bitterly, *"j'ai cru pour la premiére fois que mes plans allaient se realiser."* It was not a view that Gubbins shared, but with exquisite courtesy he sympathized with the stricken Chief of Staff, praising the gallantry and dedication of the Polish Army in their fight against hopeless odds and promising that Britain would fight on until Poland was once more free. He left no doubt that as far as he was concerned it was a point of honour.

By the time Gubbins and Wilkinson got back to Kosow the advance party was already on the point of leaving and after a hasty meal, their last on

Polish soil, the remaining members of the Mission set off with Gubbins in the lead. The British convoy was immediately caught up in the traffic, both military and civilian, men, women and children all heading south. At one stage the column came to a dead stop, and Gubbins and Wilkinson went ahead to see what was happening. The block consisted of no more than a dozen trucks and cars jammed together, their drivers slumped in exhaustion or apathy, unable to sort themselves out. By a process of persuading and cajoling, the blockage was disentangled but not before a Polish officer had drawn his pistol on Wilkinson.

"Who are you, giving orders to Poles? What are you doing in Poland?"

The officer was soon placated but as Gubbins remarked bitterly, walking back to their car, what *were* they doing in Poland? What had Britain done to help the Poles?

Two hours later the last member of No. 4 Military Mission had crossed into Roumania – all now in civilian clothes, much to the disgust of General Carton de Wiart. Splitting up and following different routes, the party set off for Bucharest. There they gradually assembled on the lawn in front of the British Legation, travel-stained and with baggage that made no pretence of being diplomatic, while arrangements were made to house them until they could leave for home.

Gubbins was lunching with the Yugoslav Military Attaché when he learnt of the murder of Calinescu, the Roumanian Prime Minister. This abortive *coup*, engineered according to German propaganda by the British Legation, made it more urgent to get the members of No. 4 Mission out of the country. Thanks to the infinite resource of Lieutenant-Colonel Geoffrey MacNab, the Military Attaché and, it must be said, the strength of the pound sterling on the Black Market, passages were booked for the main party on SS *Constanca*, a luxury liner leaving for Alexandria via Istanbul the following night. Gubbins stayed on in Bucharest for a further week to help General Carton de Wiart write up the official report of the Polish campaign.

7

THE MI(R) MISSION IN PARIS

The final draft of the despatch on the Polish campaign was finished. General Carton de Wiart, a conspicuous figure in any circumstances, insisted he was travelling *incognito* when with Gubbins and the Service attachés he boarded the Simplon-Orient express at Bucharest. They arrived in London on 4 October.

By this time all the good jobs with the British Expeditionary Force had been filled; nor was there a suitable appointment in the War Office for someone of Gubbins' rank. The Polish campaign had not brought much credit to the Military Mission. General Carton de Wiart's perceptive despatch was received with varying degrees of scepticism, since it seemed inconceivable that the German panzer tactics could succeed against such a sophisticated defence as the Maginot Line. Moreover the work of the Mission had been confined to normal military liaison and the so-called 'left-wing' element, now languishing in Cairo and due to return by sea, was still unblooded. Gubbins' discussions with the Poles during his visits in June and August had been confined to general views on guerrilla warfare and no joint plans had been made; to have raised the question of stay-behind parties once the campaign had started might have seemed defeatist. In any case the situation had developed too rapidly to have contemplated joint planning. It was a disappointing story and the General Staff's scepticism was reflected in the fact that the names of the members of the Mission Mentioned in Despatches were not gazetted until 31 January, 1941.

In the circumstances, Gubbins jumped at Holland's suggestion that he should continue working for MI(R) in a joint endeavour to establish contact with Polish and Czech underground forces. These clandestine activities were understood to be under the direction of the Polish and Czech General Staffs now established in Paris. Consequently, on 20 November, Gubbins set out for Paris as head of a reconstituted No 4 Military Mission to the Polish and Czech Armies in France. He took with him Captain Lloyd-Johnes, leaving Peter Wilkinson as rear link in MI(R).

There was sufficient routine work – translating and transmitting to

London voluminous studies by the Poles on various aspects of the recent campaign – to justify the presence of No 4 Mission, but the French military authorities remained sceptical and suspicious that Gubbins was more concerned with covert activities than with normal military liaison. These suspicions were confirmed by the fact that when visiting the Hotel Regina, the Polish headquarters, Gubbins spent much of his time with Colonel Stanislav Gano of the Polish *Deuxième Bureau*. He and Gano had met in Warsaw that summer and during their discussions about irregular warfare they had become firm friends.

Naturally, Gano kept Gubbins fully briefed about the evolving resistance in Poland. In theory it was controlled from Paris by the Polish government-in-exile, led by General Sikorski as Prime Minister; in reality, however, the difficulty of communication meant that effective control lay in the hands of the Commander of the newly constituted Home Army and his regional subordinates. Therefore Gubbins could best help the Poles by securing material aid, most urgent of all being radio transmitters and automatic pistols. He returned to London to see what could be arranged.

At this period the only source of secret wireless equipment was the SIS. Gubbins indented for eight sets for the Poles, only to be told that two might be available by early February, 1940; no more could be expected before the late spring. In any case the SIS type of transmitter was technically unsuitable for the Poles' needs. As for automatic pistols, the British Army had never had any use for them and none could be provided from War Office stores. Instead, the Poles were offered .38 revolvers, whose bulk and shape were unsuited to clandestine use and which fired rimmed ammunition not available in Central Europe. The Poles, amazed at the British failure to supply such simple items, concluded that it was more likely due to unwillingness than inability.

Then there was the question of transport. The Poles expected the British to deliver any material destined for the Home Army to Polish agents in Budapest and Bucharest. MI(R) had no secret channels of its own, transport arrangements in Eastern Europe being exclusively in the hands of the SIS. While in London Gubbins called on Laurence Grand. At first Grand seemed happy to help: "We can send in wagonfuls, my dear Colin, wagonfuls." But he was unwilling to divulge the capacity of Section D's secret supply lines, and wanted to know in detail the quantities and measurements of the material involved – information that Gubbins was unable to supply. In fact, the situation was resolved with the help of Holland. It was arranged that Wilkinson – under a false name – should liaise directly with the Balkan section of D's organization which at that time was headed by George Taylor. Taylor was not only one of the ablest members of Section D but he also had a considerable respect for Gubbins, a respect which came to be reciprocated.

Yet, even so, the secret channels operated by Section D could take only a trickle compared with the thousand kilos per month handled by the clandestine courier service set up by the Poles from Budapest.

The Czechs' requirements were less immediate. They had an advantage over the Poles in having had six months to organize their underground network before war broke out. Between March and September, 1939, they had stockpiled a considerable quantity of arms and explosives. The Czech National Committee had not yet been recognized by the Foreign Office as the representative government-in-exile and, so far as the British were concerned, the main Czech asset was their intelligence service under Colonel Moravec, who had escaped to England in March, 1939, and was now operating under the wing of the SIS.

All attempts by MI(R) to get in touch directly with Moravec were blocked by the SIS, on the understandable grounds that such contact might not only complicate relations with the Czechs but might prejudice security. Gubbins decided to short-circuit the SIS and in early December, 1939, he took Wilkinson with him to meet General Ingr, the C-in-C, at his headquarters in Paris. It emerged at this meeting that the Czechs had both material and agents, primarily based in Belgrade, and a regular courier service running from Yugoslavia across Austria. There being some five thousand Czech nationals living in Yugoslavia, they had the advantage of a favourably disposed Yugoslav government. Moreover, in Paris, the Czech General Staff had a secret radio link with the Protectorate which passed up to forty telegrams a day independently of Moravec's intelligence link. Thus, while keen in principle to get any arms and material they could lay their hands on, the Czechs showed little enthusiasm for the limited sort of aid that Gubbins could offer them. However, Gubbins was able to confirm that it was commonly agreed between the Czech headquarters in Paris and the headquarters of the Home Army that for the foreseeable future Czech resistance should remain no more than a potential threat and that it should conserve its forces for a general uprising at the appropriate time.

For the four winter months he was in Paris, Gubbins lived a life of comparative luxury. His flat on the top floor of 88, Rue de Varennes belonged to an absentee American, was well furnished and overlooked the garden of the Musée Rodin. Besides a housekeeper who was an admirable cook, Gubbins was provided with a large Renault saloon and a driver, Corporal Dickinson, who also acted as his soldier servant.

In contrast to the long hours worked at the War Office, Gubbins finished in good time for a bath and a cocktail at the Ritz or Crillon Bar, followed by dinner at a variety of restaurants, and occasionally a night-club patronized by the White Russian community. On one occasion Wilkinson accompanied him: they drank pink champagne and when the band leader came to play at their table Gubbins in his lieutenant-colonel's uniform gave a lusty performance of *Ochi chornye* and *Stanka razin*, to the astonishment of the other patrons.

However, by the turn of the year, Gubbins started to feel restless. The essential liaison with the Poles and Czechs had been established and their requirements stated in general terms: so far as the MI(R) side of his work was concerned, there was little left for him to do. For various reasons, not least the antipathy of the French authorities, he had made no effort to carry out the conventional duties of a liaison mission, for example by visiting the Polish and Czech training units which had been set up under French command, nor had he visited the Polish divisions in the rear of the Maginot Line. Meanwhile the crucial function of the Mission in its MI(R) role, the procurement of material and its delivery to despatch points in Eastern Europe, was being organized in London in cooperation with Section D. If MI(R) was to have any direct influence over the activities of the Polish and Czech Secret Armies, it was essential to step up the volume of supplies.

Early in the New Year, at Taylor's suggestion, Gubbins sent Wilkinson to inspect existing arrangements in Belgrade, Budapest and Bucharest. On his return he reported that Section D's representatives were unlikely ever to be in a position to meet the Poles' and Czechs' requirements on any significant scale and that if No 4 Military Mission was to fulfil its MI(R) function it would need to set up its own organization. The simplest solution, which was also favoured by HM representatives in Budapest and Belgrade, was for an assistant military attaché to be appointed, answerable to MI(R), whose main task would be the support of the Polish and Czech Secret Armies. This arrangement offered considerable advantages to MI(R), not least the use of Foreign Office communication facilities independently of SIS, but, before they came into force, Gubbins had been recalled to London, and on 23 March, 1940, Wilkinson, now an Acting Major, took charge of No 4 Military Mission.

8

THE NORWEGIAN CAMPAIGN

Although the German assault on Norway on 9 April, 1940, was carried out with a speed and precision that took the Allies by surprise, it had been known for weeks that the Germans were preparing an invasion. Moreover we, too, had plans to send an Expeditionary Force to Narvik, and had earmarked two divisions for this operation which was planned for 20 March. When, however, on 12 March, the Finns concluded an armistice with the Soviet Union, the majority of the troops involved were allowed to proceed to France. Nevertheless, contingency planning continued and, in particular, MI(R) was instructed to make plans for amphibious raids on Norway's western seaboard. Holland immediately summoned Gubbins from Paris and put him in charge of preparing and training the selected assault troops.

Gubbins decided that a normal infantry battalion was too large, and an infantry company too small; moreover, neither was equipped or trained for the purpose. Consequently, when Holland submitted his proposals to the CIGS on 13 April, he recommended that the Lovat Scouts should be reorganized and specially trained to operate as raiding parties. The Commanding Officer, Lieutenant-Colonel Leslie Melville, strongly objected to his regiment being dismembered in this way. When the project was discussed further with the Director of Staff Duties (DSD) on 15 April, Holland produced a draft establishment, prepared in MI(R), for special units to be known as Independent Companies, which would be armed and equipped to operate in a totally independent role for periods of up to one month. This proposal was accepted, and volunteers for as many as ten Independent Companies were called for from units in the United Kingdom which had completed their training and were waiting to be sent to France. Gubbins was the obvious choice to command this scratch force.

On 20 April formal approval was given to these arrangements and five days later No 1 Independent Company, formed from 52 Division, moved to Scotland, where it was joined by Gubbins and his headquarters staff. On 27 April they embarked at Rosyth in HMS *Arethusa* but were recalled to Scapa the following day, re-embarked in RMS *Orion* and SS *Royal Ulsterman* and eventually sailed on 1 May for Mo. Gubbins meanwhile was ordered to report to HQ North-West Expeditionary Force in London.

Here, on 2 May, Gubbins received his orders from the Force Commander, General Massy. He was to assume command of SCISSORSFORCE, comprising Nos 1, 3, 4 and 5 Independent Companies, and was given the task of preventing the Germans occupying the towns of Bodö, Mo and Mosjöen. Massy, mindful that the Independent Companies were only lightly armed, instructed Gubbins not to attempt frontal engagements, but to harass the enemy's flanks and lines of communication. He also promised that eight Indian Army officers, with experience of mountain warfare, would be attached.

Nos 3, 4 and 5 Independent Companies duly embarked at Gourock in SS *Ulster Prince*, and were joined by Gubbins and his headquarters staff late on 4 May. At 9.30 am the following morning *Ulster Prince* sailed for Bodö.

The headquarters element of SCISSORSFORCE was roughly comparable in size to the headquarters of a regular infantry brigade, and Gubbins was previously acquainted with most of his staff. His Brigade Major, Captain Urquhart, was a regular Sapper; his Intelligence Officers consisted of Captain Andrew Croft and Lieutenant-Colonel Quintin Riley, RNVR, both Arctic explorers and holders of the Polar Medal who had originally been recruited and trained by MI(R). An unexpected supernumerary was Major Kermit Roosevelt, Scots Guards, nephew of President Theodore Roosevelt. He had served in the British Army in the First World War and had again volunteered his services in the Second. He was a valuable addition to the team, described by Croft as someone "six foot two inches tall, who looked flabby, but had the courage of a lion and a heart of gold and was much respected by the troops".

Gubbins was no less fortunate in his Company Commanders: May, Stockwell, Newman, Patterson and Peddie; and in his eight Indian Army officers. Some of the latter acted as staff officers and advisers at headquarters while others commanded platoons; all were first class and with their previous battle experience set an admirable example to the young Territorials in the Independent Companies. The Independent Companies consisted entirely of volunteers, mostly drawn from the Territorial Army. Each Company comprised twenty officers and 270 other ranks, organized into three platoons each of three sections. Each platoon was commanded by an officer. Each company had Royal Engineer and Signals personnel under command as well as a support section consisting of Bren guns, one Boyes anti-tank gun and some two-inch mortars. Although only lightly armed, they could operate for several days at a time in an independent role. However, their lack of heavy automatic weapons made them unsuitable for holding fixed positions or for employment in conventional rearguard actions.

During the three day voyage from the Clyde to Bodö, Gubbins wrote no less than five different operational orders; his final plan was for No 3 Independent Company and SCISSORSFORCE headquarters staff to go ashore at Bodö, while he himself, accompanied by Andrew Croft, sailed with Nos 4 and 5 Independent Companies direct to Mosjöen.

Land was sighted shortly after midnight on 8 May and everyone came up on deck. It was bitterly cold and a mixture of sleet and snow was falling. Nevertheless, despite the low cloud, the snow-covered hills were clearly discernible in the Arctic twilight. Nos 4 and 5 Independent Companies disembarked early that morning, the men so laden with their Arctic clothing and equipment they could hardly move. One of the Indian Army officers remembered hearing an angry shout from the bridge of one of the destroyer escort: "Get to hell off this ship, I've got to get moving before the bombers arrive". Drawn up on the quayside, awaiting embarkation, was a Company of French *Chasseurs Alpins*. Gubbins had been counting on this detachment to provide the ski troops to support his infantry, and he learned with dismay that they were being withdrawn on direct orders from Paris. The Company Commander, Captain Coche, told him that the Germans were some twenty miles south of Mosjöen, but that Norwegian resistance was crumbling, their troops apparently stunned by the rapidity of the enemy advance from Namsos. "In a panic" Gubbins noted tersely in his war diary. However, he learned from the local Norwegian commander, who had come down to greet the arrival of the British troops, that a detachment of the Royal Norwegian Army, consisting of seventy men and six machine guns, had temporarily halted the Germans at a village called Fallingfoss on the road to Grane. Taking Major Newman, Commander of No 5 Company, Gubbins set off for Fallingfoss where he urged the Commander of the Norwegian detachment to hold on until he could be relieved by No 5 Independent Company. He left one of the Indian Army officers to reconnoitre a new position south of Mosjöen covering the main road and the light railway from Grane; and returned to order up No 5 Independent Company. Fortunately, the Germans seemed in no hurry to follow up and No 5 Independent Company, though strafed and dive-bombed from the air, took up their defensive position without enemy interference. Early next morning a patrol of some sixty unsuspecting German cyclists was ambushed by a platoon of No 5 Company, commanded by Captain Prendergast, Indian Army, and nearly all were killed or wounded. It was not long before the German main body appeared and Gubbins ordered a general withdrawal. Prendergast, outflanked by Austrian mountain troops, withdrew five thousand yards or so. However, a second platoon, commanded by Captain Somerville, Indian Army, although surrounded by the enemy, succeeded in holding on to their position covering the railway until 9 pm that evening. Once night fell they too withdrew. No

5 Independent Company had done well in this first encounter with the enemy. However, the Independent Companies were not equipped for conducting a conventional rearguard action, and in mountain warfare were clearly no match for the Austrian ski troops operating on their flanks. The road from Mosjöen to Mo, down which Gubbins was expected to withdraw carrying out a series of delaying actions, was still covered in snow and negotiable only by ski troops. The situation of the two Independent Companies was rapidly becoming critical and Gubbins ordered their phased withdrawal to Mosjöen. By 10 pm this had been completed, but in the meantime Gubbins had decided that Mosjöen must be evacuated and that the only way out was by sea. Enemy air raids had emptied Mosjöen harbour of all shipping by day, and it was not until late on the evening of 10 May that Gubbins learned from his Norwegian interpreter that a coastal vessel of some 600 tons, the *Erling Jahl*, was lying ten miles down the fjord in readiness to evacuate the Norwegian garrison from Mosjöen. On board Gubbins found the Norwegian District Commander who had welcomed him the previous day, and persuaded him to transfer to a smaller ship. He then chartered *Erling Jahl* for five thousand krone and ordered the master to proceed up the fjord without delay to embark the Independent Companies at Mosjöen.

At about 1 am on 11 May *Erling Jahl* docked at Mosjöen. No 4 Company was ready to embark, but it was growing light and, fearing an air attack, Gubbins ordered the vessel to return to her anchorage down the fjord. With Andrew Croft, he then set off to round up No 5 Company which had taken up a position north of the town. It was 5 am before they returned. After fighting all the previous day and marching and countermarching all night in the sleet and snow, No 5 Independent Company "were exhausted, many having to be carried on board".[1] At 6 am the *Erling Jahl* sailed for Sandesjöen at the mouth of the fjord, where she lay up until the evening when two destroyers came to escort her. Gubbins and his staff transferred to HMS *Cossack* and the small convoy reached Bodö early on 12 May.

The whole expedition had lasted little more than seventy-two hours.

For Gubbins it had been an invaluable experience, giving him an insight into the characteristics of the Independent Companies, who had come well out of their first adventure. They had been sent to Norway to harass the flanks and lines of communication of the advancing Germans. In the only action of this sort − Prendergast's ambush − No 5 Independent Company had put up a good performance. However, the unexpected rapidity of the German advance, covering the 150 miles from Namsos to Mosjöen in seven days, and the virtual collapse of organized Norwegian resistance, rendered it impossible for the Independent Companies to be employed in a harassing role. "I did not expect much from the Independent Companies," wrote Auchinleck, Commander Land Forces, to General Dill, the newly appointed

CIGS. "To be a successful guerrilla, you must, I think, be a guerrilla in your own country."[2] In the circumstances, this was not altogether fair comment, and Auchinleck's subsequent decision "to coalesce them into a unit of light infantry, under Gubbins, and put them under the command of 24th Infantry Brigade" was to employ Independent Companies in a role for which they had already demonstrated that they were neither trained nor equipped.

On 14 May Gubbins received orders from Force Headquarters at Harstad that the Independent Companies were to be brigaded with 24th (Guards) Infantry Brigade under the command of Brigadier William Fraser. The immediate task of the Independent Companies was to keep the enemy at bay long enough for an airstrip at Bodö to be completed. While this may not have been a prospect which Gubbins altogether relished, at least he had a reasonable expectation of being able for the first time since his arrival in Norway to function from his own headquarters, which he had established in the school house of a hamlet called Hopen, ten miles east of Bodö. Here he was in direct communication with SCISSORSFORCE which was disposed as follows: No 1 Company, which it will be remembered had been sent direct to Mo, was now under command of Lieutenant-Colonel T. B. Trappes-Lomax, Scots Guards, who had been appointed Commander 1st Bn Scots Guards. No 2 Company had only arrived on 14 May and was for the time being at Bodö. No 3 Company was at Rognan, at the head of the Saltfjord which runs inland from Bodö, waiting to be relieved by the 1st Bn Irish Guards. No 4 Company was guarding the Saltfjord at Straumen Island, opposite Bodö. No 5 Company was resting at Bodö.

Meanwhile, Brigadier Fraser had felt uneasy at the prospect of sending his Brigade HQ, with the 1st Bn Irish Guards, to reinforce the garrison at Mo. Mo was at the end of a long, narrow fjord and, so long as the Germans had air superiority, the maintenance of the garrison was at best a risky business. Moreover, while the road from Mo to Bodö remained snowbound, it might prove difficult to disengage and withdraw from Mo if the enemy mounted a serious attack. Accordingly, on 14 May, he flew to Force HQ at Harstad, where his appreciation of the situation was accepted and orders given that his HQ and the Battalion should proceed to Bodö.

The Irish Guards were already on their way in small boats to Skaanland where they were to be embarked in the Polish M/V *Chobry*. Meanwhile Fraser, aboard HMS *Somali*, stopped at Bodö for a short meeting with Gubbins before re-embarking for Mo to brief Trappes-Lomax about the new arrangements. A few hours out, however, HMS *Somali* came under heavy air attack and was so badly damaged that she was forced to return direct to Scapa, carrying with her the unfortunate Brigadier. Two weeks previously, when Fraser had been slightly wounded during the attack on Narvik, the command of the Brigade had automatically devolved on Trappes-Lomax as senior Battalion Commander. It was impossible on this occasion to follow this procedure: first because Trappes-Lomax was now at Mo over a hundred miles from Brigade HQ, and secondly because Gubbins, now an Acting Colonel, was the senior officer in the composite force consisting of 24 Infantry Brigade and the Independent Companies. Thus it came about that on 15 May Gubbins assumed command of 24th (Guards) Infantry Brigade.

Almost immediately the arrangements which he had discussed with Fraser at their short meeting were upset. On 15 May, a few hours after leaving Skaanland with a destroyer escort, *Chobry* came under heavy air attack; a direct hit killed the Commanding Officer of the Irish Guards, his Adjutant, eight officers and one hundred men; all the Battalion's stores and equipment were lost. Gubbins and the Brigade Major, Walter Barttelot, Coldstream Guards, anxiously awaiting the Irish Guards at Bodö, were to learn that the force had been obliged to return to the base depot at Harstad to be completely re-equipped.

Two days later, on 17 May, the 1st Bn South Wales Borderers, comprising the third major unit of the Brigade, left Harstad on board HMS *Effingham*, the Admiral's flagship. The following day, travelling at speed, *Effingham* struck an uncharted rock. Although it subsequently proved possible for No 2 Independent Company to salvage some of the Battalion's vehicles, including several Bren carriers, the South Wales Borderers lost all their stores and, like the Irish Guards, were obliged to return to Harstad to re-equip. Being temporarily deprived of two out of three of his regular infantry battalions within seventy-two hours of taking command, Gubbins was fortunate indeed to have his Independent Companies to fall back on.

On 15 May, at SCISSORSFORCE HQ, Gubbins received Auchinleck's preliminary orders. These were signalled, with a promise that they would be amplified in a letter which would be sent by hand of Brigadier Gammell, his Chief of Staff. Unfortunately Gammell, aboard HMS *Effingham*, was forced to return to Harstad.

Auchinleck had clearly been impressed by Fraser's representations on 14 May. In the letter to Dill (already quoted) he had written: "The enemy bombers, if unmolested, can offset the value of sea power in these narrow waters... and can make the maintenance of small forces almost impossible unless we can provide an adequate counter in the air and on the ground." These arguments were to be echoed by Trappes-Lomax on several occasions, and Gubbins, too, was under no illusions about the difficulty of the task confronting the Scots Guards at Mo. He would have left at once for Mo had it not been for Gammell's impending visit. As it was, he spoke by telephone to Trappes-Lomax and gave him the gist of Auchinleck's orders. In reply, Trappes-Lomax said that, as there had been a diminution in enemy activities, he had decided to pull in No 1 Independent Company and incorporate it in the defence of Mo as a supernumerary infantry company of the Scots Guards.

When Gammell still failed to turn up, Gubbins informed Trappes-Lomax that he proposed to visit Mo next day. Trappes-Lomax asked him to telephone before he set out, saying that since they last spoke the situation had taken a turn for the worse and the Scots Guards' left flank was being threatened. He therefore asked whether C Company of his Battalion, which was carrying out guard duties at Bodö, might be returned at once. Far from reassured by Trappes-Lomax's report, Gubbins decided that he must see the situation for himself without delay. He gave instructions for the return of C Company and set off by car at 8.30 that evening, 18 May.

Mo was about 130 miles by road from Bodö, an uncomfortable drive at that time of the year. To start with, the road ran eastward along the north side of the Saltfjord and Skerstadfjord. At the head of the latter, where it was some three miles wide, there was a ferry which carried a few vehicles at a time to Rognan. From Rognan the road ran south up the valley of the Saltely to the tree line, thereafter crossing an open plateau still lightly covered with snow and ice; it was a bleak moorland landscape, affording no cover from enemy air attack during the long Arctic daylight. The snow-line proper was reached about thirty miles south of Rognan and for the next twenty miles traffic was restricted to a single track cut through snow-drifts, which were in places over twenty feet deep. This so-called snow-belt was at first sight a formidable obstacle and was to become something of an obsession with Colonel Trappes-Lomax, but by the middle of May its importance was apt to be exaggerated. After a stretch of open moorland, on the far side of the snow-belt, the road descended the narrow Rana valley to Mo.

Trappes-Lomax, like Gubbins, had served throughout the 1914-1918 war. He had held various staff appointments and in 1935 was chief instructor at the Royal Military College, Sandhurst. It was a conventional career which had led in 1939 to command of the 1st Battalion Scots Guards.

Gubbins' journey took seven hours; at 5 am he was received courteously by Trappes-Lomax, and by the Commander of the Norwegian contingent, who were awaiting his arrival. Gubbins expressed his regret that the unforeseen circumstances which had prevented Brigadier Fraser from returning to Norway and resuming his command had resulted in his being placed, although not a Guards officer, in command of the 24th (Guards) Brigade. He then went on to repeat Auchinleck's orders that Mo was to be held indefinitely and he asked Trappes-Lomax for his comments. These were that Mo without further support was untenable in present circumstances. Gubbins was impressed by these arguments, especially since they had been endorsed by Brigadier Fraser. Moreover, he was aware that owing to the temporary loss of the 1st Bn Irish Guards, and of the South

Wales Borderers, there was no likelihood of reinforcements reaching the Mo garrison in the foreseeable future. Accordingly, in Trappes-Lomax's presence, Gubbins telephoned to General Auchinleck at Harstad and secured his reluctant permission to abandon Mo. However, Auchinleck emphasized that it remained of the first importance to delay the enemy's advance northwards at least until the airfield at Bodö, which was near completion, was fit for service.

The enemy was not pressing his attack, and in Gubbins' opinion there seemed no reason for an immediate withdrawal. Trappes-Lomax, on the other hand, was eager to be off and in these circumstances Gubbins decided to accept the judgement of the man on the spot. The Mo garrison – known as TRAPPESCOL – comprised the 1st Bn Scots Guards, with No 1 Independent Company under command; one troop of field artillery with twenty-five pounder guns; one troop of anti-aircraft artillery armed with Bofors AA guns; one section of Royal Engineers and one section of Royal Signals. The Norwegian contingent was not under British command, but it was obvious that its withdrawal would have to be covered by 1st Bn Scots Guards, and Gubbins agreed that the sooner it was on its way the better. With Gubbins' approval therefore Trappes-Lomax issued immediate orders that the withdrawal should commence at 10 am that morning with the Norwegian contingent starting one hour earlier. There would be considerable administrative difficulties in maintaining TRAPPESCOL from 130 miles away, but Gubbins now knew from his own experience that the road was passable. He was understandably irritated by Trappes-Lomax's all too apparent lack of confidence in his ability to improvise an overland supply line across the snow-belt, and his irritation increased when he discovered that TRAPPESCOL had actually got four days' rations instead of the two which Trappes-Lomax had declared. However, once he had settled as many of the administrative arrangements as he could, he gave Trappes-Lomax written orders authorizing him to abandon Mo and set off to return to Hopen.

Ten miles north of Mo, in a hamlet called Rosvold, Gubbins met C Coy of 1st Bn Scots Guards on its way south from Bodö to rejoin the Battalion at Mo. Their motor-buses had experienced no difficulty crossing the snow-belt, and were in fact two hours ahead of schedule. The Company disembussed and took up a defensive position astride the road to cover TRAPPESCOL's arrival from Mo.

In his communications with the CIGS, Auchinleck had never made any secret of his anxiety about the situation at Mo. "If I have to let go at Mo, I will have a shot at getting it back as soon as I can," he had written on 15 May.[3] Nevertheless he was clearly put out by Gubbins' immediate recommendation to withdraw. "Bodö must be reinforced," he wrote to Dill, "particularly as the Mo detachment is being outflanked and must retreat, so Gubbins says. Why our soldiers cannot be as mobile as the Germans I don't know, but they aren't apparently. Anyhow I have had to accept Gubbins' recommendation, but have told him to resist all the way and fight hard."[4] Gubbins later described TRAPPESCOL's withdrawal as "precipitate". The bulk of stores and equipment was abandoned and no attempt made to destroy it; the troop of 25-pounders left behind all its cable and signals equipment; No 1 Independent Company, which was still in contact with the enemy south-west of the town, was given no orders to break off its action and the first indication its Commander had of the general withdrawal was when the Company of Scots Guards on his flank started to retire. B Company, Scots Guards, under Captain John Elwes, which was also in contact with the enemy but out of touch with Battalion HQ, was left to its fate, Trappes-Lomax later remarking to Gubbins that he never expected to see it again. It was only thanks to the local knowledge of a Swedish captain who had attached himself to the Company as a volunteer and to Elwes' resourcefulness that it succeeded in rejoining the Battalion the following day.

On his return to Hopen in the late afternoon of 18 May, Gubbins and his HQ staff concentrated on improvising means of provisioning TRAPPESCOL south of the snow-belt. Nevertheless he felt uneasy about the situation, and the following morning, at about 1 am, accompanied by Barttelot, he set out again to drive south. They reached TRAPPESCOL HQ at about 9 am on 19 May. Gubbins was disturbed to learn that the rearguard had broken off contact with the enemy and was now retiring northwards, having abandoned the position at Rosvold which he himself had reconnoitred the previous day. In the circumstances Gubbins, according to the SCISSORSFORCE war diary,[5] felt obliged to issue written orders that the Scots Guards were to oppose the enemy's advance to the utmost. On the other hand, according to Barttelot's account, Gubbins had had a discussion with him and Trappes-Lomax and there was general agreement that the withdrawal should continue. When, at about 11 am, Gubbins returned to Hopen, he left Barttelot to organize the withdrawal of the Norwegian contingent, No 1 Independent Company and the Field Ambulance Company by motor-coach across the snow-belt; with these Trappes-Lomax included the troop of field artillery, which he considered useless without their signals and cable equipment. Both Trappes-Lomax and Barttelot understood that the Scots Guards were to follow on next day to a position near Storjord on the northern side of the snow-belt. There was no contact with the enemy during 19 May and the Scots Guards continued gently withdrawing. By midday the heat was oppressive and the exhausted guardsmen threw away much of their Arctic clothing and equipment. TRAPPESCOL HQ was finally established in an inn two or three miles west of the town of Krokstrand with the Battalion holding a position a few miles south at Messingsletten Bridge. 1 Bn Scots Guards' situation report of 19 May, envisaging further withdrawal, caused Auchinleck considerable disquiet and he signalled Trappes-Lomax in very strong terms: "You have now reached a good position for defence. Essential to stand and fight .... I rely on Scots Guards to stop the enemy."[6] Auchinleck's anxiety was only partly relieved by a message from Gubbins, who telephoned the GSO1 at Force HQ (Colonel Dowler) to say that he had spent the day with Trappes-Lomax and was quite happy about the situation. Dowler told him about Trappes-Lomax's latest situation report and about Auchinleck's signal to Trappes-Lomax and reiterated the C-in-C's insistence on a fighting withdrawal. Gubbins replied that he fully understood and "during the day had pointed out to Trappes-Lomax that he did not altogether agree with his plan".[7] At midnight, still far from satisfied, Auchinleck spoke to Gubbins. He repeated the points which Dowler had made and the war diary records: "He understands what I want, I think, and is going to Mo to see Trappes-Lomax again. Again I told him to remove any officer not fit to command and replace him at his discretion."

On the morning of 20 May Gubbins received the letter[8] Auchinleck had written on 16 May and which Gammell had been unable to deliver. It now contained the following postscript dated 19 May:

"This was sent by hand of Gammell who was in *Effingham*; the instruction in it still holds good. Trappes-Lomax's last message merely says he is out of contact with the enemy and proposes to continue his retreat. Can he not stand and fight? The enemy cannot be *much* stronger than he is and he seems to be in ideal country for defence – a narrow valley with almost impassable hills on either side. The enemy must be stopped and I am sure he can be. When we have stopped him I want you to consider re-taking Mo. I am doing my utmost to send you reinforcements. You are at liberty to remove any commander of any rank whom you think is not resolute or willing to fight.
(signed) C. J. Auchinleck, Lt. Gen."

Somewhat rattled by the turn that events were taking, Gubbins set out again for Krokstrand, taking with him, this time, Captain Urquhart, Brigade Major of SCISSORSFORCE. However, before leaving he sent a reassuring situation report to Force HQ:[9]

"I have withdrawn 1st Independent Company from Scots Guards command to Saltdalen area as they have had heavy fighting and must be refitted.

"Visited Scots Guards yesterday 19 May and am on way down again now. Yesterday all quiet, but CO Scots Guards anxious to get back quickly behind the 'snow-belt' which commences about thirty miles south of Rognan, and is some twenty miles wide.

"OC Scots Guards should have no difficulty in holding up enemy for some time. If forced to retire from south of 'snow-belt' I can almost certainly lift him entire in two nights to north end of it where excellent defensive positions exist. I would use buses ....

"The road Rognan-Mo is for some distance very exposed, and liable to bombing. Surface is not good and road does constitute defile for greater part of its length.

"Will send further report as aircraft now overhead and destroyer must leave."

Despite this understandable attempt to reassure Auchinleck that he had everything under control, Gubbins soon found his own misgivings amply confirmed. After crossing on the Rognan ferry he was appalled by the number of stragglers he met north of the snow-belt. The officers and men — mostly RAMC, RE and RA — whom he stopped said that they had orders to find their own way back to Bodö. Gubbins immediately ordered No 1 Independent Company to place a stragglers' post on the Rognan ferry, and he and Urquhart turned back other men telling them to rejoin their units. Gubbins was particularly indignant when he came across the troop of 25-pounders "by the side of the road, out of range of the enemy". He considered it disgraceful that they should have been withdrawn north of the snow-belt since, even without their cable and signals equipment, the troop could have played a useful part in holding up the enemy advance as, indeed, it was to do five days later, firing over open sights.

The signal from Auchinleck ordering the Scots Guards to stand and fight did not reach Trappes-Lomax until 6 am on 20 May. Without waiting to consult Gubbins, Trappes-Lomax sent a long signal back to Force HQ giving no less than seven reasons why he could not comply with Auchinleck's order and stating that he proposed to proceed with his plan to retire across the snow-belt to Storjord. "I consider it far the wisest course to fight a series of rearguard actions commencing at Storjord and so conserve the Force to help defend the Bodö Peninsula."[10]

This was a travesty of the orders which Trappes-Lomax had received from Gubbins, who arrived about lunchtime and was understandably incensed that Trappes-Lomax should have sent a reply of this sort direct to Auchinleck without first consulting him. In order that there should be no misunderstanding he gave Trappes-Lomax a written order that there was to be no withdrawal unless the safety of the Scots Guards and attached troops was seriously endangered. He took the precaution in Trappes-Lomax's presence of telephoning Force HQ informing them of what he had done. Despite this direct order, some sort of cognitive gap seems to have remained between Gubbins and Trappes-Lomax. The latter, aware that his Battalion had come straight from public duties in London and was both untrained and unfit to fight a successful rearguard action, saw no point in risking lives trying to hold difficult defensive positions south of the snow-belt when more favourable terrain existed on the northern side. Moreover he seemed to have been unaware that, as substantial reinforcements were in process of landing at Bodö, it was desirable to hold the enemy south of the snow-belt in order to give time to deploy these reinforcements to cover the Scots Guards' eventual withdrawal.

Although Gubbins had refused point-blank to countenance any further withdrawal, Trappes-Lomax seems to have been unable to accept this direct order at its face value. In his war diary, Brigadier Fraser describes the situation as follows:

"As a result of this conference (with Gubbins) Walter Barttelot, who saw Trappes-Lomax immediately after it, understood that the order to stop the enemy had been modified and that the role of the Battalion was now to delay him as long as possible by occupying a series of rearguard actions; and that Trappes was empowered to withdraw if he considered that the safety of his troops was at stake."[11]

Before leaving, Gubbins ordered Trappes-Lomax to disband TRAPPESCOL HQ and resume command of his Battalion, and sent Major Leslie Graham, the second-in-command, back to prepare a new Battalion position at Viskiskoia, five miles south of Storjord, which he himself had reconnoitred the previous day and chosen as his main defensive position north of the snow-belt.

After Gubbins had left, Trappes-Lomax summoned his Company Commanders and gave orders for the occupation of three successive rearguard positions, involving a withdrawal in each case of about four or five miles. Each position was to be held by two Companies, and Trappes-Lomax stressed that, if heavily attacked, Company Commanders were to withdraw without further orders. His intention was that after the third position had been abandoned the whole Battalion was to 'embus' and move north of the snow-belt to the position south of Storjord which Graham had been sent to reconnoitre.

Auchinleck was to prove as good as his word about sending reinforcements. Two Companies of the 2nd South Wales Borderers and the HQ 24th Infantry Brigade arrived at Bodö on 20 May. Two companies of the 1st Bn Irish Guards were on their way by 'puffer' (as the small Norwegian coastal vessels were known) and the remaining two Companies were aboard a destroyer, and bringing with them General Auchinleck's GSO1, Colonel Dowler, to confer with Gubbins. Gubbins now had under command the equivalent of nearly two Brigades; provided he could deploy these reinforcements in time, there seemed no reason why a force of this size should not be able to put up tough resistance to the advance of the German main body, now reported to be assembling at the railhead at Mosjöen. Gubbins considered it essential that the Scots Guards should hold the enemy south of the snow-belt for another ninety-six hours. Equally essential for the success of his plan was the immediate return of the requisitioned motor coaches which Trappes-Lomax had retained south of the snow-belt for the purpose of evacuating his Battalion.

The destroyer carrying the first contingent of the Irish Guards and Colonel Dowler docked at a quarter to one in the morning of 22 May. Although they had spoken several times on the telephone, this was Dowler's first meeting with Gubbins and he formed an excellent impression. "I feel that the operations about Bodö could not be in better hands," he reported to Auchinleck.[12] On the strength of Dowler's "excellent report" Auchinleck, on 22 May, made a number of important decisions. He agreed to let Gubbins have a Company of French anti-tank guns immediately, while promising him the remaining five Independent Companies when they arrived from Scotland. For administrative convenience, he formed the troops operating on his southern front into a new formation, known as BODOFORCE, which he put under Gubbins' command. Finally, after discussion with Dowler, he decided that the time had come to remove Trappes-Lomax from his command. However, before this relief could be effected, Gubbins was faced with a new emergency.

The optimism engendered at Force HQ by Dowler's reports had not been shared by Trappes-Lomax who held that the categoric orders he had received to stand fast did not preclude him from improving his dispositions. When Gubbins had left Krokstrand on 20 May, Trappes-Lomax had pulled back the rearguard about five miles into the first of the three defensive positions and next morning, there having been no reaction from the Germans, had moved Battalion HQ to a new location five miles south of the snow-belt. During the afternoon the forward two Companies of the Scots Guards had become lightly engaged by enemy patrols and during the night had withdrawn under the orders of the Company Commanders. Passing through the second defensive position, as arranged, these two Companies had occupied the third and final position just short of the snow-belt.

On 21 May Gubbins sent Major Baily, one of the attached Indian Army officers, to Trappes-Lomax with verbal orders that under no circumstances were the Scots Guards to retire without his permission and that the requisitioned motor coaches should be returned to the Brigade transport pool forthwith. With reinforcements on the way, Gubbins was fairly relaxed about the general situation, particularly since the Scots Guards had reported (inaccurately) that they were still holding the Messingsletten line and that the enemy was not pressing his attack.

Having stopped briefly at Storjord to brief Graham, Baily did not reach Scots Guards Bn HQ until midnight on 21 May. The next morning Trappes-Lomax seemed to have come to the conclusion that, considering the state of his Battalion, which was exhausted and demoralized by constant enemy air attack, to attempt to hold on for another thirty-six hours south of the snow-belt was to risk a major disaster. He told Baily that it was impossible to hold on to his present position and repeatedly complained of the difficulties facing his men in the kind of warfare in which they were engaged and for which they were untrained. According to Baily, he seemed particularly worried about the high snow plateau between his position and Storjord. In any case, during the early afternoon, he handed Baily a copy of his operation orders for an immediate disengagement and withdrawal to Storjord. He did not ask for comments and appears not to have answered when Baily enquired whether a copy of these operation orders had been sent to Gubbins.

Meanwhile, during the morning of 22 May, after Dowler had re-embarked, Gubbins concentrated on the arrangements for moving the Irish Guards from Bodö to the Rognan area. However, he sent Urquhart, the Brigade Major, forward to make sure that Trappes-Lomax was carrying out his orders. Urquhart telephoned Gubbins during the late afternoon and told him that that night Trappes-Lomax intended to withdraw the Scots Guards across the snow-belt. Gubbins recognized that this premature withdrawal not only ruined his plans for the defence of Storjord but, unless he took immediate action, might jeopardize the safety of his entire force. Although deeply shocked by Trappes-Lomax's action, Gubbins decided that to countermand the withdrawal at this late stage might well precipitate the disaster which Trappes-Lomax dreaded, and instead he set himself the task of damage limitation.

All that morning the BODOFORCE staff had been trying to improvise transport for the Irish Guards, who were disembarking at Bodö throughout 22 May and being dribbled forward by every available means — civilian buses, trucks, trawlers, ferry boats. There was clearly no time to prepare the defensive position in the Storjord area through which the Scots Guards would have withdrawn. Instead Gubbins decided to take up a reserve position at Pothus, half way between Storjord and Rognan, with the Irish Guards and No 2 Independent Company. Pothus was not such a satisfactory position since it was only ten miles south of Rognan and the defenders would be fighting with their backs to the fjord. Moreover, although most of the small parties of Irish Guards had managed to find their way forward as far as Rognan by evening of 22 May, there was no way of getting them further forward than Pothus in the time available.

The reserve position at Viskiskoia, which Graham had prepared, was dominated on the right flank by a high hill and Gubbins had planned that this would be occupied by No 3 Independent Company before the final withdrawal of the Scots Guards across the snow-belt. Owing to the Scots Guards' retention of the motor transport, No 3 Company had had to march up the Salt valley from Pothus and had arrived too late and too exhausted to deny this dominating feature to the enemy.

The final withdrawal of the 1st Scots Guards during the evening of 22 May was uneventful, the buses moving across the snow-belt at half-hour intervals. The enemy made no attempt that evening to follow up, and by midnight the Battalion was in the rear position covering the bridge over the Viskisnoia River with No 3 Independent Company on its right flank, sent up by Gubbins on 19 May to protect the withdrawal.

At about 1530 hours on 23 May Gubbins arrived at Bn HQ bringing with him Auchinleck's signal relieving Trappes-Lomax of his command. Trappes-Lomax did not deny that his decision to withdraw had been contrary to the orders which Gubbins had given him but he claimed that the safety of his Battalion was at stake. Gubbins could not overlook the fact that Trappes-Lomax's untimely withdrawal had endangered the entire force and, as Commander of BODOFORCE, he could not condone such conduct. He ordered Trappes-Lomax to hand over to Major Graham and to report to Force HQ at Harstad. Then, with Graham, he went forward to see the situation for himself.

The news of Trappes-Lomax's dismissal had spread rapidly. He was a good regimental officer and a popular CO; there is a poignant entry in the 1st Scots Guards war diary for 23 May:

"This crushing blow took place in the middle of an enemy attack and it is hardly to be wondered that the morale of both officers and men was still further shaken by the loss of a CO, for whose personality and ability everybody had the highest respect and in whom everyone had the greatest confidence."[13]

By the afternoon of 23 May the engagement had become general, and Gubbins and Graham on their way forward came under heavy mortar and machine-gun fire, much of it from the high ground on the right flank. Gubbins recognized that the Scots Guards were exhausted and demoralized and he saw little prospect of their standing and fighting. In the words of the

1st Scots Guards war diary: "The men were utterly exhausted and a certain demoralization had set in, in consequence of fatigue, loss of kit, a succession of rearguard actions, and continuous menace from the air, which invariably disclosed every position to the enemy and enabled him, without interference, to harass the battalion and base his plans on certain knowledge."

At midnight the Scots Guards passed through the 1st Irish Guards who heard the slow shuffling tramp of tired men. They came down to the roadside and in silence watched the lines of tattered men as they passed. The twin battalions had often passed each other on the march, but this time there was no jeering, no Irish guardsman shouted, "Get up off your knees", no guardsman replied, "Having a good rest, Nick?"[14]

It was clear that if the enemy advance was to be checked the force which Gubbins had now assembled at Pothus must undertake a sustained rearguard action. It was therefore decided that, under Gubbins' direction, an experienced infantry officer, Major Hugh Stockwell, Royal Welch Fusiliers, commanding No 2 Independent Company, should assume command of all fighting troops in the area. The enemy was engaged at first light on 25 May, and there ensued a tough infantry battle lasting thirty-six hours, at the end of which the enemy had made no significant advance.

On the evening of 25 May Gubbins had been summoned to Bodö from his forward HQ at Rognan to meet Colonel Dowler who, with the last company of the 2nd South Wales Borderers, arrived from Harstad in HMS *Beagle* in the small hours of 26 May. Dowler told him in strictest confidence that the War Cabinet in London had decided three days previously that "certain equipment, troops, ships and guns, now in Norway was urgently needed for the defence of UK". He was therefore to prepare for evacuation. This meant that instead of being required to delay the enemy until Auchinleck had taken Narvik, the new task of STOCKFORCE, as Stockwell's command was now known, was to delay the enemy only for long enough to cover the withdrawal of BODOFORCE in readiness for evacuation which, it was planned provisionally, should take place between 1 and 3 June.

When he got back to Rognan at mid-morning on 26 May Gubbins found that the enemy was pressing hard and threatening the flanks of the Pothus position with his mountain troops. In the new circumstances he decided at midday to order a phased withdrawal to Fauske, some forty miles east of Bodö on the north side of the Rognan fjord. So bitter was the fighting round Pothus that it was not until the middle of the afternoon that Stockwell, with the timely assistance of two Gladiator aircraft from the airstrip at Bodö, was able to begin to disengage; from early evening onwards he fought a fierce rearguard action round the two demolished bridges over the River Salt. It was fourteen miles from Pothus to Rognan and during the withdrawal the troops came under heavy mortar and air bombardment. Nevertheless the rearguard companies of the Irish Guards fought extremely well, destroying the forward ammunition dump and blowing up bridges and jetties as they withdrew. The second stage of the withdrawal was particularly precarious since it involved ferrying STOCKFORCE, numbering about four thousand men, with their guns and vehicles, from Rognan to Finneid, ten miles down the fjord. With the help of Lieut-Commander W. R. Fell, who was in charge of small boat operations, Gubbins had assembled ten 'puffers' and a large ferry boat and these made repeated runs from Rognan to Finneid, a journey lasting an hour each way. Inevitably, a considerable quantity of stores and ammunition had to be abandoned at Rognan; demolition charges were laid with time fuses set to explode when the evacuation was completed. Embarking the troops and loading guns and vehicles under air attack proved difficult and, not surprisingly, the evacuation took longer than planned. Moreover, a quarter of an hour before these demolition charges were due to explode, the engine of the large ferry boat caught fire. There were a thousand troops on board who tried unsuccessfully to put out the fire, some of them using their steel helmets filled with water, and it was only at the last moment that Commander Fell, manoeuvring his 'puffer' with great skill, succeeded in towing the ferry off. Even so it was less than fifty yards distant from the jetty when the charges exploded, showering the troops with burning timbers. By the time the two-man demolition party had escaped in a rowing-boat, the ferry had already come under fire from German cyclist patrols which had entered the town just as it was pulling out. It was, to say the least, a close-run thing. Having crossed the fjord, STOCKFORCE re-formed north of Fauske and during the night of 25 May any supernumerary troops were dribbled back to Bodö.

While all this was going on, Gubbins was preparing his evacuation plans and, by the time STOCKFORCE was in position at Fauske, these plans had been finalized and submitted for approval to Force HQ. In a pencilled note to Auchinleck, Gubbins had written, "I would be very grateful indeed if evacuation could be arranged 31 May at latest as I rather doubt if I can hold till 1 June. If impossible, however, we just have to do our best." Before this message was received, Auchinleck had despatched Dowler to Bodö for the last time, to inform Gubbins that BODOFORCE would be evacuated by destroyer on three successive nights, starting during the night of 29/30 May.

The stubbornness of STOCKFORCE's rearguard actions and the systematic removal or destruction of 'puffers' and other small craft was successful in temporarily halting the enemy at Rognan, and gave Gubbins breathing space. On 29 May he issued his embarkation orders. Nos 1 and 4 Independent Companies and the administrative headquarters staff of BODOFORCE were ordered to concentrate at Bodö ready to embark on two destroyers which were due to take them off that night. Meanwhile the Scots

Guards at Hopen were told to take up a defensive position so that the 1st Irish Guards and Nos 2 and 3 Independent Companies could abandon their rearguard position north of Fauske and, withdrawing through the Hopen position, proceed straight to Bodö. The withdrawal proceeded according to plan and half an hour after the bridge at Hopen had been blown the first German cyclist patrols arrived and were engaged by the Scots Guards. For the next twenty-four hours the enemy did not press his attack and Nos 2, 3 and 5 Independent Companies were taken off in three destroyers during the night of 30/31 May. The withdrawal of the 1st Scots Guards was covered by the 2nd South Wales Borderers, and enemy cyclists and machine guns had once again to be held off, but no serious pressure developed. The final rearguard, consisting of one company of Scots Guards and one company of South Wales Borderers with four 25-pounder guns, took up a position some four thousand yards east of Bodö to cover the embarkation of the rest of 24th Infantry Brigade which took place on the night of 31 May/1 June. Gubbins himself left with HQ 24th Infantry Brigade in the last destroyer.

To avoid alerting the enemy, it had been impossible to burn the abandoned stores and material, but guns and motor vehicles which could not be loaded on to the destroyers were tipped into the sea. Gubbins also did all he could in the short time available to destroy civilian as well as military stocks of petrol. He sent Andrew Croft on several missions deep into the surrounding countryside to drain outlying filling stations, and on the last night Croft and Quintin Riley were left behind at Bodö to drain and destroy the main petrol depot on the northern outskirts of the town. After completing this mission, these two officers succeeded in escaping by fishing boat to Narvik, 130 miles distant.

It was fortunate that during the three days of evacuation low cloud prevented enemy air activity; casualties were minimal and none of the destroyers was sunk. Nevertheless the credit for this most successful evacuation must go to Gubbins who displayed a technical skill and sureness of touch which did not escape the notice of General Auchinleck. Auchinleck wrote in his final report, "The swiftness and efficiency with which the evacuation was carried out reflects great credit on Brigadier Gubbins and his staff".[15] In a private letter to the CIGS dated 3 June, he gave a list of officers who had done outstandingly well. At No 5 was: "Gubbins has, I think, been first-class. Should be a divisional commander or whatever the equivalent may be in the New Army!"[16]

After spending a few days at Harstad winding up the affairs of BODOFORCE, Gubbins travelled home in RMS *Lancastria* and by 10 June he was back in Scotland. It was widely acknowledged that he was one of the few officers who had come well out of the Norwegian Campaign and his outstanding services were rewarded by his immediate appointment to the

Distinguished Service Order. Aged forty-four he was at the very top of his form and his recent experiences had left him full of confidence in his ability to handle major units in battle.

Although the French had not yet surrendered, the evacuation of the BEF with its loss of arms and equipment had led to a complete reorganization and with General Ironside now in command of GHQ Home Forces, Gubbins seemed certain of a good appointment in the 'New Army'. However, any personal ambitions which Gubbins may have felt when reporting to the War Office on his return were tempered by his strong sense of loyalty to Colonel Holland, the head of MI(R), who had, after all, been the original sponsor of the Independent Companies. Whatever his personal inclinations may have been, and there is some evidence to suggest that he had hoped, if not for an active command, at least for a senior training appointment, with the Germans now poised to invade England during the summer months, Gubbins seems to have shown no hesitation in accepting Holland's proposal that he should form and command MI(R)'s latest brain-child. This was a secret guerrilla force to operate behind the enemy lines in the event of a German invasion.

9

THE AUXILIARY UNITS 1940

By mid-June the numbing incredulity produced by the Dunkirk evacuation and the arrival of German forces on the Channel coast had given place to a sense of frantic urgency to prepare a virtually defenceless Britain for an invasion which at the time appeared inevitable. As the self-styled experts on subversion, Section D and MI(R) had been instructed to create, under the direction of GHQ Home Forces, the nucleus of a resistance organization, to which volunteers — military or civilian — might rally. When Section D's enthusiastic, and sometimes dramatic, efforts to obtain recruits aroused the suspicions of local military authorities and protests to HQ Home Forces, General Ironside, the Commander-in-Chief, decided that all clandestine guerrilla and subversive operations must henceforth be coordinated under military control. Gubbins, who it will be recalled had served on Ironside's staff in North Russia and in whom, after his exploits in Norway, the War Office had full confidence, was the obvious choice.

"I had in fact been given a blank cheque but was there any money in the bank to meet it? Everything would have to be improvised. Time was the essence... at the shortest we had six weeks before a full-scale invasion could be launched; if we were lucky we might have until October, after which climatic conditions would give us a respite ... but the immediate circumstances necessitated the highest degree of decentralization from the start. There would be no question of coordinating these forces into large units or grouping them for battle; they must be very small units, locally raised, and able to melt away after action. So there was no need for transport, and wireless too was out of the question. The highest possible degree of secrecy must be maintained... not only because ordained by higher authority but for the personal security of those men who were to be left behind. GHQ Home Forces would give me their order of priorities as to probable invasion areas where we should try and develop first. These underground forces must have some general title for daily military purposes but it must be such as to give no indication whatever of their role and of such uninteresting and general nature as to excite no interest. This bothered me quite a lot.

"Finally: a small staff of serving officers for our HQ for minimal training, administration and supply duties; half a dozen operational officers to raise and command the units in the top priority areas. A headquarters somewhere in the quiet mid-west, reasonably accessible with a really good training area round it, and far from all other military formations and installations. A couple of sections of men, say a sergeant and eight privates, also serving soldiers, for each area to help its development − i.e. for continuing training, construction of hide-outs etc. How to recruit the men for the units; what their armament should be, and how to get it."

By the end of June a headquarters had been set up in Whitehall Place opposite the side entrance to the War Office. Relying for his staff and early unit commanders on those who had served under him in Poland and Norway, Gubbins put Peter Wilkinson in charge of organization and plans and Bill Beyts, 6th Rajputana Rifles, who had been one of his attached Indian Army officers in Norway, in charge of training. XII Corps Observation Unit, which had been established by General Andrew Thorne, the GOC, and was commanded by Peter Fleming, became the first Auxiliary Unit, followed closely by an East Anglian Unit under Andrew Croft.

The base of the Auxiliary Units organization rested on a cadre of intelligence officers, ranking as captains, many of whom already had local connections. To them fell the task of recruiting likely civilians from the Home Guard, swearing them to secrecy under the Official Secrets Act, and organizing them into patrols of from three to five men. Each member of the patrol received general training in guerrilla tactics and the use of explosives, and each patrol was given one or more special targets, for which they were expected to operate from specially prepared and positioned hide-outs located in woods, farm buildings, cellars, even a deserted badger's set. Peter Fleming was to describe the domestic economy of these hide-outs as bearing a general resemblance to the Lost Boys' subterranean home in the second act of Peter Pan. If invasion came, their task would be to harass enemy communications and rear areas with ambushes, demolitions and acts of terrorism as opportunity arose.

However, although the role of the Units was approved and supported by GHQ Home Forces, their presence was understandably unpopular with local Home Guard commanders, and positively repugnant to some senior military commanders who not only disliked their role but, perhaps with more justification, regarded it as ineffective. This disapproval was shared by one or two of the Regional Commissioners; one of them, in an awkward interview with Wilkinson, threatened to arrest any member found operating in his area. In Eastern Command, relations had already become strained when Edward Beddington-Behrens, one of Gubbins' most enthusiastic supporters, had strode theatrically into the presence of the GOC, hurled a Molotov cocktail through the open French window and, in a flash, incinerated the General's favourite peach tree. Similarly, a spectacularly successful attack on HQ 1 Division at Steyning did not endear the Auxiliary Units to Major-General Bernard Montgomery who had previously declared the perimeter of his headquarters to be impregnable. It often required Gubbins' personal intervention to resolve the problems arising from these excesses of zeal, and from his association with these irregular forces his reputation among the military *bien-pensants* undoubtedly suffered further damage.

Nevertheless, recruiting proceeded apace throughout the summer and, by the end of August, more than a dozen intelligence officers had been appointed and trained, while, along the whole of the south coast and as far north as the Humber, there was a network of partially trained and equipped Auxiliary Units. While priority in equipment was given to the most threatened areas in the south, recruiting had also been carried out on the east coast of Scotland and in South Wales. In the early days, largely to try to preserve the security of individual patrols, much of the training in explosives had been given by members of the headquarters staff – no hardship in the glorious summer of 1940 to spend two or three nights a week in the country holding demolition classes and taking part in night exercises. Things were not moving fast enough, however, and in August it was decided to throw security to the winds and to establish a central training school at Highworth, near Swindon. Coleshill House, an Inigo Jones masterpiece, was a large property, its stables and outhouses providing offices and classrooms, and a main store for the arms, explosives and other equipment which were at last becoming available from army and secret sources. Courses were held every weekend for some two dozen members of Auxiliary Units: poachers and peers, chief constables and clerks, kipped down together on the floor of a makeshift dormitory in a hayloft. Resident staff enjoyed greater comfort in the servants' bedrooms at the top of the house, and everyone messed together in the servants' hall. Daylight hours were spent in demonstrations of weapons, explosives and field craft, the hours of darkness in night exercises. In all these activities Gubbins took a leading part; he never missed a weekend course and displayed a remarkable capacity for remembering names and for sizing up the individual members of these heterogeneous groups; his enthusiasm and energy made a very favourable impression on the students.

No less important was the procurement of arms and equipment, much of which in the early days had to be scrounged. There were four main sources: the War Office for rifles, which were in very short supply, grenades and gelignite; MI(R) for sticky bombs and phosphorus Molotov cocktails; Section D for time pencils and for the infinitely precious plastic explosive which could only be used for demonstration because of its scarcity; finally, through confidential contacts dating from the Polish Mission, poachers' pistols, some with silencers, some with folding stocks, all designed for ease of concealment and for silent killing. It was not easy, sources such as the War Office and GHQ Home Forces being disinclined to deprive their own forces, but, fortunately, 500,000 Springfield rifles which President Roosevelt had persuaded the US Army to release from First World War stocks began to reach England in July. A fairly generous allotment reached Auxiliary Units, to become their basic weapon – a great improvement on the shot gun or pitchfork. Jefferis and Macrae of MI(R) produced what explosive devices they could, but their output was small and tended to be too sophisticated for general use. As for Section D, one of Gubbins' early tasks had been to take over Grand's civilian stay-behind organization, hastily and unofficially set up earlier and proving a source of embarrassment to all concerned. This remit did not improve relations between Gubbins and Grand. Nevertheless, to Grand's credit, he gave orders that Section D's technical establishment (Station XII) at Aston House, near Stevenage, should do everything possible to help Auxiliary Units. Gubbins found them an invaluable source of material assistance:

> "They had apparently an unlimited stock of plastic, would make up and pack explosive charges for us to our specifications if we could find a couple of packers, would help with Molotov cocktails and sticky bombs for anti-tank work, and had already produced, and held in great numbers, a type of Polish-invented time-fuze, which I had brought back from one of my pre-war trips to Warsaw – the famous pencil fuze which later became standard for the British Army.
>
> "I received also a small windfall for our force from a friend in the United States, son of a former American ambassador here and a passionate anglophile, who had cabled me out of the blue asking if he could help our country in any way, and I had replied: pistols and sub-machine guns. A packing-case duly arrived at our HQ at Coleshill addressed simply to Colonel Gubbins, c/o The War Office, containing a couple of Thompsons and a nice selection of automatic pistols with ammunition to match.
>
> "Stranger things happened in those strange and desperate times, not always to our advantage, and I will mention one unexpected set-back.
>
> "I knew that all weapons in private hands at the commencement of

the war had been called in by the police on orders presumably from the Home Office, and I naturally thought that this would provide a most useful source of supply. To our astonishment and suppressed rage we discovered that everything that could have been of use to us had been disposed of irretrievably. I visited two county police stations myself to see if I could get hold of something; in Leeds I found that these weapons had been thrown into the lake in Roundhay Park, and at another station ... that they had been dumped into the sea – presumably again on orders from the Home Office."

With every week the efficiency and scale of Auxiliary Units increased: hide-outs and secret observation posts were constructed and stocked with food; caches of arms and explosives were organized; an embryonic system of short-wave radio communication was in process of being set up to link the intelligence officers with adjacent patrols and eventually with rear headquarters at Highworth; and in the critical days of September, along the east and south coasts of England from John O'Groats to St David's Head, some three thousand men organized in patrols were standing-to and training with enormous enthusiasm, determined in Winston Churchill's words 'to perish in the common ruin rather than to fail or falter in their duty'.[1]

On 25 August the Prime Minister wrote a minute to the Secretary of State for War:

"I have been following with much interest the growth and development of the new guerrilla formations ... known as Auxiliary Units. From what I hear these units are being organized with thoroughness and imagination, and should, in the event of invasion, prove a useful addition to the regular forces. Perhaps you will keep me informed of progress."[2]

By the end of September, however, it became clear that Hitler did not intend to invade in 1940 and, for someone of Gubbins' experience, there was not much left to do in Auxiliary Units. While at Southern Command and when he succeeded Ironside as Commander-in-Chief Home Forces on 29 July, General Sir Alan Brooke had on several occasions congratulated Gubbins on their progress. Nevertheless, in spite of a recommendation for promotion on his return from Norway, no alternative employment for Gubbins was in sight when, in November, 1940, he was offered secondment to the newly formed Special Operations Executive with the rank of Brigadier.

So far as Gubbins was concerned, the formation, training and equipment of Auxiliary Units was a triumph of improvisation and personal leadership. So far as their role in the event of a German invasion was concerned, it was his opinion that

"they would have justified their existence: to what degree would have been entirely dependent on the circumstances. But my judgement is based heavily on the fact that they were costing the country nothing either in man-power or in weapons.... These patrols in their left-behind missions, out of all contact, entirely on their own, with their caches of arms and stores would have given some account of themselves in the invasion areas but their usefulness would have been short-lived, at the longest until their stocks were exhausted, at the shortest when they were caught or wiped out. They were designed, trained and prepared for a particular and imminent crisis: that was their specialist role."

10

SOE: 1940/1941

Once there was no possibility of a British Expeditionary Force returning to the Continent in the foreseeable future, subversive warfare began to be taken more seriously by the Service Chiefs and, more important, attracted Mr Churchill's attention. As early as 27 May the War Cabinet endorsed a Chiefs of Staff recommendation "that this form of activity was of the very highest importance, that a special organization would be required, and the plans to put these subversive operations into effect, together with the necessary preparations and training should be proceeded with as a matter of urgency".[1]

Beaumont-Nesbitt, encouraged by Holland, put in a strong plea that the War Office should direct these activities on paramilitary lines. Sir Alexander Cadogan, Permanent Under-Secretary at the Foreign Office, would have been content to let the War Office do it, but, at C's instigation, put in a counter-claim on behalf of Section D. However, the strongest bid came from Dr Dalton, the Minister of Economic Warfare, who argued that subversive warfare was not a job to be handled by regular soldiers and, more plausibly, that since opposition to the Nazis was most likely to occur in left-wing anti-Fascist circles, it was sensible to put the new organization under a Labour Minister, particularly one who was already engaged in waging economic warfare.

Dalton's arguments, reinforced by certain domestic political considerations, prevailed. On 22 July, 1940, a Minute[2], initialled by Neville Chamberlain, Lord President of the Council, created a Special Operations Executive to coordinate sabotage, subversion and secret propaganda against the enemy overseas. The Special Operations Executive (SOE), for which the Minister of Economic Warfare, Dr Hugh Dalton, was made responsible, initially consisted of three branches: SO1 for propaganda; SO2 for subversion; and SO3, which did not survive infancy, for planning.

The Prime Minister did not particularly care for Dalton, but nevertheless was attracted by the possibilities open to SOE and enjoined him to "set Europe ablaze". This was "easier to command than to achieve. Indeed ... he sometimes came nearer to setting Whitehall ablaze".[3] In order to safeguard the Foreign Office's interest Cadogan approved the appointment of his private secretary, Gladwyn Jebb, to be the chief executive officer of the new organization. The SIS, for their part, was hostile from the outset and justifiably apprehensive that, if even a quarter of Dalton's wilder schemes took shape, its vestigial remaining links with Hitler's Europe were likely to be compromised beyond repair. C, therefore, nominated Frank Nelson, who had previously been in Basle as head of Colonel Claude Dansey's special section of the SIS, to SO2 in the hope that he would keep 'these amateurs' under control.

Dalton had originally intended that SO2 should be a civilian organization − the 'Fourth Arm' he had called it − but he soon realized that some of the activities envisaged for SO2 were of a quasi-military nature, requiring the services of a professional soldier. Gubbins had already caught Dalton's attention when both had been guests at a dinner party at the Polish Embassy in November, 1939. On this occasion Gubbins, just back from Poland, had inveighed against the Treasury for holding up the delivery of Hurricane fighters, urgently needed by the Poles, while haggling over which government should pay the shipping charge. It was one of Gubbins' favourite stories, and it appealed to Dalton, a great supporter of the Poles and at that time a member of the Labour Opposition. Consequently, when Gubbins' name was suggested, Dalton was enthusiastic.

"I had to fight for his body against the C-in-C Home Forces, but with the backing of the DMO (Director of Military Operations) ... I got him."[4]

Gubbins' decision to go to SOE is surprising because he had little confidence in sabotage and subversion as such; had in fact a somewhat old-fashioned sense of propriety; and knew very well that certain of SOE's projected activities fell into what in those days was regarded as an equivocal category. Admittedly there was a financial inducement: the salary offered by SOE was better than Army pay, and Gubbins, with very little private means, had a boy still at boarding-school. Also Dalton had promised him immediate promotion to Brigadier. However, it was not much to be a 'Baker Street brigadier' and Gubbins must have known that had he hung on for another six months or so, Brooke would almost certainly have given him a brigade, if not the division for which he been recommended on his return from Norway. The Scots Guards affair cast a shadow, but there was no question of it having blighted his career.

It is true that he felt a strong sense of obligation to the Poles, but this was scarcely a sufficient ground for putting his Army career at risk, and his decision to join SOE can only be attributed to a conviction that, if properly coordinated with regular operations, guerrilla warfare on the mainland of Europe might prove decisive in what might otherwise be a single-handed struggle against Hitler. In this scenario, an organization like SOE would clearly have a major role. Gubbins may well have believed that with his unique MI(R) background this is where his duty lay, at any rate for the time being. He did not demur when told by the War Office to hand over command of Auxiliary Units, and, accompanied by his secretary, Margaret Jackson, and by Peter Wilkinson as his GSO2, on 18 November, 1940, he reported for duty at the SO2 HQ. The War Office had honoured Dalton's promise and he found himself once again an acting Brigadier, though this time "specially employed and not paid from Army funds".

To begin with, SO2 had used Section D's offices at 2, Caxton Street, but when the blitz began in earnest, there was an urge to seek more substantial accommodation. In November, shortly before Gubbins' arrival, the headquarters had moved to 64, Baker Street, which in peacetime had been the head office of Marks & Spencer. Unfortunately, there was no room in this building to accommodate Gubbins and his staff, who were relegated to Berkeley Court, a block of apartments opposite Baker Street Station, where they occupied two gloomy family flats.

Soon after taking over as CD, Nelson had dismissed most of the former staff of Section D and MI(R) while retaining the services of George Taylor and Tommy Davies as his two assistants. Taylor had recently returned from the Middle East where he had been sorting out the remains of Section D's Balkan organization; Nelson made him his chief of staff, responsible for SO2's operations and organization world-wide. Assisted by Bickham Sweet-Escott, previously head of Section D's Balkan section, in November, 1940, he was still staffing SO2's country sections. Prominent among his early recruits were Charles Hambro, a leading merchant banker and Chairman of the Great Western Railway, who had a special interest in Scandinavia, and Harry Sporborg, a partner in Slaughter & May, the City solicitors. Gubbins, with his previous links with Czechs and Poles, was welcomed as another important addition to this team. Tommy Davies, who, it will be remembered, had been a member of the original Polish Mission, was responsible for training, supplies and services, and for virtually everything not directly operational. Another early recruit, John Venner, a leading chartered accountant, was to remain the organization's finance officer throughout the war, and played a vital role in SO2's activities.

On arrival, Gubbins' first act was to take over from Davies responsibility for training, including the Section head, Major J. S. Wilson, whom Davies had brought with him from MI(R). Wilson, with Wilkinson and Perkins of the former Polish Mission, supported by Margaret Jackson and Vera Long as personal secretaries, formed the nucleus of Gubbins' section in Berkeley Court.

Dalton had promised Gubbins that he would be appointed Director of

Operations but had left it to Nelson to define his relationship to Taylor, whose direct responsibilities included a number of purely subversive projects in French Morocco, West Africa, South America, the Iberian Peninsula, the Balkans and the Middle East; like the clandestine activities of SO2's representatives in New York, Stockholm, Berne, Madrid and Lisbon, they were specifically excluded from Gubbins' control. As we shall see, the anomalies of his position caused some misunderstanding with the Chiefs of Staff and the Joint Planners for whom "Director of Operations" implied wider responsibilities than Gubbins had so far been given. However, since he and Taylor were old friends and used to cooperating with each other in Section D, the confusion in Baker Street was less than might have been expected. Nor, so long as there were virtually no operations for Gubbins to direct, was there much risk of friction with the heads of country sections, although some of these viewed his appointment as a threat to their future independence, while others genuinely doubted whether regular soldiers were temperamentally suited to conduct the sort of subversive operations for which they conceived that SO2 had been created. Rather than seeking to have his position clarified, Gubbins felt sufficiently self-confident to await developments. However, there were two matters which demanded his urgent attention if the organization was not to go the way of Section D. First, it was essential that SO2's objectives and priorities should be carefully tailored to conform with directives handed down by the Chiefs of Staff. Secondly, he realized that, instead of the current free-for-all in which country sections more often than not approached Service Ministries direct with their various operational requirements, standardized procedures must be adopted which were more acceptable to the three Services, and in future all joint operations involving the delivery of agents or *matériel* by sea or air must be coordinated and handled by an operations section directly responsible to himself. It was with these two requirements very much in mind that, in December, Gubbins secured the services of Major R. H. Barry, Somerset Light Infantry, to be head of his Operations Section. Barry, a 32-year old Wykehamist, was an officer of outstanding ability. He was an Army interpreter in French and German, a graduate of the Staff College, Camberley, had served in France at HQ BEF, and more recently as an instructor at the wartime Staff College at Minley Manor. With a short intermission, he was to remain with SOE for the rest of the war, in due course becoming Chief of Staff when Gubbins was appointed CD.

The Chiefs' of Staff first directive to SOE dated 25 November, 1940[5], had been issued a few days after Gubbins' arrival in Baker Street. It reiterated that while there was no intention to build up a British Army comparable in size with the German Army, it was nevertheless intended to provide a striking force on the Continent when the morale of the enemy had been

1. Helen (Nonie) Gubbins, Colin's mother (centre), with her five sisters.

2. Colin in his teens.

3. Killiemore House as it is today.

4. Second-Lieutenant Gubbins in 1914.

5. Captain Gubbins in 1918.

6. With General Ironside (second from left) on the River Dvina at
Archangel, 1919.

considerably weakened. Consequently, "undermining the strength of spirit of the enemy forces, especially those in the Occupied territories, should be the constant aim of our subversive organizations." The directive continued that, in the long view, the way should be prepared for the final stage of the war when, by coordinated and organized revolts in the Occupied countries and by popular risings against the Nazi party inside Germany, direct and decisive military operations against Germany might be possible. Meanwhile, priority was to be given to cutting enemy communications and subverting enemy morale. Second priority was to be given to organizing cooperation with our own troops in operations against Italy and Tunisia. Only third priority was to be given to similar operations in Scandinavia and North West Europe.

Although this directive had been prepared in consultation with Jebb and Nelson, it took insufficient account of the realities of the situation. Only in Poland and Czechoslovakia, neither of which was given priority in the directive, were there underground movements capable of cutting enemy communications on any significant scale or, in due course, of organizing a general rising. SO2 had inherited no agents in Italy or Tunisia from either Section D or MI(R); attempts to organize courier lines to Italy from Switzerland were proving extremely difficult; and there was no likelihood, for many months to come, of being able to undertake clandestine operations in Italy, or of providing support for regular operations in North Africa. Only in Scandinavia, in Gubbins' opinion, was there a reasonable chance of meeting the requirements of the directive; but planning and mounting such operations were primarily the responsibility of Hambro and Sporborg who were in charge of the Scandinavian country sections.

The truth was that, partly due to Dr Dalton's exaggerated claims, SOE had become the victim of a widely held fallacy that Occupied Europe was smouldering with resistance to the Nazis and ready to erupt if given the slightest support or encouragement. In reality in these early days, most people in Occupied Europe were still stunned by defeat and, except for a few ardent patriots, asked for nothing except to be left in peace. Compared with the horrors of invasion, the German Occupation, though disagreeable and humiliating, was as yet by no means intolerable, and most people were content for the time being to remain neutral, if only to survive.

The exceptions were the Poles. Facing extermination under German and Soviet occupation, the Polish nation depended for its survival on an active underground resistance. Notwithstanding Dr Dalton's vague claims, what later became known as the Polish Home Army was at no time an offshoot of SO2 but (when it chose) took its orders from the Polish government-in-exile. However, close personal links had been forged by Gubbins and members of the Polish mission in Paris with the officers of the Polish General

Staff dealing with home affairs. On arrival in England this staff section, now known as the Sixth Bureau, finding itself dependent on the British authorities for the provision of arms and explosives, training facilities and, above all, long-range aircraft, turned to SO2 for help. The latter, facing mounting criticism for its lack of results, seized on the Polish Home Army as an example of what could be achieved by well-organized resistance groups in Occupied Europe. In fact, in the winter of 1940, the Polish connection was perhaps SO2's principal asset and Gubbins was not alone in trusting that the success of the first flight to Poland, due to take place early in the New Year, might satisfy Dalton's demands for instant action, besides going some way to confound the scepticism of SO2's critics in Whitehall.

From the outset Dalton had wanted to play an executive role in SO2. He saw the organization's first task as being to mobilize left-wing opinion throughout Occupied Europe into a mass movement that would rise and overthrow the dictators. It was a simplistic goal which overrated the power of rational social democracy to overcome national and ideological prejudices, not to mention political aspirations which would sometimes prove incompatible with British war aims and inimical to agreed British strategy. Dalton was apt to attribute the lack of enthusiasm shown by country section heads to conservative prejudice against this left-wing constituency which, he maintained, was merely waiting for the call to arms. It was a fallacy widely held by the readers of the Left Book Club. "Too little political gumption and biases against the left,"[6] was his verdict on the senior members of SO2. Dalton had seen active service on the Italian front during the First World War and his prejudice against businessmen and Civil Servants did not extend to regular soldiers. In any case Gubbins was very much in favour, having been so to speak the fruit of a victory over the War Office which had not wanted to let him go to SOE. Like everyone else, Gubbins at times found Dalton exasperating, but admired the singleness of purpose with which he fought SOE's battles in Whitehall and certainly did not share the view of some of Dalton's Etonian contemporaries that he was a traitor to his class. Besides, they both liked and admired the Poles. As a token of his regard, General Sikorski invited Dalton, accompanied by Gubbins and Jebb, to spend Christmas, 1940, visiting Polish army units in Scotland. Dalton enjoyed this outing, liked tramping about the heather and the frequent opportunities for hearty exchanges with Polish soldiers. It was typical of him later to remark that he thought the Poles had been gratified when he and Jebb had changed into dinner jackets for a reception, while Gubbins, not for the last time defiant of the army clothes regulations, had worn the kilt. However, of more lasting importance, Dalton had had for the first time the chance to comment when Gubbins expounded the theories about guerrilla warfare which he and Holland had developed in MI(R). His discussions with

Gubbins and Jebb during the Scottish trip resulted in a significant modification of Dalton's views about the capability and, indeed, the future role of SO2.

Gubbins took little part in the first flight to Poland as most of the arrangements had all been made before he arrived in Baker Street. On its return to London after the fall of France, No 4 Military Mission had been reorganized and its 'left wing' element disbanded. However, during the summer of 1940, while Gubbins and Wilkinson were engaged in organizing Auxiliary Units, MI(R) had resumed contact with the Polish General HQ now established at Hotel Rubens in Buckingham Palace Road. When, in due course, MI(R) was absorbed by SO2, the officer dealing with Polish affairs, Captain H. B. Perkins, was transferred to the new organization. Larger than life in every dimension, Perkins, who had joined the original Polish Mission in Warsaw in 1939, was to serve under Gubbins for the rest of the war, remaining one of his most loyal and trusted supporters.

Shortly after his arrival in Britain, General Sikorski, anticipating a breakdown in communication with Occupied Europe, had relieved General Sosnkowski of his responsibility for the Home Army and had delegated full powers to Colonel Rowecki, the local commander in Warsaw.[7] Meanwhile, the VI Bureau had selected and trained a small group of officers who had volunteered to act as couriers and return to Poland by parachute, and to this end had also enlisted SO2's support in their attempts, hitherto unsuccessful, to convince the Air Ministry of the feasibility of regular liaison flights to Poland. These were beyond the normal range of the obsolescent twin-engined Whitley aircraft which were all that could be spared at this time for special operations. However, partly in acknowledgement of the outstanding contribution made by Polish fighter pilots during the Battle of Britain, the Air Ministry, in the late summer of 1940, agreed to modify one of the Whitley aircraft for long-range flights by fitting an auxiliary fuel tank in the fuselage amidships.* In peacetime, Perkins had owned a small engineering works in southern Poland and he and the VI Bureau, in cooperation with the RAF, drew up the specification for cylindrical containers attached to parachutes which could be released from the aircraft's bomb-bays. These containers, designed to carry arms and explosives, were constructed by SO2's technical section.**

The first flight had originally been scheduled to take place before

* Because of this excessive load, the modified aircraft had usually to be 'bounced' during take-off in order to enable it to become airborne – a technique considered to be extremely risky.

** With a slight modification, suggested by the Polish Home Army to improve their portability, these containers became SO2's standard equipment for the duration of the war and were also adopted by the Airborne Division and the Commandos.

Christmas but there was a last-minute postponement while further modifications were made in order to extend the aircraft's range. However, after two false starts, the operation was finally carried out on the night of 15 February. Three parachutists were successfully dropped in the neighbourhood of Bielsko and, after a flight of some fourteen hours, the aircraft returned safely to base. Although dropped eighty miles short of the agreed reception point, and in a part of Poland annexed by the Germans in 1939, all three couriers succeeded in reaching Warsaw.*

It was an outstanding achievement on the part of Flight-Lieutenant John Austin, RAF, and his British aircrew, but neither in Baker Street nor at Polish HQ were the enormous difficulties of the air operation fully appreciated. Nor was it foreseen that over twelve months would elapse before it proved possible to repeat the flight. On the contrary, planning started both in London and in Warsaw for massive air support of the Home Army with the prospect of mounting a full-scale airborne operation when the time was ripe. Dr Dalton, elated by this first liaison with Occupied Europe, was particularly reluctant to accept that, despite its success, the lesson to be drawn from this first operation was the sheer impossibility of supplying the Polish Home Army from bases in the United Kingdom, still less of supporting a general rising. Nor was it a conclusion that the Poles could readily accept. If Gubbins took a more realistic and professional view than Dr Dalton, he nevertheless could not afford at this stage to discourage the Poles from planning future operations on the grandest scale.

Unlike the Poles, whose government-in-exile had been immediately recognized by the Allies, the Czech National Committee, headed by President Beneš, was not accepted as a representative government until mid-1941. On the outbreak of war, a Czech General Staff had been established in Paris and a small Czech contingent integrated into the French Army. However, President Beneš had stayed in England where he had taken refuge from the Germans in 1939. From there he could remain in touch with the Protectorate by means of the radio link established by the Czech Intelligence Section which, since March, 1939, had been working under the aegis of the British SIS. In the aftermath of the German invasion in 1939, the Czechs had improvised an underground organization based on the traditional Sokol movement – a sporting and gymnastic league which had flourished as a symbol of Czech nationalism under Austrian rule and was a unique feature of Czech society between the wars. To begin with, the underground organization was very loose-knit, but after the Germans had

* One of them subsequently returned to London in 1942, travelling overland via Lisbon.

disbanded the Czech Army, military officers had taken command and, on the outbreak of war, had brought the whole organization under the nominal control of the Czech General Staff in Paris.

It will be recalled that, in the early months of the war, Gubbins and members of No 4 Military Mission had approached the Czech General Staff, although the Czechoslovak forces were formally under French command. In reply to Gubbins' enquiries, the Czechs had indicated that their underground movement required no immediate help from the British since there was already concealed in the Protectorate a substantial quantity of arms and explosives and both radio and courier communications were, for the time being, presenting no difficulty.

After the fall of France, however, the Czechs, like the Poles, found themselves dependent on the British to provide the aircraft needed to maintain physical contact with their homeland. When Gubbins arrived in Baker Street SO2 had not as yet formed a Czech section. However, early in the New Year President Beneš invited Dalton and Gubbins to luncheon; General Ingr, Moravec and Wilkinson were also present. In discussion, it was agreed that some two dozen volunteers from the Czech armed forces now in the United Kingdom should be trained by SO2 and subsequently held available for clandestine operations in the Protectorate. It was further agreed that an essential pre-condition of any future operations was the establishment of a secure radio link with the Protectorate entirely independent of Colonel Moravec's intelligence network which must in no circumstances be compromised. A volunteer was soon found and trained, but, owing to the notoriously adverse weather conditions in Central Europe, it was not until April that, after several false starts, he was dropped 'blind' not in Bohemia, as he should have been, but in Austria. Nevertheless, he succeeded in reaching Prague and came on the air.

By the time this operation, code-named BENJAMIN, had been completed, the nights had become too short to risk further long-range flights. This curtailment was a source of great frustration to the Poles. However, although for form's sake they pretended otherwise, the Czechs were not altogether displeased: they had demonstrated their willingness to play their full part in the secret war against Hitler without compromising their all-important intelligence network or committing the underground to activities likely to provoke reprisals; moreover it might be assumed that the formal relations now established with SO2 would prove a useful step towards the recognition of their National Council. At the least, Beneš, who viewed everything from a political angle, had good reason to be satisfied.

In its relations with both Poles and Czechs, SO2 was dealing at arm's length with existing underground organizations, while the necessary detailed briefing and local knowledge was provided by the Polish and Czech authorities in London. The task of the Polish and Czech sections of SO2 was thereby greatly simplified.

No such advantage was enjoyed by the French section. The existence of the Unoccupied Zone provided many Frenchmen with an illusion of independence and, although there were plenty of ardent patriots, many of them at this stage owed their first loyalty to Marshal Pétain. Consequently, there was no organized underground resistance either in the Occupied or Unoccupied Zone comparable to that which existed in Poland, or even in the Protectorate. Moreover, since most able-bodied Frenchmen resident in the United Kingdom had rallied to the Free French movement in 1940, SO2's F (French) Section was finding great difficulty in recruiting organizers and radio operators and, inevitably, these consisted for the most part of individuals unwilling to serve under de Gaulle. Consequently, SO2 and, in particular, F Section, was distrusted, and its declared intention of organizing resistance in France separate from, or even in competition with, the Gaullist movement was greatly resented by the General and was to prove a continuous source of friction. Happily, better relations existed at the operational level.

In January, 1941, SO2 was given the task of attacking German aircrews belonging to *Kampfgeschwader* 100, a bomber squadron stationed at an airfield near Vannes in Brittany. SO2 had no suitable agents available and Gubbins asked Colonel *Passy*, de Gaulle's Chief of Intelligence, for four volunteers to undertake the mission which was code-named SAVANNA. After receiving rudimentary parachute training, the redoubtable Captain Bergé and his team were briefed and despatched, not by F Section which was responsible to Sporborg, but by Gubbins' new operational section headed by Barry. Intelligence sources had reported that the aircrews were accustomed to travel nightly to and from the airfield in two motor coaches, which it was now proposed to ambush and destroy. There was, however, a last minute intervention by the Chief of the Air Staff who wrote to Jebb: "I think that the dropping of men dressed in civilian clothes for the purpose of attempting to kill members of the opposing forces is not an operation with which the Royal Air Force should be associated."[8] Portal's scruples were overcome, but as a result of his intervention the parachute drop did not take place until the middle of March. By then the German aircrews had changed their routine and the attack had to be abandoned. Although it failed in its objective, SAVANNA demonstrated that it was possible to drop small parties 'blind' even in Occupied France, without being detected; that individuals could travel long distances by railway without undue risk and that, having completed their assignment, agents could be collected by submarine at a pre-arranged rendezvous and brought safely back to England. More important, SAVANNA established Gubbins' interest in France, previously the sole responsibility of Sporborg. Further, it was agreed that, in view of the unsatisfactory relations which existed between F Section and the Free French, the new Free French Section (R/F) which SO2 was about to form, should be operationally responsible to Gubbins and Barry, although the overall direction of French affairs should remain with Harry Sporborg.

Encouraged by the experiences of SAVANNA, Gubbins agreed to undertake a second *coup-de-main* operation using Free French parachutists trained by SO2 and, once again, transported by the RAF. This was known as JOSEPHINE B and consisted of an attack on the Pessac Power Station. It took place on 7 June and was entirely successful. SAVANNA and JOSEPHINE B had demonstrated SO2's capacity to carry out commando-type operations against designated targets in France using parachutists drawn from the Free French forces in the United Kingdom.[9] However, although such *coups-de-main* produced welcome short-term results, it was clear that they were irrelevant, and might even prove detrimental, to SO2's principal task of organizing sabotage and building up the clandestine resistance which might, at some future date, be used to support an allied invasion. In fact, F Section had already taken the first step in this direction when it dropped its first agent in the neighbourhood of Châteauroux in Unoccupied France on the night of 5 May, followed six weeks later by the first supply drop in the neighbourhood of Limoges. But, so far as his section was concerned, Gubbins was reminded that training must now have the first priority and that supervising SO2's day-to-day operations as well as efforts to establish closer working relations with the Chiefs of Staff Joint Planning Section could now safely be left to Barry.

Gubbins was fortunate in taking over Jack Wilson as head of his training section. A former Deputy Head of Police in Calcutta, Wilson had an unrivalled experience of counter-subversion. Moreover, after his retirement, he had become Chief Instructor of the Boy Scout Training Centre at Gilwell. In 1940 he had been recruited by MI(R) to train the Independent Companies which Gubbins was to command in Norway, and when MI(R) was dissolved, Davies had arranged for his transfer to SO2.

SO2's basic training programme owed much to the MI(R) *Handbooks on Guerrilla Warfare* which Gubbins and Jefferis had compiled in the spring of 1939. Moreover, the War Office as a temporary measure had agreed that small parties of SO2's students could receive their paramilitary training at Lochailort, originally an MI(R) establishment and now a Commando Training School. So far as SO2 was concerned, this arrangement was unsatisfactory since for reasons of security it was usually desirable that national groups, and some individuals, should be trained separately. SO2 had, therefore, decided to form its own paramilitary training school, and Wilson had been instructed to requisition a number of houses in the Arisaig area within easy reach of Lochailort. These were mostly shooting lodges and holiday houses, each large enough to accommodate a dozen or more students and instructors in fairly austere conditions. To begin with, Lieutenant-Colonel J. W. Munn, RA, formerly an instructor at Lochailort, was put in charge of this complex.

After completing paramilitary training, the next stage was a parachute course at Ringway (now Manchester airport) where the newly formed Parachute Regiment was based and where the RAF had a parachute training unit. In the early days the training provided by the RAF was rudimentary to say the least. Three or four students at a time, accompanied by a conducting officer, were put up at local hotels where, being foreigners, they rarely failed to attract considerable attention. The following day the students were driven to Ringway to learn the drill for jumping through a hole in the fuselage of a mock-up Whitley. They spent the afternoon packing, under supervision, one of the parachutes which they would use the next day, when they had to make three or four live jumps over nearby Tatton Park. Anyone who landed without injuring himself in the process qualified as a parachutist and was duly awarded his 'wings'.* However, for security and other reasons, these arrangements were shortly to be superseded by a more rigorous training which included residence for a week or more at a special SO2 parachute school at Dunham House near Manchester. Here polylingual groups of students were treated by a somewhat idiosyncratic commandant as though they were English public school boys: the accent was on character building and trenchant — sometimes misleading — reports were sent to Baker Street on a student's character and capability.

With very few exceptions, all students were obliged to undergo paramilitary and parachute training since this provided a useful first assessment of an agent's suitability. Subsequent training depended on the nature of an individual's particular mission, and was planned in close consultation with the country section concerned. Selected agents were sent to a school of unattributable sabotage which SO2 had inherited from Section D; others went to be trained as radio operators. In the early summer of 1941 a complex of so-called 'finishing schools' was set up in the Beaulieu area of the New Forest, to give general training in 'clandestinity' and secret service techniques. Finally, most country sections were allotted houses of their own which they used for more specialized briefing and indoctrination and sometimes as holding units. The responsibility for these latter establishments, which were spread throughout the Home Counties, was usually shared between the Training Section and the country section

---

* This description is based on Wilkinson's experience in January, 1941, when he was the first member of the Baker Street staff to qualify.

concerned; however, there was no uniform practice. Over the years this modest framework developed into a vast and unique training organization at home and overseas which covered almost every aspect of subversive and irregular warfare. It was undoubtedly one of SOE's most impressive achievements and was universally admired.

As can be expected, Gubbins took a keen interest in all aspects of training. He personally interviewed the commandants and many of the senior instructors, recruiting a number of officers who had formerly served under him in Auxiliary Units. As soon as he could, he himself qualified as a parachutist; later he took part in skiing courses at Aviemore, as well as in amphibious exercises at Arisaig. These excursions provided him with an agreeable release from Baker Street and gave him the chance to study the type of agents being recruited by the various country sections, their quality and their motives in volunteering for special operations.

Various senior SOE officials, notably Gladwyn Jebb, had been in fairly continuous contact with the Chiefs of Staff at policy-making level. Nevertheless, the Chiefs of Staff were far from happy about the coordination of SOE's activities − about which they knew virtually nothing − with their general strategic plans. Accordingly, in the New Year, they had seconded Lieutenant-Colonel R. D. Guinness, RE, to Baker Street as the so-called Director of Plans. However, Barry's arrival and the setting up of an Operations Room had led to a parallel − though less formal − relationship between Gubbins and the Chiefs of Staff organization at the working level. The situation was further complicated by the fact that Guinness' planning section was not under Gubbins' direction.

In March, 1941, SO2 was approached by the Forward Operational Planning Section (FOPS) of the Joint Planning Staff, and asked to report on the military, and above all the logistical, implications of making use of resistance movements in Occupied countries. Gubbins, with Barry and his staff, embarked on a number of studies which included plans for subversive operations in 1941 and, in the longer term, for the arming of patriot forces throughout Europe. Some of the points contained in these studies were incorporated in a FOPS paper (JP(41)444)[10] which was submitted to the Chiefs of Staff. This paper concluded that to support patriot forces, even if the final phase of hostilities was as early as 1942, would require the full-time use of over two hundred aircraft; whereas to transport men and material for a general uprising would require six months' full-time effort by Bomber Command. Such a commitment to SOE was clearly unacceptable to the Chiefs of Staff, who observed rather sourly that, in any case, there was no certainty that SO2 would be in a position to make good its claim to provide patriot forces on a significant scale, still less to control them so that their activities supported rather than interfered with conventional operations. Gubbins and Barry were not discouraged by this rebuff, and in the latter half of July produced an SO2 memorandum. This paper accepted that for the time being it was unrealistic to contemplate providing air support for a full-scale rising in Poland or Czechoslovakia, and set out more modestly and in greater detail the logistic requirements for the support of resistance activities in North West Europe. Dalton endorsed this memorandum which he submitted to the Prime Minister with the somewhat dubious claim that SOE was ready to "set in motion large-scale and long-term schemes for revolution in Europe". In due course Churchill referred SO2's memorandum to the Chiefs of Staff, and Jebb and Gubbins were invited to attend when it was taken on 14 August.[11] Its rejection was predictable, if only because the German invasion of the Soviet Union on 22 June had reversed the balance of manpower, thus removing the prime justification for the support of patriot forces. Nevertheless, the Chiefs of Staff accepted that subversion and sabotage should be encouraged but they remained doubtful about the potential value of secret armies and deferred further discussion until the War Office had reported on the availability of arms to equip such forces. Poland and Czechoslovakia were not discussed, and it was tacitly accepted by everyone, except by the Polish and Czech governments-in-exile and by SOE, that significant British support for any Polish or Czech national uprising was unrealistic and could no longer be considered in future plans. As for North West Europe, though admitting the possibility of forming secret armies, the Chiefs of Staff were sceptical of their value in the face of German repression. The only positive outcome of the meeting was a promise by the Chief of the Air Staff to expand the Special Duties flight into a squadron. 138 Squadron, later commanded by Group Captain 'Mouse' Fielden formerly Captain of the King's Flight, was duly established at Newmarket on 25 August. There was, however, a proviso that intelligence missions had priority over special operations.

It was a frustrating summer for Gubbins, and indeed for the whole Baker Street fraternity — the 'Baker Street irregulars' as they were dubbed in Whitehall. SOE's future role was still unclear; even its continued existence was uncertain. Beside the usual Whitehall busybodies and the frankly envious, there were some senior officers who genuinely disapproved, on grounds of ethics or expediency, the sort of action which Dalton and SOE were committed to pursue. Gubbins, too, had reservations, preferring a direct policy towards the creation of resistance groups and secret armies rather than the setting-up of cells to promote the subversion and terrorism favoured by some of the more fanatical members of SOE. Quite apart from these ethical and politico-military considerations, there was a genuine clash of interest with the Royal Air Force, since by 1941 it had become clear that irregular operations could only be supported on a significant scale at the expense of the bomber offensive. The clash of interest with the SIS was no less grave. Justifiable fears were expressed that the widespread recruitment of resistance groups throughout Europe, as envisaged by SOE, would at best cause confusion; would by their very nature almost inevitably be penetrated by the enemy; and could hardly fail to complicate, if not compromise, the task of the intelligence organizations.

It was also felt, with some truth, that Dr Dalton had been entrusted with the control of SOE very largely for reasons of political expediency and that in the summer of 1940 the role of his organization had not been thought through. SOE's independent status was becoming increasingly unwelcome to the Foreign Office, the War Office, the SIS and the Air Ministry — powerful, and sometimes unscrupulous, enemies. Dr Dalton's vision and drive had done much to put SOE on the map but his loud voice, his abrasive personality, and the rhetorical and often extravagant claims he made on its behalf, did not on the whole inspire confidence in Whitehall.

So far this narrative has confined itself to operations for which Gubbins was directly or indirectly responsible. However, this was by no means the sum of SO2's activities during the first six months of 1941.

Gubbins' previous connection with the Poles and Czechs was not the only asset which SO2 inherited. It had also taken over from Section D a network of agents in Hungary, Yugoslavia and Roumania which had been built up by George Taylor during the winter of 1939 for the purpose of interdicting German imports of oil and grain from Roumania. After the fall of France, SO2 Cairo became responsible for directing and supplying this network.

At a meeting of the War Cabinet on 13 January, 1941,[12] Dalton had obtained Mr Churchill's somewhat sceptical endorsement of a plan for sabotaging German rail and river communications in neutral countries in Eastern Europe. To put this plan into force, George Taylor was despatched to Belgrade with wide-ranging powers. After the Axis invasion of Yugoslavia, Taylor found himself interned in Italy with the other members of the British Legation, but not before SO2 had played a minor part in the overthrow of Prince Paul, the Regent of Yugoslavia, in favour of the young King Peter. Little was known in London of the extent of SO2's involvement and reports reaching Baker Street were almost certainly exaggerated, but Dalton made the most of them. Operation RUBBLE, on the other hand, was an undoubted success. In March, 1941, several British freighters, caught in the Swedish port of Gothenburg and loaded with extremely valuable cargoes of steel ball-bearings, were hijacked, taken through the Skagerrack, and handed over to the Royal Navy, at a pre-arranged rendezvous, to be escorted safely to British waters. This exploit, in which the Operations section had played no part, was directed by Charles Hambro who shortly afterwards received a well-earned knighthood. RUBBLE was probably the most lucrative operation ever undertaken by SOE and Dalton had every right to boast of its success.

Less happy was the outcome of Operation RELATOR which Jebb and Gubbins put to the Chiefs of Staff on 3 February. This involved making secret preparations in Spain to organize guerrilla warfare if the Germans invaded the Iberian Peninsula. It was proposed to use not only British officers but also Republican refugees and other anti-Franco elements. The plan got a frosty reception from General Dill, the CIGS, and was effectively vetoed by Sir Samuel Hoare, HM Ambassador at Madrid, who pointed out that if these preparations came to the notice of the Spanish authorities, it might well precipitate the invasion they were designed to prevent. It was reluctantly agreed that contingency planning might continue, and a small party of Spanish-speaking officers was trained and sent to Gibraltar to await events. Here they languished until Hitler's invasion of the Soviet Union removed any immediate threat to the Iberian Peninsula. Gubbins had been only marginally involved in this operation, but he had the thankless task of defending it, which did no good to his reputation either with the Chiefs of Staff or with the Foreign Office.

Meanwhile, a new situation had developed in the Eastern Mediterranean. British military planning had taken little account of the Balkans; it had been assumed that the British confrontation with the Italians would take place either in North Africa or in Abyssinia. Indeed, at that time the Joint Intelligence appreciations discounted a German invasion of Greece, except as "a security measure to remove the threat to the Roumanian oil supply". The activities of both Section D and later SO2 had therefore been confined by the Chiefs of Staff and by the Foreign Office, fearful of offending neutral opinion, to covert sabotage of rail and barge traffic between Roumania and the Third Reich. Any preparations for overt subversion, let alone guerrilla warfare, in the event of a German invasion had been expressly forbidden. However, with Taylor's arrival in Belgrade to take charge of the situation, most of these restrictions were lifted; but by then it was too late.

In his enthusiasm, Dalton had promised the War Cabinet that SO2 would not only destabilize the regime in Roumania, but would also effectively block the River Danube at the Iron Gates, a project which had so far defeated both Section D and SO2 even with the covert assistance of the Yugoslav army.

Both the Chiefs of Staff and GHQ(ME) accepted that SO2's plans, like many others, had been overtaken by the German invasion of the Balkans. However, GHQ's expectations had been raised by the success of G(R), an offshoot of MI(R) which General Wavell had established at GHQ, in mobilizing indigenous guerrilla support during the Abyssinian campaign. When a British expeditionary force was sent to Greece SO2 was asked to provide active support. As might have been foreseen SO2, which still had an entirely civilian staff, was unable even to contemplate meeting this requirement. Urgent telegrams were sent to Baker Street with the result that the YAK Mission headed by Peter Fleming was hastily diverted from recruiting dissident Italian prisoners of war and despatched to Greece. This small party made its way to the Monastir Gap and did what it could to harass the German advance. It was no more than a gesture on the part of SO2 though one of the Mission was killed during the subsequent evacuation. GHQ(ME) made no secret of its disappointment with SO2's performance, and General Wavell, previously a supporter, joined in the recriminations. Indeed, recriminations were the order of the day; the Army, still smarting from its enforced withdrawal from Greece and Crete, was busy seeking scapegoats wherever it could.

Gubbins, it will be recalled, had no direct responsibility for operations in the Balkans. However, former colleagues in the War Office had warned him early in June that trouble was brewing in Cairo, a warning that was confirmed by Wilkinson who had just returned from Crete. Disturbing news had also reached Dalton. On 26 May he noted in his diary: "Eden showed me a private wire from Wavell to Dill saying that special operations in the Middle East was 'a racket'."[13]

Further complaints continued to be received and in July Nelson flew out to Cairo taking Sweet-Escott with him and leaving Hambro in charge of Baker Street. The most recent allegations of impropriety were found to have emanated from a disconsolate junior member of SO2's Cairo staff whose husband had recently been taken prisoner, and proved to be greatly exaggerated. Far more disturbing was the remarkable zeal with which, in Wavell's absence, his Chief of Staff, General Arthur Smith, had pursued these innuendos at a time when the enemy was advancing on Alexandria and it might have been expected that the critical military situation would have demanded the Chief of Staff's full attention. Less surprising was the discovery that ambitious officers in GHQ, foreseeing that the burgeoning resistance in the Balkans might one day develop into significant paramilitary operations, were determined that this development should in future be under the control of GHQ and not left in the hands of untrained civilians.

Recognizing that the character of special operations in South East Europe had radically altered since the German invasion, Nelson had decided, before he left England, that he must make changes in Cairo. As the new head of SO2 he had chosen Terence Maxwell, a banker who had recently graduated from the Staff College, and to conciliate SO2's military critics Nelson now agreed that in future Maxwell should be assisted by one or two senior officers seconded from GHQ(ME). Gubbins had initially welcomed this development as conforming with the MI(R) concept that guerrilla action should take place under the general direction of the theatre commander, and he was reluctant to perceive that this was the thin end of the wedge, the first of the many attempts by GHQ(ME) to take over SOE(ME) which was still bedevilling relations two years later when he himself became CD.

It is arguable that had Gubbins been allowed to go to the Middle East when the Germans first marched into Yugoslavia, he would have taken charge of the situation and put SO2 on a military footing. In consequence, much of the subsequent difficulties and disasters which befell SOE's Cairo station might have been avoided. Dalton, however, would not hear of it. He was well aware how much SO2 depended on Gubbins' relations with the military authorities and on Gladwyn Jebb's contacts with the Foreign Office. Indeed, during 1941, it was largely the professional reputation of these two men that saved Baker Street from being dismissed by Whitehall as a bunch of lunatic and potentially dangerous amateurs. In any case, Gubbins still had a full-time job to do in London.

By now Gubbins and his staff had outgrown their accommodation in Berkeley Court, and were moved to Norgeby House, a modern office block almost opposite 64, Baker Street. Here Barry was able to set up a proper Operations Room, and Douglas Dodds-Parker, who had recently returned from Khartoum, was put in charge of it. There was predictable opposition; some country section heads were unwilling to divulge their plans (or lack of them) to Gubbins' Operations staff on the grounds of confidentiality. Others genuinely doubted the ability of army officers to handle the essentially civilian tasks of sabotage and subversion which many considered their first object. The more cynical saw the establishment of the Operations Room as an unwelcome extension of military influence in SOE. Gubbins and Barry worked hard to allay these suspicions. In any case, it could not be denied that in November, 1940, when Gubbins had arrived in Baker Street, SO2 had not had a single radio set operating in Occupied Europe, whereas during the following summer and autumn over sixty assorted agents had been despatched to North West Europe − a high proportion (twenty-seven) being destined for France. This was no mean achievement, but Dalton was far from satisfied. On 1 December, 1941, he noted in his diary, "Our last reports have been most bare, only tales of what has not been done, with most of the blame put on the weather. I told Gladwyn that just now I am particularly anxious for a successful operation or two."

Like his fellow socialist, Jean Jaurès, who had been assassinated in 1914 on the eve of the First World War, Dalton believed that with suitable political inducement the workers of Europe would rise as one, overthrow Prussian militarism and secure universal peace. It was not a vision which appealed either to Eden or to Duff Cooper, the Minister of Information. In August, 1941, wearying of what they considered to be Dalton's intrusions into their affairs, they joined forces and secured the abolition of the Propaganda Section (SO1). It was replaced by a Political Warfare Executive in which the Foreign Office set the tone and SO2, though still responsible for delivering the 'black' printed propaganda in Occupied Europe, had only a consultative role in its preparation. Having lost the fairest jewel in his crown, Dalton was all the more determined to make the most of SO2, henceforward to be known as SOE, about whose political direction he had very definite ideas. Gubbins found some of these ideas Utopian and even ridiculous. Nevertheless, he had a more speculative mind than many of his Baker Street colleagues, dismissed by Dalton as 'too many bankers' and though no way a socialist, shared some of his Minister's prejudices, as well as his affection for the Poles. Gubbins had not previously experienced ministerial pressure and, unlike Jebb and the other Whitehall professionals, had not yet learned to exploit or discount it. He greatly admired Dalton's energy in promoting SOE, but became increasingly aware that it was only Nelson's untiring efforts which prevented the Minister from meddling disastrously in the day-to-day business of the country sections. The more he saw of Nelson, the more he respected the integrity of this shy and unassuming man. The respect was mutual and, in Taylor's absence, Gubbins became in many ways the mainstay of the Baker Street organization. Recognizing this, Dalton and Nelson both felt that his responsibilities should be widened; Baker Street's current operations were now proceeding smoothly under Barry; more than fifty training establishments of various sorts had been set up by Jack Wilson; moreover, since the German invasion of the Soviet Union, the Czech and Polish connection had lost its immediacy while the latest Chiefs of Staff directives had emphasized that SO2's future plans should be focused on North West Europe. Accordingly, in November Nelson embarked on a major reorganization: the two French sections as well as the Belgian, Dutch, German and Austrian, were added to the Polish and Czech sections for which Gubbins was already responsible. To assist him, two so-called Regional Controllers were appointed: Robin Brook, a founder member of Dalton's Private Office in Berkeley Square, was to supervise North West Europe; while Wilkinson, recently returned from the Middle East, was to resume charge of liaison with the Poles and Czechs and also to supervise the German and Austrian sections.

In order to instil some measure of corporate responsibility, as well as to smooth feathers ruffled by the extension of Gubbins' empire, Nelson seized the opportunity to institute an SOE Council, which met weekly and was attended by the Directors and other key personnel. Meanwhile, by appointing Taylor, now returned from internment in Italy, Sweet-Escott and Jack Beevor to his Private Office, Nelson ensured that the direction of SOE was kept firmly in civilian hands.

One of the most important factors affecting Gubbins' new responsibilities was the Soviet entry into the war and its impact on resistance in North West Europe – particularly in France. Stalin's call to communist sympathizers world-wide to take immediate action to relieve pressure on the Red Army had resulted in an upsurge of anti-Fascist resistance throughout Occupied Europe on a scale hitherto undreamed of by SOE. Some of these extreme left-wing groups were led by organizers recruited and trained by the Comintern before the war and some actually received orders direct from the NKVD. These professional anti-Fascists, used to years of living illegally, were very different from the moderate socialists who Dalton would have chosen to spearhead the workers' revolution, and were the latter's natural enemies. It was a pattern soon to be established world-wide and accounted for much of the antagonism to SOE displayed by both radical left-wing and extreme right-wing circles.

An equally important factor so far as France was concerned was the antipathy which existed between the supporters of Marshal Pétain and the followers of General de Gaulle. As a result of his experiences with SAVANNA and JOSEPHINE B, Gubbins was predisposed towards the Free French, though, as we have seen, relations between SOE and General de Gaulle were far from cordial. Gubbins' prejudice was strongly reinforced by his meeting with Jean Moulin, who had come secretly to London in September and had made a most favourable impression on Gubbins, as indeed on everyone else he met. Moreover, Moulin had overcome de Gaulle's reluctance to allow French resistance organizations to engage in immediate action against the Germans besides constituting a potential force to be employed at the time of liberation. Nevertheless, the Foreign Office remained adamant in its refusal to allow SOE to conduct active operations in Unoccupied France and continued to be equivocal in its attitude towards General de Gaulle. It had to be accepted that Whitehall preferred the activities of F Section's agents, which it was imagined that SOE could control, to those of the Free French which it could not. For Gubbins, whose primary task was to kill Germans, it was by no means an easy inheritance.

As for relations with the Soviet Union, Gubbins found himself opposed to the views of his Minister and many of his colleagues. In his long-standing distrust of Soviet intentions, Gubbins was even more resolute than 'the bankers'. Dalton, on the other hand, partly under pressure from left-wing colleagues in the Labour Party, supported the idea of establishing a working relationship with the NKVD. So began one of the most futile essays in allied cooperation of the whole war. In due course Colonel Ivan Chichayev arrived in London and set up his office in Bayswater, in the block of flats already occupied by Colonel Moravec and the Czech Intelligence Service.* SOE's reciprocal Mission to Moscow was headed by Colonel Guinness whose Planning section had become redundant in the reorganization. Since there was what Gubbins considered to be a forlorn hope that the Soviet authorities would allow RAF aircraft on flights to Poland to land in the USSR and refuel before returning, the Mission included Captain Richard Truszkowski, who had been with the Polish Mission both in Warsaw and in France. However, although Gubbins knew more about the Soviet Union than most of his colleagues, he had made no secret of his prejudices and was not surprised when Dalton and Nelson decided not to put him in charge of the new Soviet Liaison Section.

While sceptical about future liaison with the NKVD, Gubbins was enthusiastic about SO2's connections with the United States. Thanks to the friendship which developed between President Roosevelt and William Stephenson, head of the British Security Coordination Office (BSO) which had been established in New York at the beginning of the war, a special relationship existed between SO2 and its United States counterpart long before Pearl Harbor. Gubbins had met Colonel W. J. Donovan, whom Roosevelt had put in charge of special operations when the former had visited London in July, 1940. During a second visit the following December, Donovan had been taken by Gubbins to see SO2's paramilitary training school in Scotland which had greatly impressed him. Consequently, on his return to Washington, although the United States was not yet belligerent, Donovan had encouraged selected members of his organization to undergo training at the paramilitary school which SO2 had set up in Canada. Here many useful friendships were formed and when OSS established its London headquarters in Brook Street, Mayfair, early in 1942, close cooperation was assured and OSS was given the benefit of SO2's experience.

As before, Taylor remained responsible for SO2 activities in North and South America, but it was probably Gubbins' section which established the closest working relations with OSS. As a first step, Captain Stacy B. Loyd jnr. was attached to the Polish and Czech sections in Norgeby House. It was the first of many such attachments.

The description of Gubbins' first year in Baker Street would be incomplete

---

* Although there is no doubt that Chichayev and Moravec regularly exchanged views, at the time of the execution of Heydrich this propinquity was the subject of an official protest by Chichayev.

without some reference to the arrangements he made with the First Aid Nursing Yeomanry (FANY) through his cousin Mrs Phyllis Bingham. As a result, the FANYs were not only employed as drivers at Headquarters, but also provided the administrative staff at most of the training schools and holding establishments. Moreover, when SOE built its own radio station, this was almost entirely manned by FANY operators. From the outset FANYs had been employed in the houses where agents were held for their last few hours or nights before they were despatched to their destination, and from 1942 onwards many of SOE's female agents were also enrolled in the FANYs to insure their pension rights if they became casualties. Also for administrative reasons it became the general rule that SOE's female staff working in operational theatres and required to wear uniform should be enrolled as FANYs.

By the end of the war there were several hundred FANYs serving in SOE at home and abroad. The exploits of some of those who served as agents in France have been well publicized. However, the FANY rank and file played an unobtrusive but no less important role in SOE and all, whatever their rank or status, looked to Gubbins as their patron. He, for his part, always took a personal interest in their welfare. To celebrate the New Year, he organized at one of the training schools an all-ranks dance for members of his staff to which he invited the FANY drivers. Presided over by Mrs Bingham, it was as decorous as an end of term party at a girls' school; however, Gubbins wore the kilt and led the Scottish dancing until the small hours of the morning. At a time when senior officers were not expected to enjoy all-ranks dances, Gubbins proved an exception and his staff parties continued to be a regular feature. In staff relations, as in much else, he was ahead of his time.

11

SOE: 1942

The second half of 1941 had not fulfilled the promise of the early months. The French had proved less responsible than had been expected and a number of arrests had taken place; severe German reprisals in Norway had become a source of friction with the Norwegian government; the weather had prevented any flights to Poland during the autumn months and a second radio operator despatched to Czechoslovakia had been arrested shortly after his arrival. Dalton remained as impatient as ever about the time spent in training and preparation and left Nelson in no doubt about his disappointment with Baker Street's performance.

For Gubbins, the only bright spot at the turn of the year had been the success of operation POSTMASTER. This plan, conceived by SOE's outstation in Lagos, had been carried out by Major Gus March-Philipps, the founder of SO2's Small Boat Section. In September, 1941, with a skeleton crew which included Captain J. G. Appleyard, who was also to be killed on active service with SOE, March-Philipps had set out from Poole Harbour in *Maid Honor*, a small fishing smack, bound for West Africa. Here, in an exploit worthy of an Elizabethan privateer, he and his crew had succeeded in cutting out the 7,600-ton Italian liner *Duchessa d'Aosta* which, on Italy's declaration of war, had taken refuge in the neutral port of Fernando Po in Spanish West Africa. Despite the misgivings of the Foreign Office, the incident had only provoked a formal complaint from the Spanish authorities, and had provided the Royal Navy with an extremely valuable prize.

The first six months of 1942 were to see the replacement of Sir Frank Nelson by his deputy Charles Hambro, several unsuccessful attempts to abolish SOE as an independent organization and, in February, a change of Ministers. Thanks to the unremitting efforts of Dalton, Nelson and Jebb, there was also a marked improvement in SOE's standing in Whitehall. The development of closer relations between Baker Street and the Joint Planning section of the Chiefs of Staff was much to the credit of Gubbins and Barry. General Sir Alan Brooke's appointment as CIGS at the end of November, 1941, had delighted Gubbins. His predecessor, General Sir John Dill, had never shown much enthusiasm for irregular operations, nor had Gubbins found him particularly helpful at meetings of the Chiefs of Staff Committee. With Brooke his personal relations were already established. Moreover, having been brought up and partly educated in France, Brooke's attitude to foreigners was more sophisticated than Dill's and more attuned to SOE's point of view. Dalton gave the new CIGS dinner on 6 January, describing the meeting as "mutually satisfactory".[1] Brooke was more forthcoming in his diaries: "Dined with Dalton and discussed with him his sabotage activities in Europe... and also the question of raising local forces in Europe to be armed and equipped at the last moment .... There is a great deal to be done in this direction at present and I don't feel we are doing anything like enough."[2] Three days later Dalton had a meeting with Admiral Mountbatten, the newly appointed Chief of Combined Operations. This meeting too was constructive, Dalton noting with satisfaction Lord Louis' agreement that it was on the French industrial working class that SOE should count. The staff talks which followed soon settled outstanding questions such as the operational control of raiding parties. Moreover, Lord Louis, whose eye was often on the main object, was quick to note that SOE offered a unique and apparently inexhaustible source of special arms, explosives and other technical supplies which Combined Operations had neither the funds nor the facilities to manufacture for themselves.* SOE was also able on occasions to provide German speakers and other specialist personnel for CCO's raiding parties. Gubbins, having commanded the original Independent Companies, took a keen interest in these arrangements, not least because March-Philipps' Small Scale Raiding Force, which had been formed under his auspices while remaining under SOE's administration and general direction, now passed under the operational control of the CCO.

So far so good, but Dalton's attempts at mending his fences with the Air Ministry were less successful. It will be recalled that in August, 1941, eight Whitley and two Halifax aircraft had been made available at Newmarket for special operations. This allotment was increased in February, 1942, to ten Whitley and five Halifax aircraft. The following June the number of Halifaxes was doubled to make up for the Whitleys which were being taken out of service as obsolete.

Since the Chiefs of Staff had decided against the support of secret armies in Poland and Czechoslovakia, the number of long-range aircraft capable of flying to these two countries was kept to the minimum necessary for the support of sabotage and subversion. This limit caused great dissatisfaction to the Poles, whose pilots had fought so bravely in the Battle of Britain, and

---

* After his meeting with Mountbatten Dalton shrewdly noted, "He may become, or be presented by others, as an uncomfortable acquisitive force."[3]

who felt they deserved better of the Royal Air Force. Moreover neither Poles nor Czechs could understand the extreme reluctance of the Royal Air Force to accept their aircrews for operations to Poland and Czechoslovakia. The Air Ministry's reasons were that this would result in a loss of flexibility. At the time of the Chiefs of Staff 1941 directive to SOE it had been accepted that resistance could only be supported on any significant scale at the expense of the RAF's bomber offensive. This essential clash of interests, so often nearly fatal to SOE, was to occupy Gubbins during 1942 and 1943 more than any other issue. It was clearly impossible for allied governments-in-exile to accept the Air Ministry's ruling that the support of their patriot forces should be accorded lower priority than the bombing offensive, which many of them had good reason to believe was far less effective than the Air Ministry claimed. SOE bore the brunt of their dissatisfaction and, as SOE's Director of Operations, Gubbins' position was far from enviable. However, he continued throughout 1942 and 1943 to fight with the utmost tenacity for what he considered to be a proper recognition of SOE's requirements of long-range aircraft.

Gubbins was not, at this stage of the war, particularly involved in SOE's running battles with the Foreign Office, except when, for reasons of state, restrictive conditions were imposed, such as the ban on active operations in the Unoccupied Zone of France. His personal relations with officials such as Roger Makins and Frank Roberts, successive heads of the Central Department, with whom he had dealt over Czech affairs since the earliest days of MI(R), were excellent. Nevertheless, like other senior officers in Baker Street, Gubbins could hardly have failed to be aware that, however improved SOE's relations with the Service Ministries might become, a reconciliation between SOE and the Foreign Office was virtually impossible so long as Eden was Foreign Secretary and Dalton Minister of Economic Warfare. The Foreign Office had never ceased to regret that Halifax had agreed to SOE's independence in the first place. Eden told Cadogan, his Permanent Under-Secretary, that had he been Foreign Secretary in July, 1940, he would never have accepted it.[4] Eden distrusted Dalton's Fabian *dirigisme* and, with some justification, suspected him of wishing to interfere in foreign affairs which, given the intrinsically political character of many of SOE's activities, was almost unavoidable. He also found Dalton's loud voice and rumbustious heartiness repellent. Dalton for his part thought Eden a stuffed shirt and made no secret of it. Moreover, the themes for overseas propaganda proposed by Dalton at staff meetings of SO1 from time to time included appeals for socialist solidarity in occupied Europe. Prescriptions of this sort, in themselves often sensible, frequently clashed with the rhetoric of right-wing exiled politicians and were sometimes couched in terms which some thought had been specially calculated to irritate the Foreign Secretary and other Conservative Ministers.

Early in 1942 SOE's enemies were busy spreading rumours, not altogether unfounded, that the Prime Minister was contemplating abolishing SOE entirely and sharing its functions between the Chiefs of Staff and the Foreign Office. It was not a prospect viewed with enthusiasm by Sir Alexander Cadogan.[5] Fortunately for him, the fall of Singapore precipitated a reshuffle of the government in which Dalton was transferred – he was always careful to say 'promoted' – to become President of the Board of Trade. His replacement as Minister of Economic Warfare was Viscount Wolmer, who almost immediately succeeded his father as Earl of Selborne. Gubbins, who owed to Dalton his appointment to SOE, recognized his considerable achievements, and shared some of his prejudices – for instance his hatred of appeasement. Nevertheless, like many others in Baker Street, he felt a sense of relief that one of the main causes of SOE's unpopularity in Whitehall had been removed. Happily for his peace of mind, he was unaware that for several days the very existence of SOE had been in the balance.

Lord Selborne was aged fifty-four when he took over SOE, a small stooping figure with a deceptively mild appearance. Cadogan commented, "I dare say it will work but he is not very inspiring."[6] However, Gubbins returned from his first meeting enthusiastic. Selborne had listened in silence while he had set out his views not only about the contribution which patriot forces might make, provided their activities were coordinated with and complementary to regular operations, but also his insistence that unless more aircraft were made available all these efforts would be in vain. Selborne had clearly been impressed by the cogency and professionalism of Gubbins' presentation and Gubbins thought he seemed disposed to adopt his policy as his own, as indeed it was to prove.

Unlike Dalton, Selborne showed no desire to interfere in the everyday work of SOE. In fact, now that its activities were coming more directly under the direction of the Chiefs of Staff there was no longer so much scope for ministerial intervention. Some of the original members of the organization may have regretted the disappearance of the midnight sessions in Berkeley Square when, under Dalton's benign supervision, SOE's future was thrashed out, sometimes in terms of a socialist crusade. Gubbins had little in common with Dalton's young disciples and found these juvenile discussions exasperating. He greatly preferred Selborne's practical and incisive approach to SOE's current objectives; for, with the entry of the United States and the Soviet Union into the war, there was at last a prospect of re-invading North West Europe in the foreseeable future, and there was a definite role for SOE in support of this sort of operation.

Selborne had arrived in Berkeley Square well aware of the allegations of incompetence, and worse, constantly made about the Baker Street headquarters, and his appointment had coincided with one of the periodic waves of dissatisfaction with SOE. His own first impressions, as he told the Prime Minister, had been more favourable than he had been led to expect, but he had not the slightest intention of allowing himself to be associated with an organization which was in any way disreputable. Accordingly, one of his first acts was to arrange for John Hanbury-Williams, managing director of Courtaulds and a director of the Bank of England, assisted by Edward Playfair of HM Treasury, to enquire into the allegations against SOE. The details of the Hanbury-Williams report remain confidential, but while recommending more formal liaison with some of the departments who had hitherto been kept officially in ignorance of SOE's activities, Hanbury-Williams let it be known that in general he had found Baker Street "as much sinned against as sinning". Gubbins had noted with approval that this verdict, coupled with informal liaison arrangements with the JPS which had emerged from Dalton's meeting with Brooke, had gone a long way towards regularizing SOE's position. He particularly hoped that the appointment of Lieutenant-Colonel Dibley, a much respected former member of the Staff Duties branch of the War Office, to scrutinize Baker Street's war establishments, would once and for all dispose of the charges of extravagant use of manpower.

Only the Foreign Office remained implacable. On 25 March, after a visit with Jebb to Baker Street, Cadogan recorded that he was "not frightfully impressed" and on 8 April that "PM seems to have more or less kept his (and our) end up with Selborne last night".[7] It is true that some of Cadogan's exasperation with SOE at this time seems to have been due to Selborne's decision to dispense with Gladwyn Jebb, and the difficulty of re-absorbing the latter into the Foreign Office where his substantive rank was that of First Secretary.

Jebb's departure meant that the Foreign Office was able to exert less leverage on SOE, but it also left SOE without direct access to Foreign Office departments at working level. Gubbins did not consider this a serious handicap but on personal grounds he was sorry to see Jebb go. In the early days they had fought many Whitehall battles together on SOE's behalf. While neither at that time was particularly popular in his own service, Jebb's incisive mind and exceptionally wide inter-departmental experience, coupled with Gubbins' tenacity and military expertise, made them, for their rank and age, a formidable combination. Besides, although initially Jebb's view on SOE's role was of a Fourth Arm dedicated to sabotage and subversion, he was largely converted by Gubbins to the concept of patriot armies. Gubbins' admiration for Jebb was reciprocated: "But above all, to Colin Gubbins credit is due," wrote Jebb in his final report. "I have seldom met a man more vigorous and a more inspiring soldier, or incidentally one possessing more 'political sense'. There is no doubt that he is the lynch-pin of the existing machine, and so long as he is there it is certain that it will continue to function, whatever arrangements are come to at the top." Before Dalton's departure, while SOE's future was still in the balance, Jebb had prepared a memorandum. The areas of possible friction between the Foreign Office and SOE, which Jebb's memorandum identified, were all too familiar to the officials concerned. However, the fortnightly meetings designed to iron out these difficulties, at which the SIS was also to be represented, were to become occasions for mutual accusation as often as for constructive consultation. At the time Gubbins' main preoccupation was with France, and his comment on the 'treaty' was that SOE "was still under the crippling Foreign Office ban not to undertake violent sabotage in Unoccupied France". However, the memorandum also specified that in enemy and enemy-occupied territory SOE was to work "under the directions of the Chiefs of Staff or the responsible commander-in-chief". This provision foreshadowed the devolution of responsibility for special operations which was later to prove one of SOE's distinctive features when Gubbins became CD. The memorandum also contained the injunction that "if any organization in touch with SOE were found to be in a position to exercise political influence in the country, SOE should at once consult the Foreign Office and the Chiefs of Staff as to the line to be adopted". In the years to come, Gubbins was to find to his cost that, in seeking to satisfy both the Foreign Office and the Chiefs of Staff, SOE was bound to fall foul of both.

In the vital area of North West Europe, although detestation of the German occupation was fairly general in France and the Low Countries, agents despatched from the United Kingdom by both F and RF Sections during the second half of 1941 had reported few signs of organized resistance. However, contact had been made with several individuals, some of whom were obviously potential leaders. Of these the outstanding example was Jean Moulin, a Gaullist supporter of the first quality. In 1940 Moulin had been *préfet* of the Department of Eure et Loire, which straddled the demarcation line between the Occupied and Unoccupied Zones. He had been dismissed by the Germans in November and had gone to live in the South of France. After ten months spent encouraging support for de Gaulle throughout South-East France, he had reached London in September, 1941, after long delays, travelling on false papers via Lisbon. Gubbins, like everyone who came in contact with Moulin, including the Germans, was immensely impressed by his competence and personality. Although he saw the dangers of sabotage and terrorism at this stage in the war, Moulin saw no less clearly that the moment for active resistance could not long be delayed. It was something of a personal triumph that he should have succeeded in persuading de Gaulle, in November, 1941, not only to form a so-called National Council of Resistance, but also to sign an *ordre de mission* for him, envisaging armed action and ultimately the use of military force to take over civil power. Moreover, whatever de Gaulle's reservations, Moulin had no hesitation in accepting SOE's offers of support. The so-called 'recruitment' of Moulin was counted a major success for RF Section, and Gubbins considered that under Moulin's leadership the Gaullist movement would be capable of providing the cadre on which a future secret army might be formed.

Moulin returned to France on 2 January, and Gubbins' enthusiasm for the Free French lessened as it became increasingly clear after his departure that de Gaulle had little interest in paramilitary operations, had views of his own about the future role of his supporters in France and was extremely unlikely ever to prove amenable to direction by the British Chiefs of Staff, still less by SOE, when the time came for the liberation of his country. Besides, the General was altogether unable to reconcile himself to the activities let alone the existence of SOE's independent French section. A proposal that F Section should be absorbed into the Free French organization was unequivocally rejected by the Foreign Secretary on 20 January and even Gubbins accepted that it was clear that "we cannot build up a proper secret army in France under the aegis or flag of de Gaulle; that we must do through our independent French section, until such time as a combination is practical politics".[8] It must be admitted, however, that when he wrote this minute, Gubbins had little confidence in F Section, whose activities in 1941 had been less effective than those of the Free French. The latter had at least shown that they could mount *coups de main*.

However, the next important visitor to arrive in London was an F Section agent, Baron Pierre de Vomécourt. Though not in the same class as Moulin, de Vomécourt, who had been one of the original agents dropped by F Section near Châteauroux, was nevertheless an outstanding performer. Moreover, unlike Moulin, he had recent information about potential resistance in the Occupied Zone which was of immediate interest to the military authorities. Accordingly, as well as taking de Vomécourt to see Eden on 28 February, Gubbins also took him to call on the CIGS. Besides, the circumstances of de Vomécourt's return to London intrigued Gubbins and his account of his recruitment of his two brothers and the steps he had taken to get resistance going both in the Occupied and Unoccupied Zones increased Gubbins's confidence in F Section's capability.

Unfortunately, during 1942 most of F Section's effort was to be directed towards supporting the so-called *Carte* organization. With the benefit of hindsight it seems almost incredible that SOE failed to realize that the claims of André Girard, the organizer of *Carte*, were simply too good to be true.

However, in 1941/42 the prospect of establishing contact with the French 'Armistice Army' with its promise of activating resistance groups of up to a quarter of a million men for paramilitary tasks when the moment came was immensely attractive, not only to Gubbins but also to the Chiefs of Staff as a general prospectus. Two senior section officers, sent in specially by Baker Street, had reported favourably on the *Carte* organization and Gubbins was in no position to enquire into its leader's credentials. Buckmaster had only recently taken charge of F Section, while Robin Brook, the extremely able regional controller of Western Europe, was at that time still relatively inexperienced. Foot's description[9] of this organization's disastrous career illustrates the extent to which the headquarters staff in Baker Street depended on the judgement of its agents in the field; also its general desperation about getting anything going in France in time for the invasion of North Africa (Operation TORCH), which was already being planned, let alone the invasion of Europe which was still, though without much conviction, scheduled for 1943.

Whatever Gubbins's misgivings about the performance of the two French sections in the spring of 1942, there seemed even less likelihood of being able to organize effective resistance in Belgium and Holland. Almost every allied government-in-exile was debilitated by intrigue and faction. The Belgians were no exception, and during 1942 Gubbins was forced to spend much time sorting out Belgian affairs. Not only were there internal rows and jealousies between the various Belgian authorities in London, there was also the perennial difficulty described by Sweet-Escott "of reconciling the wishes of the Belgian authorities in London, who wanted to keep any organization there was in Belgium intact until D-Day, with the need of SOE to justify itself in the eyes of the British authorities who provided the facilities and naturally wanted quick dividends".[10] Dalton's boast to Churchill that, when supplies had been dropped, "I think you may take it that something pretty big will happen in Belgium" was a triumph of hope over experience.

Later in the year, in August, 1942, the situation deteriorated to the extent that the Belgian Government temporarily broke off relations with SOE, a *modus vivendi* not being re-established until the following November, after the intervention of the Chiefs of Staff. By then there was strong suspicion that some, if not all, of SOE's radio sets in Belgium were being operated by the Germans.

Gubbins' relations with the Netherlands authorities were more cordial and less time-consuming. But even when, in April, 1942, the so-called 'Plan for Holland' was drawn up and approved by the Netherlands government-in-exile, the inexperience and incompetence of SOE's Dutch country section, the over-confidence of the Dutch authorities in London, and the desperate optimism so characteristic of allied governments-in-exile combined to facilitate the Germans' very competent and successful handling of their Operation NORDPOL. This counter-intelligence operation led to the capture of no less than forty-three Dutch parachutists and their radio sets, and gave the *Abwehr* the chance to mount an elaborate deception plan which lasted for nearly two years. When the extent of the enemy's penetration of the Dutch resistance organization was reported to the Chiefs of Staff in December, 1943, it nearly proved fatal to SOE, whose survival depended once again on the personal intervention of the Prime Minister. But this is to anticipate. In the spring of 1942, Gubbins, ignorant of the disasters which had already overtaken the first Dutch agents, remarked that he was agreeably surprised that things were going so well in the Netherlands.

Of all Gubbins' acquisitions under the November, 1941, reorganization, he probably found Norway the most agreeable. His participation in the Norwegian campaign in 1940, when commanding the Independent Companies, gave him a keen personal interest in Norwegian operations. However, the Chiefs of Staff, in their 1941 directive, had relegated the status of Norway to that of a country in which a British offensive was unlikely, and therefore it was considered unworthy of intensive airborne support. This ruling put the Norwegians on a par with the Czechs and Poles in terms of the allocation of aircraft. There were, however, two important differences. First, from time to time and unpredictably, Norway caught the Prime Minister's attention as possessing the sort of seaboard which invited small boat raids. He therefore gave Norway higher priority than that accorded by his Chiefs of Staff. Secondly, unlike the Poles and Czechs, Norwegian resistance was not entirely, or even largely, dependent on air support. The Small Boat Service – known as the Shetland Bus – had been established at Lerwick as early as 1940. Crewed by Norwegian seamen and administered by SOE, the Shetland Bus continued to function with great success throughout the war. Moreover, news had reached SOE early in 1941 that a promising secret organization known as Milorg was already in existence. As so often happened when resistance organizations were directed by former regular army officers, Milorg's leaders, while ready to call out their men to support an act of invasion did not believe that the sort of sabotage and subversive operations prescribed for Norway by the Chiefs of Staff had sufficient military importance to justify the ruthless German reprisals which would certainly be provoked. It was a point of view with which Gubbins personally had much sympathy, though he was forced to point out to Milorg that there were at least four sabotage targets in Norway which were of considerable strategic importance, apart from the Prime Minister's periodic preoccupations with hit and run raids. Those differences of opinion did not seriously disturb SOE's relations with the Norwegian authorities and, in

February, 1942, Gubbins appointed Jack Wilson, previously in charge of SOE training, to take charge of the Scandinavian Section which under Wiskemann, the previous sectional head, had hitherto been directly responsible to Hambro and Sporborg. It was to prove one of Gubbins' most successful appointments, and it was followed by the arrival in March of Skinnarland, a prominent member of the Norwegian resistance, who was an engineer at the Norsk Hydro plant at Rjukan in South Norway. Norsk Hydro was one of the priority targets for sabotage as it was known to manufacture heavy water (HO) essential for German experiments to produce an atom bomb. Skinnarland was given three weeks' training and was then parachuted back to Norway with orders to remain at his post and await instructions. He was destined to play a key role in Operation GUNNERSIDE in the following February, when a group of Norwegian parachutists succeeded in putting Norsk Hydro out of action for many months − perhaps SOE's most brilliant success in the whole war. But this too is to anticipate.

While the Scandinavian country section could safely be left in Jack Wilson's hands for the time being, Gubbins found it necessary to turn his attention once again to Central European affairs. At the initial meeting between Dalton and Beneš in 1941, it had been agreed that SOE should train a small contingent of Czech troops for special operations. The SIS was unwilling to allow Moravec to jeopardize his existing radio links which were being used to carry valuable intelligence traffic, and before any action could be taken it was necessary to establish independent radio communications with the Protectorate. Several air sorties to Czechoslovakia in the spring of 1941 had proved abortive because of bad weather and during the summer months the hours of darkness were too short to permit flights to Central Europe. The Czech authorities were not particularly worried by these failures, nor by the decision of the Chiefs of Staff that it was impossible to provide air support for general risings in Central Europe. There were ample supplies of arms and explosives in the Protectorate; their armament industry, fully mobilized by the Germans, provided Czech workers with innumerable opportunities for the undetectable (and unverifiable) sabotage approved of by the Chiefs of Staff in which their underground organization claimed to excel. There had never been any question of the Czech Home Army attempting the sort of paramilitary operations favoured by the Poles, at any rate until the time was ripe for a general rising. Nevertheless, with Russia's entry into the war, Beneš began to worry lest the relatively passive role adopted by the Czech resistance might count against the Czechs' territorial claims in the post-war settlement. In short, they could no longer rely on the reputation for subversion and sabotage which they had gained when under Austrian domination before and during the First World War; some spectacular gesture was needed, whatever the cost.

In September, 1941, Gubbins was informed that President Beneš had sanctioned a terrorist attack on some prominent personality in the Protectorate, possibly on the *Reichsprotektor* Reinhard Heydrich himself. Colonel Moravec enquired whether SOE would help in this project by providing facilities for training and supplying any special weaponry that was required. Gubbins had no hesitation in agreeing, but decided to restrict the knowledge of the Czech approach, and above all of the identity of the probable target, to a very small circle. There was no need for him to seek ministerial approval and there is no evidence that he consulted Dalton at this stage. Acts of terrorism fell within SOE's charter and, as a senior official of the *Sicherheitsdienst*, Heydrich was a legitimate target. Moreover, in the last resort Beneš and the Czech government were free to do what they liked in their own country without having to seek British approval. However, Gubbins pointed out to Moravec that an assassination of this sort was a purely political act which, even if unsuccessful, would result in wholesale reprisals for which, in his view, there was insufficient military justification. Later on Gubbins revised this opinion on learning that Heydrich, before coming to Prague, had made a special study of resistance elements in North West Europe, his elimination therefore becoming of direct interest to SOE.

By the time that Selborne took over from Dalton, independent radio communication with the Protectorate had been re-established; two agents had been selected by the Czechs, trained and equipped by SOE and dropped in Bohemia by the RAF, and the assassination was due to take place at the first opportunity. Gubbins therefore lost no time in putting Selborne in the picture, making it clear that the odds were against the operation succeeding and that absolute secrecy was essential. There is no reason to think that Selborne informed the Prime Minister of SOE's implication until news reports were received that the attack had succeeded to the extent that Heydrich had been seriously wounded. The SIS was certainly aware of Czech intentions and may or may not have informed the Foreign Office. It also seems likely that the Russians were forewarned, if not by Beneš, at least by Moravec who was in regular contact with Ivan Chichayev, the NKVD resident representative in London.

Although ANTHROPOID, as the operation was code-named, had been planned and executed entirely by the Czechs, SOE's Czech section had provided essential support and the two agents had been transported to Czechoslovakia by the RAF. The reprisals were even more terrible than Gubbins had predicted and effectively liquidated organized Czech resistance for the rest of the war. This is not the place to try to assess the importance of ANTHROPOID which was certainly one of the most sensational operations in which SOE was involved. It is, however, interesting that Gubbins appears to have seen no particular objection to SOE being implicated in a political assassination, the sort of operation that Eden later stigmatized as "war crimes business" though admittedly Heydrich was by any standard a special case. Nor did he seek ministerial approval or disclose the true nature of the operation until it was too late for anyone to interfere. As it transpired, news of SOE's part in Heydrich's assassination was received with approval by the Prime Minister, and Mr Churchill was reported to have winked when President Roosevelt subsequently asked him whether the British authorities had been involved. Nevertheless, although Gubbins wrote to Moravec congratulating him on the success of the operation, it was not until many years after the war that SOE's involvement was publicly acknowledged. Meanwhile Beneš had his own reasons for not wishing the responsibility of the Czech government in London to become known. The secret was well kept.

The spring of 1942 also saw one of the few serious approaches by a German resistance group. Dr Willem Visser t'Hooft, later to become head of the World Council of Churches, visited London in May bringing with him from Switzerland a memorandum written by Baron Adam von Trott zu Solz, addressed to Sir Stafford Cripps. Trott, who was to be hanged with many of his friends and collaborators following Stauffenberg's abortive attempt to assassinate Hitler on 20 July, 1944, had been a Rhodes scholar at Balliol College, Oxford, in the early 1930s. He was a young man of great charm and intelligence, with a wide circle of English friends, including not only Cripps, but also Lord Lothian, Lady Astor and her son David. He had stayed at Cliveden in the summer of 1939, had had conversations with both Neville Chamberlain, the Prime Minister, and with Lord Halifax, the Foreign Secretary, and had been conspicuous in his efforts to avert the outbreak of war between Britain and Germany. However, some of his pre-war activities, not least his ardent German patriotism, had been misunderstood, and he was viewed with extreme, though in fact wholly unjustified, suspicion by the intelligence authorities in both Britain and the United States. In any case, his memorandum of April, 1942, contained features quite unacceptable to British public opinion which, at this stage of the war, was neither disposed to distinguish between good and bad Germans nor interested in plans for the resurgence of a post-Nazi Germany. The Bishop of Chichester, while visiting Stockholm, had received parallel approaches from two German evangelical clergymen, Pastor Schonfeld and Dietrich Bonhöffer also representing what later came to be known as the *Kreisauerkreis* (after Helmut von Moltke's country estate at Kreisau). The rejection of these approaches by the British authorities is described in Christopher Sykes' biography of Trott, *Troubled Loyalty*. It is fruitless to speculate what might have been the outcome of a positive decision, but it is interesting to record Gubbins' reaction to these events. SOE was naturally one of the departments consulted about Trott's memorandum. Gubbins, never very confident in dealing with German affairs, least of all with 'good' Germans, agreed reservedly with the Foreign Office and the SIS (which had had its fingers badly burnt in the Venlo incident in 1939) that there should be no response to these approaches and no reply sent to Trott's memorandum enquiring about the British attitude to post-Nazi Germany. The fact that Trott was a junior member of the *Auswärtiges Amt*, and Moltke a serving officer in the *Abwehr*, and that both individuals made frequent visits abroad, only possible with official sanction, did not inspire confidence. Moreover Trott's pre-war association with the so-called "Cliveden Set" certainly counted against him. It is ironical that many of the views on the shape of post-war Europe contained in Trott's memorandum, which Gubbins never saw, bore a remarkable resemblance to those later put forward by the Bildeberg Group with which Gubbins was later to be so closely associated.

It is conceivable that the British government missed an opportunity of curtailing the war by its failure to respond positively to the *Kreisauer Circle* in 1942 but, so far as SOE was concerned, Gubbins shared the view of his German section that the only element in Germany with sufficient strength to overthrow Hitler, the SS, and the Party at large, was the German Army itself. He recognized that the time might come for the revolt of the *Reichswehr*, for example when the Continent was invaded, but he was certainly right in deciding that the time was not ripe in the early summer of 1942.

In fact, however, he had given the matter little serious thought. For want of trained personnel Gubbins had not been able to delegate enough of his new responsibilities, was trying to take on too much detailed work himself and had far too little time to spend on thinking about the long-term implications of supporting European resistance, let alone the resurrection of a democratic Germany. He was overwhelmed with current problems not least on account of his constant anxiety that, when the time came for the cross-Channel invasion, SOE would be found unprepared. He was well aware that only the most tentative beginnings had been made in France and he was haunted by the knowledge, not generally shared in Baker Street, that it would be a year or eighteen months before any resistance groups were ready for action and if, as was still assumed for planning purposes, the invasion took place in 1943, it seemed all too likely that SOE's contribution would be too late. This sense of desperation caused Gubbins to approve several ill-considered projects in France, among them a Polish operation with the code name ADJUDICATE.

A Polish cavalry officer, Captain Dzierzgowski, had been parachuted by EU/P, SOE's civilian Polish section, into the Unoccupied Zone of France, at the instigation of Professor Kot, to see if there were any Poles living there whose services could be enlisted for sabotage and subversive operations indicated by SOE. The circumstances of Dzierzgowski's secondment, and even more the fact that he was to work under British direction, caused a major row to develop between the Polish Ministries of Defence and the Interior, into which Gubbins was inevitably drawn since SOE dealt separately with both. Although Dzierzgowski survived a number of personal adventures, including breaking his leg on landing and allegedly operating his transmitter while still in hospital, his mission was almost entirely valueless from SOE's point of view and for political reasons had to be disavowed by SOE, though he received the Military Cross for his efforts.

Gubbins cannot altogether be absolved from responsibility for the Dzierzgowski débâcle. Like the *Carte* incident it was in large part the consequence of the frustration experienced by SOE in the spring of 1942 at being unable to get in touch with resistance elements in France whose existence was beyond question. The Dzierzgowski incident did only temporary damage to Gubbins' relations with the Polish General Staff, hitherto impeccable, and in any case the latter in the spring of 1942 had more substantial grievances.

By the time Selborne took over from Dalton almost all the governments-in-exile were more or less dissatisfied with their relations with SOE, which they blamed for Whitehall's lack of enthusiasm for European resistance movements. Now that there was talk of an invasion of the Continent in the foreseeable future, they multiplied their attempts to find ways of by-passing Baker Street. Although these intrigues caused Gubbins and his staff a considerable amount of unnecessary work, only one of them posed any serious threat to SOE's continuation as an independent organization. It was sad, but not altogether surprising that it should have been Gubbins' old friend, General Sikorski, the Polish Prime Minister, who provoked this crisis.

Despite the relative success of the initial flights to Poland in February, 1941, the winter of 1941/42 had proved disappointing, adverse weather or aircraft unserviceability preventing any successful flights taking place until February. The Poles blamed SOE and the Air Ministry jointly for the latter's adamant refusal to constitute a Polish flight, manned by members of the Polish Air Force, reserved exclusively for flights to Poland, though individual Polish and Czech pilots and navigators had been posted to 138 Squadron the previous autumn.

When Hitler declared war on the United States, Sikorski made immediate plans to pay an official visit to Washington to demonstrate the independence of the Polish government in London. High on his agenda was the Polish requirement for three Liberator aircraft which Colonel Donovan had somewhat casually promised Sikorski during his visit to London in the

7. With his son Michael in India.

8. Over a nullah in India.

9. Nonie Gubbins with Michael and Rory.

autumn of 1941. Ignoring the fact that Liberator aircraft could not undertake night sorties until fitted with exhaust flame suppressors which had not yet even been designed, the Poles imagined that the possession of these aircraft would enable them to undertake immediate regular flights to Poland independently of both SOE and the Air Ministry. Second on General Sikorski's agenda was a more general grievance. Since their arrival in England, the Polish General Staff had felt frustrated by the evident unwillingness of the British Chiefs of Staff to consult the Poles about future strategy, or to discuss seriously the part envisaged for the Polish Home Army when the time was ripe for a general rising. Sikorski hoped to find the United States planners more forthcoming.

Sikorski's flight was not uneventful for in mid-Atlantic an unprimed explosive device, alleged to be of SOE origin, was discovered (some Poles said it had been planted) in the aircraft's lavatory by Retinger, one of Sikorski's more controversial personal advisers. Notwithstanding this incident, duly investigated by both British and Polish security authorities and never satisfactorily explained, the party arrived safely.

The warmth of Sikorski's welcome in Washington, not perhaps wholly unconnected with the importance of the Polish ethnic vote in the forthcoming Congressional elections, the accessibility of members of Congress and officials, and the sympathy and apparently infinite patience with which the Polish case was listened to in Washington was a very agreeable change from the indifference displayed by British Ministers and officials in Whitehall. On their return to London, stimulated by their enthusiastic reception in Washington and as yet unaware of the gap between Congressional promise and performance, Sikorski and his advisers prepared a memorandum for Mr Churchill. This paper advocated the immediate formation of an Allied General Staff. Its tasks were described as being to plan and direct the invasion of Europe and to "prepare plans for the future insurrection of the conquered countries in coordination with the general war plan, and particularly with the plans connected with landings on the Continent".[11] This was too much for SOE to swallow, and Gubbins was embarrassed, to say the least, that Sikorski should have sent Churchill this memorandum without consulting or even informing him. Although almost all the governments-in-exile were to some extent frustrated and disappointed with SOE's performance and had been suspicious of Dalton's motives, the Sikorski memorandum did more than anything else to rally support for SOE. The Chiefs of Staff, not only irritated but fearful that they were about to be exposed to a series of more or less similar approaches from other allied governments, authorized Brooke, the CIGS, to tell Sikorski that his proposal was unacceptable since SOE existed to undertake precisely the tasks he had described. The speed and indeed the strength of the Chiefs of Staff's reaction rebounded to SOE's credit among the other allied governments, particularly those like the Czechs and French who by no means relished the prospect of a joint staff dominated by the Poles directing their resistance effort; on the whole they preferred SOE with all its shortcomings. The Poles' elation over the warmth of their reception in Washington had gone to their heads and they had not behaved well even though their frustration with the British authorities was understandable. By any standards they had treated SOE generally, and Gubbins in particular, with less than their usual courtesy. Gubbins was nonetheless delighted with the outcome of the incident which had resulted in a firm declaration of Chiefs of Staff support for SOE. However, to make up for any loss of face which Sikorski might have suffered, he instructed his hard-pressed planning section to collaborate with the Polish General Staff in producing a forecast of the arms, clothing and other supplies which the Home Army would need in the event of a general uprising, a Herculean and patently futile task.

Although the indignant Poles had lost little time in informing almost all the other allied governments-in-exile of the gist of the Chiefs of Staff's reply to Sikorski, in June the Chiefs of Staff decided to go further and to send copies of this communication formally to all the allied governments in London. The information about SOE's functions was also given a fairly wide distribution in Whitehall. From now on SOE was squarely on the map.

With the worst of the early struggles now over, early in May Nelson decided to resign. It came as no surprise. For the past two years he had been under continuous strain and harassment, and by the time of Selborne's arrival in Berkeley Square he was very nearly played out. Gubbins had worked closely with him and greatly admired his self-effacing devotion to duty, and the way in which he had worked himself almost to death on SOE's behalf. On the other hand he had reached the conclusion that Nelson was neither by temperament nor training the right man to lead an increasingly paramilitary organization, about to engage in active support of regular operations in Europe. Nelson had played an indispensable role in curbing Dalton's excessive enthusiasm, but he lacked the panache and possibly the vision to expound SOE's potential importance convincingly to military commanders in the field. In recent months it had been noticeable that he had tended to leave it to Gubbins, Jebb or Hambro to present SOE's case to the Chiefs of Staff. His personal entourage, men who had been with him from the start such as Taylor and Sweet-Escott, were devoted to him. Nevertheless, true to the popular conception of the head of a secret organization, he had remained an austere and somewhat remote figure to the rank and file. Dressed in the uniform of a wingless Flight Lieutenant, later a Wing Commander, in the RAFVR, he was sometimes passed unnoticed by members of his staff in the passages of Baker Street.

Charles Hambro, who succeeded Nelson, had a very different personality and background. Having captained the Eton cricket eleven in 1915, he had gone almost straight from school to France, joining the Coldstream Guards and winning a Military Cross for conspicuous gallantry. On demobilization he had joined his family bank, starting what was to prove a brilliant career in the City. Appointed a director of the Bank of England at the early age of thirty, he had assumed numerous responsibilities. Notable among these, at the time he succeeded Nelson, was the chairmanship of the Great Western Railway. This appointment, of vital importance in wartime, meant that he was unable to give his full attention to SOE's affairs though he often worked even longer hours than Nelson did. Hambro had joined SOE in 1940, about the same time as Gubbins, and as head of the Scandinavian section had been responsible for several successful operations. In the reorganization of November, 1941, when Gubbins took charge of SOE's activities in Western Europe, Hambro had been appointed Nelson's Deputy, which relieved him of operational responsibilities and allowed him for the time being to work in Baker Street on what was virtually a part-time basis.

Changes at the top in a secret organization, in which much depends on personal loyalties, tend to be particularly unsettling. Coming so soon after Dalton's departure, Gubbins viewed the transition from Nelson to Hambro with mixed feelings and some misgivings. With Nelson he had known where he stood, had been able to discuss frankly SOE's many teething troubles, and in turn had been relied on for professional advice which had almost invariably been accepted. With Hambro he felt on less sure ground. If Nelson sometimes had given the impression of being a plodding professional Hambro was nothing if not a brilliant amateur — and remained so throughout the sixteen months he was CD. As Jebb remarked to Dalton, "Hambro lives by bluff and charm".[12] Gubbins on the whole distrusted brilliant amateurs, was initially suspicious of Hambro's charm and at times slightly resentful of the easy assurance with which the latter delegated the too difficult problems, treating Gubbins as an extremely competent general manager. Nevertheless, from SOE's point of view, it was a successful partnership and although circumstances, particularly in Whitehall, were far more favourable than in Nelson's time, it was under Hambro that SOE lost its slightly dubious reputation emerging, if not as a Fourth Arm, at least as a respectable and efficient auxiliary service. Hambro lacked Nelson's foundation of professional secret service experience on which to base his judgement and, with his many outside commitments, had far less time than Nelson to study SOE's problems in depth. He consequently had a tendency to act on the last advice he had received. Whenever possible Gubbins took care to submit his proposals in writing for Hambro's written approval, having found that the latter's verbal agreement sometimes led to misunderstanding.

The Chiefs of Staff marked the change-over from Nelson to Hambro by providing SOE with an up-to-date directive. Issued on 12 May, 1942, and entitled *SOE Collaboration in Operations on the Continent*,[13] it left no doubt about the organization's future role. The directive itself made it clear that this role was in any case merely of secondary and peripheral importance, not of a sort which entitled SOE to the top priority in meeting its future requirements of manpower and material, a priority which it had hitherto tended to take for granted. SOE was directed to try to build up and equip paramilitary organizations in the areas of projected operations while taking care to prevent premature risings; the task of patriot forces was to cut enemy communications of all kinds and prevent the arrival of enemy reinforcements during the initial assault which, it was envisaged, would take place in 1943. Not only were Baker Street's activities relegated to the "important but not essential" category but the time-scale might have appeared to someone not acquainted with the characteristics of organized resistance as being urgent rather than immediate. Compared with its predecessor, the 1942 directive downgraded the importance of SOE's tasks, though these remained precisely of the sort that Gubbins had always envisaged for resistance movements in support of regular operations. However, there was no doubt that if the invasion were to take place in 1943, time was extremely short.

A supplementary directive, issued at the same time as the directive for *Operations on the Continent*, and foreshadowing Operation TORCH which had not yet been approved by the Joint Chiefs of Staff, enjoined SOE in conjunction with OSS to prepare the ground for negotiated agreement with the French authorities in North Africa to ensure the entry and favourable reception of allied forces. Moreover SOE was authorized to tell the French authorities that, if a secret agreement was reached, they would be under no obligation to serve under de Gaulle. The prime responsibility for subversion in North Africa was later to be allotted to OSS, but in May, 1942, as far as Gubbins was concerned, the North African commitment was an additional responsibility which he was far from confident of being able to meet.

The growth of SOE's operations and the variety of tasks now allotted to it made it impossible to rely indefinitely on the SIS for radio communications with the field and for the provision of forged documents. These were strangleholds by which the SIS, since the days of Section D, had hoped to contain the extent of subversive operations and prevent them compromising the activities of intelligence agents. There had been few justified complaints about the efficiency with which the SIS had handled SOE's radio communications, but in the early days there were probably well-founded suspicions in Baker Street that the SIS was reading some of SOE's agents' traffic. By the spring of 1942, with the possible exception of Claude Dansey, who was almost paranoid where SOE was concerned, no one in Broadway

Buildings had the time, even if they had the inclination, to read decrypts of SOE traffic. Nevertheless it was symbolic of SOE's coming-of-age when Gubbins was told to set up a radio system exclusively for the use of SOE.

One of his first acts was to recruit Colonel F. W. Nicholls, Royal Signals, who was both an acknowledged expert on clandestine communications and, no less important, a friend and former colleague of the head of the SIS Signals establishment. Nicholls and Gubbins were old friends; they had first met in India in the 1920s and had kept in touch ever since, Gubbins looking upon him with respect as one of the leading authorities on secret communications. He had hoped to enlist his services in 1940 to develop an ultra short-wave radio network for Auxiliary Units. Nicholls, who joined SOE in November, 1942, and became Director of Signals in 1943, was given instructions to set up a home station entirely independent of the SIS and capable of transmitting up to fifteen kilowatts in an emergency. It is interesting to note that, throughout his service with SOE, Gubbins gave the design and production of communications equipment and the training of W/T operators the highest priority. It was the mark of the professional soldier.

Although glad to be shot of its responsibilities for handling SOE's radio communications, the SIS was somewhat reluctant to give up its monopoly in the production of forged documents, fearing that the possibly indiscriminate use of forgeries by resistance groups would alert the Germans and sooner or later compromise intelligence activities. However, by 1942 they were clearly unable to meet the requirements of the French Maquis. Gubbins had little difficulty in obtaining agreement to approach the Poles for their permission to expand the Polish unit already working at their training school at Briggens in Hertfordshire. In turn SOE provided extra photo-litho equipment, a paper making machine (which was indispensable) and some British engravers. From these modest beginnings, Station XIV, as it was called, became an extremely efficient unit printing hundreds of sets of false papers for the French resistance in the months leading up to D-Day. An unsolicited testimonial to the efficiency of SOE's radio station and printing press came from no less an expert than Colonel Dewavrin (*Passy*), head of the Free French Second Bureau, who remarked in his memoirs that SOE's technical services were superior to those of the SIS.

This by no means comprehensive account of Gubbins' activities is intended to give some idea of the scope of his responsibilities in the first half of 1942. Not only was he involved in discussions of policy and future strategy at the highest level with the Chiefs of Staff and with many of the leaders of the allied governments-in-exile, but in an organization which was rapidly expanding, and recruiting often inexperienced and untrained officers, he was frequently obliged to supervise the detailed work of the country sections. It was no exaggeration to say that he had become the mainspring of SOE, and it came as something of a shock to Selborne when, late in April, there was a move on the part of the War Office to appoint Gubbins as head of the British Military Mission to Moscow. It was an appointment which according to the Secretary of State for War was supported by both the Prime Minister and the Foreign Secretary. Had he been offered an active command — even in the rank of colonel — Gubbins might have been tempted to leave SOE. But although he was experiencing perhaps the most frustrating six months of his time in Baker Street, he was not in the least attracted by the prospect of a liaison job, particularly with the Russians. Fortunately, Selborne vigorously opposed this appointment and finally succeeded in enlisting the support of the Prime Minister, who confirmed that Gubbins was indispensable to Baker Street. The Chiefs of Staff, provoked by the Sikorski letter into a more ready appreciation of SOE, were also persuaded to oppose the appointment, which was dropped.

However, Gubbins, well aware of the extent to which he was damaging his own army career by electing to remain on the 'specially employed' list, was anxious lest the careers of other regular officers serving under his command should likewise be prejudiced. Dick Barry had originally been seconded to SOE for a year and, about this time, the War Office informed Gubbins that he should return to regular duty. Barry's successor was Group Captain C. McK. Grierson, a regular RAF officer who took over under the symbol of AL (Air Liaison). If it had been hoped that, by appointing an RAF officer to succeed Barry, the Air Ministry would more easily be persuaded to increase the allotment of aircraft for SOE's operations, these hopes proved vain. Moreover, unlike Barry, Grierson spoke no French or German and had little experience in dealing with foreigners. Since Grierson also knew nothing of the complexities of country section work or the technical aspects of SOE activities, in June, 1942, Gubbins transferred Wilkinson to a newly-formed Planning Section to assist him.

At the same time Gubbins reinforced his own private office, hitherto consisting only of his personal assistant, Margaret Jackson. Lieutenant-Colonel Charles Harington, Cheshire Regiment, (later Lieutenant-General Sir Charles, C-in-C Middle East 1963-65), Major Arthur Nicholls, a Reserve Officer in the Coldstream Guards, who was later to be awarded the George Cross for conspicuous gallantry in Albania, and Captain Hugh Saunders, Royal Artillery, were all recent graduates of the Staff College. With their arrival, and that of Lieutenant-Colonel M. Rowlandson, Royal Artillery, Norgeby House took on an altogether more military complexion, though there were pockets of resistance. Staff studies were prepared for such diverse subjects as the *ad hoc* committee on Equipment for the Allied Forces, and the project known as "The Moon is Down". The former, set up by the Chiefs of Staff in December, 1942, is self-explanatory, but "The Moon is

Down" is worth mentioning as being typical of the sort of bright idea which used to involve SOE's staff officers in so much unnecessary work. This scheme, originally conceived by Professor Lindeman in November, 1941, echoed John Steinbeck's novel of the same name, and envisaged dropping arms indiscriminately throughout Occupied Europe. Gubbins endorsed the view of his Planning Section that random schemes of this sort would constitute a gross misuse of the very limited resources available for specific special operations.

On the whole SOE was concerned with more weighty matters during the summer of 1942. Gubbins did not play a leading role in drawing up the SOE-OSS Agreement of June, 1942[14], which it fell to George Taylor to negotiate. The Agreement provided that in Western Europe the responsibility for special operations should be shared equally between SOE and OSS; the British were to have primary responsibility in the Balkans, the Middle East, India and West Africa, while the Americans were to have primary responsibility for China, Korea, Finland, the Pacific and, above all, North Africa. It was North Africa that was of particular interest to Gubbins.

Although the COS directive of May, 1942, had assumed that SOE's activities in North Africa would be in support of a military operation, Anglo-American agreement on the scope of the operation was not reached by the Combined Chiefs of Staff until the last week in July. Gubbins had therefore barely three months to make his arrangements.

Fortunately, Guinness, who had been relieved in Moscow by George Hill, was available in Baker Street to take over from Barry the liaison with the TORCH planners when the latter took up his appointment on the Operations staff of AFHQ. Nevertheless, Gubbins kept the arrangements under his personal control. He knew that the performance of the SOE teams involved in TORCH was of critical importance to the whole concept of irregular forces acting in support of invading armies. There was general agreement that the head of the SOE detachment at AFHQ should be a fairly senior regular soldier. After some hesitation, Gubbins chose Colonel Munn, the head of his Training section. It was not one of his more successful appointments, but it was a clear case of there being "either no one else or someone else". Unfortunately, Munn had had no previous experience of country section operations, still less of the intricacies of French politics of which the North African variety was particularly complex. To make good the former deficiency, Douglas Dodds-Parker, who had set up and run the Operations Room in Baker Street, was included in Munn's team; while, as politico-intelligence officers, he had David Keswick, and 'Mouse' Glyn who, when based on Lagos, had had experience of running extremely successful subversive operations against Vichy-controlled administrations in West and Central Africa. A colourful description of the early days of Massingham, as

SOE's detachment was called, is contained in Douglas Dodds-Parker's *Setting Europe Ablaze*.

Back in London Massingham's activities took up most of Gubbins' time. The fact that SOE in North Africa was supposed to play a subordinate role to OSS, and that the American and British authorities differed in their attitude towards de Gaulle, led to SOE's often unjustified suspicions about the good faith of their OSS colleagues, suspicions which were doubtless reciprocated. Moreover the politico-intelligence assessments of David Keswick were frequently at variance with those not only of the Americans but also of the British SIS and the received wisdom of the Foreign Office. That Keswick often proved correct in his usually gloomy predictions irritated Foreign Office officials to the point that they were about to demand that the political section of Massingham be shut down, or at least that Keswick should be recalled, when Admiral Darlan was shot. The fact that his assassin, Lieutenant Fernand Bonnier de la Chapelle, had been recruited as an instructor by SOE and issued with a pistol by SOE looked like precipitating a first-class international crisis. SOE's enemies were quick to accuse Hambro and Gubbins of gross irresponsibility or worse. Nor indeed was the situation at all clear in Baker Street where in the absence of hard information, the general sentiment was that Darlan's death was the best thing that had happened since Heydrich's assassination the previous May; if Massingham had organized it, the more power to their elbow. Nevertheless, the lack of information from Massingham and the confusion surrounding the incident was both damaging to SOE and a source of continuous embarrassment to Selborne, Hambro and Gubbins, who were unable to provide satisfactory answers to urgent enquiries from Ministers and from the Chiefs of Staff. Consequently, early in the New Year, Selborne and Hambro decided that the quickest solution was for Gubbins to fly out to Algiers to see what had happened and to decide what had to be done with Massingham as a result of Darlan's death. Gubbins realized before he left on 21 January, 1943, that Munn would almost certainly have to go.

During his stay in North Africa, Gubbins visited the whole of the First Army front, saw all the SOE posts and also visited all British and American Corps, Divisional and some Brigade Commanders. On his return to Army HQ he had another long meeting with General Anderson who asked him to draft a directive on the functions of SOE detachments, which was issued by HQ First Army on 12 February. Gubbins found his trip to Algiers extremely rewarding. There was much to be learnt from the experiences of the officers who had been attached to the British and US Corps during the landings. On a wider scale he was able to form firsthand impressions of the French political scene which were invaluable in the months to come; so were his impressions of the US Army and the functions of an integrated headquarters. He had been able to discuss special operations with General Eisenhower, the Supreme Allied Commander, and together with Colonel Donovan, who had arrived from Washington, he laid down a pattern for SOE and OSS's cooperation with regular forces in theatres of active operations which remained essentially unaltered for the remainder of the war. It was altogether a refreshing interlude, and it was with a sense of achievement that he boarded his aircraft at Maison Blanche for his return flight to England on 9 March. SOE was about to enter a new and potentially far more rewarding phase in its existence.

12

SOE: 1943

One of Hambro's first acts on becoming CD had been to appoint Gubbins as his Deputy for Operations (DCD/O), and, after some initial opposition from the War Office, Selborne had secured his promotion to Acting Major-General on 22 December, 1942. His opposite number, the Deputy for Administration, was Sir John Hanbury-Williams whom, it will be recalled, Selborne had commissioned to report on SOE on taking over from Dalton. Owing to Hambro's many outside activities, much of the responsibility of the day-to-day running of SOE had fallen on these two men. During the autumn of 1942 it had grown increasingly obvious that Gubbins was over-committed, and that pressure of work made it imperative for him to reorganize his original Section and shed more of his direct responsibilities.

Giving Jack Wilson a free hand in directing Scandinavian affairs had already proved an outstanding success. In February, 1943, the Norwegian resistance carried out their attack on the Norsk Hydro Heavy Water plant at Rjukan. This operation, known by the code name GUNNERSIDE, was probably the most important act of sabotage carried out by either side during the Second World War. The target, recognized as being of the highest priority, was only entrusted to SOE as a last resort after the disastrous failure of a glider-borne attack, mounted by COHQ during the previous November. Operation GUNNERSIDE has been described in great detail elsewhere. As with the assassination of Heydrich, the detailed planning of the operation – in particular the problem of obtaining access to the target – had had to be left to local initiative. Nevertheless, SOE could and did claim a spectacular success which helped to carry Gubbins and his colleagues over the disastrous six months which followed.

While Gubbins had been in Algiers discussing collaboration with OSS and SOE's future role in the Mediterranean with General Eisenhower and his Chief of Staff, Bedell-Smith, arrangements were being finalized for the secret meeting between Churchill and President Roosevelt, scheduled for mid-January at Casablanca. The subjects under discussion at this Conference included matters of far-reaching consequence for SOE: not only the future strategy for 1943 and 1944 but the perennial problem over the status of de Gaulle, towards whom the United States' attitude remained equivocal to say the least. The Casablanca Conference was also the occasion for Roosevelt's declaration enforcing 'unconditional surrender' on the Axis powers. This statement, concurred in by Churchill, effectively prevented SOE's representatives in neutral countries from offering the slightest encouragement to emissaries from anti-Nazi groups in Germany.

So far as Gubbins personally was concerned, the most alarming decision was that every effort should continue to be made to mount some form of SLEDGEHAMMER – a limited cross-Channel operation – in August, 1943. It was no secret in Baker Street that the British planners had tacitly accepted as long ago as October, 1942, that there was no prospect of undertaking a major cross-Channel invasion in 1943. Consequently SOE's French sections were counting on at least twelve months in which to lay their plans. Since TORCH had given the Germans the excuse to invade the Unoccupied Zone of France, the Foreign Office ban on operations in Central and Southern France had been lifted and F Section had made contact with a number of individual resistance groups. The *Carte* organization, on which so much effort had been lavished in 1942, had proved useless at the time of TORCH, and any lingering hopes raised by its leader, Girard, were dashed when, towards the end of March, 1943, the *Abwehr* moved in and liquidated the entire network.

Although other F Section circuits were nascent at this time, they were most unlikely to be ready for active operations by mid-1943, and Darlan's brief interregnum in Algiers had proved particularly damaging to their credibility. The Free French groups, potentially far more numerous than F Section's adherents, suffered from what was to prove a fatal organizational defect. Although bound to appear confident, particularly when dealing with the Chiefs of Staff and Service Ministries, Gubbins worried constantly through the spring of 1943 that when the time came SOE would be unable to fulfil its commitments.

Besides the apparently insoluble problems presented by the prospect of SLEDGEHAMMER, which was not finally abandoned by the Prime Minister until April, 1943, another matter arising from the Casablanca Conference directly concerned Gubbins. This was the decision to constitute forthwith an Allied Inter-Service Planning Staff to prepare the cross-Channel invasion in 1944. This Staff, known as COSSAC, was set up at the end of January in Norfolk House, St James's Square, under the direction of Lieutenant-General F. E. Morgan. Morgan was two and a half years older than Gubbins and had been commissioned from Woolwich into the Royal Artillery in 1913; from Gubbins' point of view there could hardly have been a better choice. He lost no time in briefing Morgan on SOE's activities in

France, and in setting up within SOE, under Brigadier F. E. Mockler-Ferryman, a new directorate responsible for operations in Western Europe and for liaison with COSSAC. Nevertheless, there was no disguising the fact that SOE's efforts in North-West Europe were potential rather than actual, and the inherent unpredictability of special operations made Mockler-Ferryman's task far from easy in dealing with the hard-headed, highly professional staff officers in COSSAC's planning section. On the other hand, Gubbins saw to it that from the very outset General Morgan and his staff were left in no doubt that, with or without SOE's support, a considerable degree of spontaneous resistance was bound to occur at the time of the cross-Channel invasion, and that SOE was more likely than any other agency to be able to direct this patriotic activity into useful channels. Consequently, whether they approved of irregular warfare or not, Morgan's staff was soon persuaded to recognize SOE with all its limitations as an independent auxiliary force, working under COSSAC's general direction. It says much for the personalities concerned that this partnership fructified and persisted long after COSSAC had been dismantled. But it is indisputable that Gubbins' special relationship with Morgan was of crucial importance in giving a lead.

Although the prospects in France looked bleak at the time of Mockler-Ferryman's appointment, the tide had in fact already turned. The success of the TORCH landings, the German surrender at Stalingrad, Alexander's victories in North Africa and the prospects of access to the almost unlimited resources of the United States combined to cause an incredible improvement in the climate of resistance throughout Occupied Europe during the first six months of 1943. A symptom of this change of fortune was the growing number of young men who decided to take to the hills in preference to being conscripted to forced labour in Germany. During the winter of 1942/43 few of these youthful *Maquisards* could safely be incorporated in the clandestine circuits being organized by SOE. The majority, whose murderous innocence made them splendid material for a future *levée en masse*, were forced meanwhile to live illegally, and providing for their material support became a major preoccupation for the Free French authorities in London who naturally turned to SOE for help. Meanwhile, besides the immediate problem of their subsistence, SOE had to devise means of harnessing and directing this patriotic potential or at least trying to prevent the *Maquisards* from getting in the way of regular operations when the time came for the invasion. The solution put forward by SOE planning staff was to drop by parachute small uniformed groups (later known as Jedburghs) at or about the time of the invasion.

Mockler-Ferryman was still relatively inexperienced in clandestine techniques and Gubbins had not yet sufficient confidence in the professionalism of some of the individual country section officers to let them conduct their operations without his personal supervision. Some at least of SOE's circuits in North-West Europe were strongly suspected of having been penetrated by the Germans — an acceptable risk given the circumstances and the characteristics of resistance work — but many such contingencies required Gubbins' personal attention and decision. It had been a disagreeable surprise when the *Abwehr* had closed in and destroyed the *Carte* organization, though it had long been suspected that it had been penetrated. Nevertheless hope still lingered in F Section that there might be a nucleus on which a new organization could be built. Meanwhile, in the Free French Resistance, security risks were greatly accentuated by de Gaulle's insistence for political reasons on centralizing their organization under Jean Moulin, despite the technical objections of RF Section which had been forcefully reiterated when Moulin had been brought out to London for consultation and a short rest in February and March, 1943. On 21 June disaster struck, and Moulin and most of his senior colleagues were arrested at Caluire, a suburb of Lyon. It was only because of Moulin's heroism in remaining silent under torture that the organization that the Free French had so laboriously built up over the previous twelve months was not entirely liquidated. This catastrophe, coinciding with mass arrests in late June and July of members of F Section's PROSPER circuit, which had wide ramifications in Paris and its environs, occurred at the worst possible time; SOE's future was once again under review by the JIC and Chiefs of Staff, and this catalogue of disasters, conscientiously reported by Hambro and Gubbins, did not improve the Chiefs of Staff's opinion of SOE as a reliable organization.

In any case, a new Chiefs of Staff directive, dated 20 March, 1943, had given top priority to subversive operations on the Italian islands, on Corsica and on Crete. Moreover operations in the Balkans came ahead of resistance in France, Poland, Czechoslovakia, Scandinavia and the Low Countries. Once again, except in the Balkans, the SIS was given operational priority over SOE. As for operations on a wider scale, the directive stated that resistance activities should focus on current sabotage and guerrilla warfare rather than on preparations for future uprisings for secret armies. Only in the Balkans should the fullest exploitation of guerrilla warfare take precedence over sabotage. SOE was invited to produce a paper analysing its capacity to fulfil these tasks and at the end of the year to report how far the directive had been carried out.

As might be expected, SOE's main complaint was about the shortage of aircraft available to support these requirements — an insufficiency which was highlighted by the conclusions of the *ad-hoc* Committee on Equipment for Patriot Forces which submitted its report to the Chiefs of Staff at the end of March. Predictably the Committee's first conclusion was that unless current delivery facilities were considerably increased, full value would not be obtained from resistance groups at the crucial moment. The Chiefs of Staff's invitation to report on SOE's capacity to carry out the new directive provided Gubbins with an opportunity, once again, to state SOE's claim for additional aircraft, and he kept his planning staff extremely busy in the second half of March preparing the necessary memoranda. Selborne, Hambro and Taylor were more optimistic than Gubbins that SOE's representations would bear fruit, on the grounds that guerrilla activity in the Balkans, sponsored and supported by SOE Cairo, had already been favourably noticed by the Prime Minister and the Chiefs of Staff, and was unquestionably tying up a significant number of enemy divisions, though at this stage in the war more Italians than Germans. Moreover, the allocation of ten additional Halifax aircraft for the support of guerrilla forces in Yugoslavia, Greece and Albania – though still inadequate to meet their needs – was thought to augur well for the future.

Gubbins took a more pessimistic view. In France, which was his main concern, resistance was nowhere near as active as in the Balkans. Nevertheless, now that the tide of war seemed to have returned in favour of the allies, and German repression in the former Unoccupied Zone was making it increasingly difficult for Frenchmen of any political colour to remain sitting on the fence, SOE's prospects looked brighter than they had ever done before. However, not only was there a chronic shortage of aircraft, but the Chiefs of Staff explicitly, but unreasonably, desired SOE to dampen down resistance activities until a cross-Channel invasion was ready to take place in 1944. When Gubbins and his staff tried to explain to the JPS that resistance either increased or diminished and vanished, and to talk of damping it down was wholly unrealistic, this inherent instability was seized on by the Joint Planners as an additional reason for preferring the so-called certainties of the bombing offensive and the blockade which at least could be switched on and off as circumstances demanded. In due course the point was taken to the extent that a JPS paper of 10 June, in referring to resistance groups, recognized that "although it may be possible to defer full-scale revolt to the right moment, SOE ... cannot restrict their support. It is the very nature of the organizations they establish that they should multiply themselves and it is in every way desirable that SOE's support should keep pace with this growth." This was an important advance since, from the inception of SOE, the Chiefs of Staff had expressed their doubts, admittedly not altogether unjustified, about the ability of the organization to bring the patriot forces they were supporting sufficiently under control for their activities to be of any positive value.

The memorandum prepared by SOE on its ability to meet the Chiefs of Staff's requirements was cautiously optimistic. It promised in due course effective contributions in Corsica, Greece and Yugoslavia, France, Poland, Norway and Holland, always provided that increased air support was forthcoming. At the same time the point was made that, with existing air resources, less than half the demands for supplies could be met even if operations were confined to Corsica, the Balkans and France.

The Chiefs of Staff were understandably reluctant to accept SOE's claims at their face value, and in any case had no intention of providing the additional aircraft that the logic of the situation appeared to demand. Their discussion of SOE's paper on 24 April was inconclusive and it was agreed to remit SOE's estimates to the JPS for further examination. By the time this examination was completed, Anglo-US agreement had been reached that the cross-Channel operation should take place in 1944 and should be given priority over operations in the Mediterranean. So far as Gubbins was concerned this decision encouraged the hope that before long the imbalance of the present weighting in favour of guerrilla operations in the Balkans would at least be partially redressed in favour of building up the burgeoning resistance groups in France.

It was encouraging, and the fruit of much hard work by Gubbins and his planning staff, that the JPS had endorsed SOE's appreciation of resistance potential in Europe. Even more satisfactory was their recommendation to the Chiefs of Staff that the Admiralty and the Air Ministry should be asked for an immediate report on ways in which SOE's demands for increased transport requirements could be met. In addition, the JPS had recommended that the Air Ministry should meet forthwith SOE's current request for an additional eighteen aircraft.

Gubbins' jubilation over these developments was tempered by his certainty that the last recommendation would lead to a direct confrontation with Bomber Command. Nevertheless, as an alternative to the long months of procrastination and indecision, he welcomed the prospect of a showdown. If SOE was to continue, it was, he thought, high time that the War Cabinet and the Chiefs of Staff made their attitude clear even though it was by no means certain that the final decision would be in SOE's favour. Whatever the outcome, he himself was bound to be involved in protracted discussions at the highest strategic level. This was a prospect very much to his taste. At the same time he was well aware that he was directly responsible for the lives and activities of SOE's operational officers, over a hundred of whom were now at work in North-West Europe, and indirectly for innumerable indigenous patriots who had been encouraged to look to SOE not only for military, and in some cases political, guidance but, owing to the exigencies of enemy occupation, for every imaginable variety of material support. It was an awesome responsibility for a middle-ranking officer in his middle forties.

The Chiefs of Staff were in no hurry to come to a decision about SOE. On receiving the JPS report, their first reaction was to recommend that the Air Ministry and SOE should get together and examine ways to increase airborne supplies. Since Grierson had been engaged in almost continuous discussion of this subject with the Air Ministry and with the RAF element of the Joint Planning Staff for the last eight months or more, as well as being SOE's representative on the *ad hoc* Committee for the Equipment of Patriot Forces, SOE may be forgiven for thinking that little ground remained to be explored. In the event any rational consideration of priorities was upset by the intervention of the Prime Minister, whose imagination had been caught by the Yugoslav guerrillas, and who urged that supplies to the Balkans should be stepped up to five hundred tons a month. In consequence it was the end of July before the joint Air Ministry/SOE report reached the Chiefs of Staff. Its conclusion – obviously unacceptable to Bomber Command – was that to fulfil the role envisaged for it by the JPS SOE would require the full-time use of a hundred and two heavy bombers. This recommendation, involving the deployment of some ten per cent of the operational strength of Bomber Command, was altogether too much for Portal, who submitted a closely argued memorandum. The Chief of the Air Staff's conclusion was that, while there was a very good case for providing aircraft to back SOE's activities in the Balkans, even at the expense of Bomber Command, it would be a serious mistake to divert any additional aircraft to supply resistance groups in Western Europe, which would not be operationally active until next year, when these bombers could be of immediate and actual value in accelerating the defeat of Germany by direct means. In short, Portal was prepared to offer fourteen additional aircraft by the end of the year, but this increment would be primarily for Balkan operations since, in his opinion, the twenty-two aircraft already available to Western Europe should be 'capable of sustaining resistance groups in a lively and vigorous condition until we can concentrate in turn on their ultimate exploitation.'

The fallacy in the CAS's argument had already been dealt with in the JPS/SOE report. Hambro returned to the charge, commenting that "the maintenance of our organizations at their present strength and day-to-day activity requires an increase in our present effort." Moreover, "the process of equipping resistance groups must be a gradual one spread out over a period", and it was quite unrealistic to envisage, as did the Chief of the Air Staff, that the supplies could be dropped at the last moment. However, Hambro decided not to force the issue since both he and Gubbins agreed that it would be futile to take on the CAS on his own ground. After a short discussion on the 27 July (which SOE was not invited to attend) the Chiefs of Staff approved Portal's recommendation. This conclusion was disastrous for SOE, and Selborne demanded that the allocation of aircraft should be discussed by the Defence Committee although the latter was in many respects a less influential body than the Chiefs of Staff. By now the gloves were off, and the CAS promptly circulated an SIS report alleging that the SOE networks in Northern France had been penetrated by the Germans and could not be relied on until they had been rebuilt on a smaller and sounder basis. While this was fair comment about some of the networks supplied by SOE, the JIC, who were instructed to look into the allegation, considered this SIS report to be exaggerated. SOE, which was, albeit belatedly, consulted by the JIC, was able to show that SIS's complaints were directed exclusively against RF (Free French) circuits, and that F Section's requirements alone could more than provide full employment for all the aircraft at present allocated for special operations in France.

Although this rather sordid intrigue between the Air Ministry and the SIS may be said to have misfired as a result of circumstances which Professor Stafford has described, its effects were damaging to SOE in that the JIC report recommended, not for the first time, that intelligence needs should have priority in France and it was for consideration whether a temporary transfer of aircraft for SOE purposes from the United Kingdom to the Middle East, at the expense of France, might not be justified. This recommendation, which was none of the JIC's business, directly supported the Air Ministry's case, and the JIC report was circulated before the meeting of the Defence Committee. At this meeting Churchill appears to have given rhetorical support to Selborne, but the conclusions were broadly those of the Chiefs of Staff; the number of UK-based aircraft for special operations to Western Europe should remain unchanged, while the number of long-range aircraft allotted to the Middle East should be increased to thirty-six. If Gubbins found the outcome disappointing after he had put so much hard work into preparing SOE's case, it was more or less what he had predicted in June. So far as SOE was concerned, the most helpful recommendation of the JIC report was that measures should be taken to improve coordination between the Chiefs of Staff and SOE; but before this recommendation could bear fruit SOE's future as an independent organization was once again put in question as a result of yet another crisis originating in Cairo.

While Gubbins had been fully engaged in discussing SOE's future at the strategic level, there had been a series of operational disasters in North-West Europe, some of which have been already mentioned. The arrest and death of Jean Moulin and most of his closest collaborators had dealt a nearly mortal blow to the Free French resistance movement; while the almost simultaneous liquidation of the PROSPER circuit was no less disastrous for F Section's hopes of establishing an effective organization in Northern France. Belgian resistance was crippled by intrigue and suspected of German penetration, and by July the rumours that SOE's Dutch organization had been deeply penetrated had hardened almost into certainty. The attitude of the Chiefs of Staff was considered by Gubbins and many members of SOE to be shortsighted. Although the activities of the SIS, Admiralty and Air Ministry were cynical to say the least, it must be admitted that there were solid reasons for the Chiefs of Staff to display caution in accepting SOE's claims at their face value. On the other hand, the Chiefs of Staff had already learnt to their cost that with all its faults SOE, or something like it, was indispensable for keeping at arm's length importunate governments-in-exile and their general staffs, of whom the most persistent were the Poles.

Ever since the summer of 1939, the Poles had cast their spell on Gubbins, appealing particularly to the romantic side of his nature. Although in neither case could the slightest blame be attached to SOE, the catalogue of disasters which occurred about this time would be incomplete without the inclusion of the arrest on 30 June of General Rowecki, the brilliant commander of the Polish Home Army who had succeeded against all the odds in welding Polish resistance groups of widely different political persuasions and prejudices into a highly efficient paramilitary force. No less catastrophic for Polish unity was the death of Gubbins' old friend, General Sikorski, who was drowned four days later on 4 July in an aircraft accident at Gibraltar. Gubbins immediately perceived the disastrous consequences of the loss of these two moderate men just when a decision had to be reached about future Polish-Soviet relations and the attitude to be adopted by the Home Army if Poland were overrun by the advancing Red Armies. In the longer term too, Gubbins realized that the inevitable Soviet demands for a revision of the Poles' pre-war eastern frontier would be bound to have a detrimental effect on the British attitude towards Polish resistance.

Besides, Sikorski's loss meant a great deal to him personally. Like many senior Polish officers, who had felt at home in Paris, spoken fluent French and were familiar with French military procedure, Sikorski had been shattered by the fall of France and had never entirely succeeded in acclimatizing himself to the British way of life. Gubbins had been one of a small circle of British friends, which included Victor Cazalet who perished with the General, whom Sikorski had trusted and consulted on a wide variety of subjects. Although it has been suggested that Gubbins was in some way to blame for some of the misunderstandings between the Chiefs of Staff and the Polish General Staff about the future role of the Polish Home Army, his friendship with General Sikorski was entirely beneficial, and the subsequent difficulties arose primarily because, after Sikorski's death, there was no one in the Polish community of sufficient stature to combine as Sikorski had done the responsibilities of Prime Minister and Commander-in-Chief.

As Prime Minister, Sikorski was succeeded by Stanislaw Mikolajczyk, the

Minister of Interior and leader of the Peasant Party. Mikolajczyk was at that time virtually unknown in British circles and lacked Sikorski's authority both in his dealings with other allied leaders, including Stalin and Churchill, and in his relations with his own ministers and generals. Gubbins on the other hand had had numerous official dealings with him when Mikolajczyk had succeeded Kot as Minister of Interior, in which capacity he had been responsible not only for the clandestine civilian administration inside Occupied Poland, the so-called *Delegatura*, but also for the mobilization and administration of Polish communities abroad. These communities included, it will be recalled, the half million Poles in North-Eastern France for whom, as long ago as 1941, HM Treasury had sanctioned a large credit to be administered by SOE. Although, as leader of the Peasant Party, Mikolajczyk was looked on unfavourably by many Polish officers, Gubbins had a high regard for his courage, integrity and common-sense. He therefore never doubted that when Mikolajczyk became Prime Minister he would remain well disposed towards SOE.

General Sosnkowski, the hero of Lwow, who succeeded Sikorski in his capacity as Commander-in-Chief, was a far more awkward customer. In the autumn of 1939 in Paris, Sosnkowski had been appointed by Sikorski, largely for political reasons, as the nominal commander of the Home Army and as such he had suffered greatly from frustration. In his official dealings Gubbins had found him obstinate, erratic and narrow-minded and had warmly applauded Sikorski's decision, forced on him after the fall of France, to supersede him. Gubbins had every reason to fear that Sosnkowski's new appointment as Commander-in-Chief would lead to friction with SOE. He had not long to wait.

One of Sosnkowski's first acts was to make a direct approach to the Combined Chiefs of Staff (CCS) in Washington about the inadequacy of support for Polish resistance, hoping to achieve better results by going over the heads of SOE and the Air Ministry than through the hierarchic channels designated by the British Chiefs of Staff. To support this *démarche*, Sosnkowski had acquainted the CCS with a plan recently transmitted to London by the Polish Home Army. This plan envisaged a situation in which the bulk of the Polish Air Force in the UK was transferred to a safe area in Poland, temporarily seized by the Polish Resistance and consolidated by the Polish Parachute Brigade from Britain in the face of the advancing Red Army. It was estimated that this safe area could be held for up to three weeks and by that time the Western allies would have overrun Germany and reached the Polish frontier before the Russians entered Poland. Although the members of the Polish VI Bureau, who were in daily, often in hourly touch with SOE, admitted that the whole plan was fantastic, there was understandable reluctance on the part of the Polish General Staff, and

General Sosnkowski in particular, to disillusion the Polish Home Army who, in their desperate situation following Rowecki's arrest, could not bear very much reality. Referring their plan to the CCS seemed as good a way as any of gaining time.

In any case, the Polish Government and the Polish General Staff, for equally understandable reasons, had consistently refused to accept the warnings of the British COS, and of the CIGS in particular, that large-scale support for a Polish uprising had never been, and could never be, an integral part of Western grand strategy. In purely military terms, the activities of the Polish Home Army, as seen from Washington and London, continued to be too irrelevant to Anglo-US strategy to justify the diversion for its support of any substantial number of long-range aircraft. General Sosnkowski's demand for six hundred sorties a year (which in practice meant over a hundred sorties per month) as the minimum Polish requirement was manifestly impossible to meet.

Gubbins was upset on learning of these Polish representations which were bound to be rejected by the Chiefs of Staff both in Washington and London. He was keenly aware of the disappointment that a negative response would cause among men, women and children in Occupied Poland who for the last four years had been fighting not only for their lives but for the future independence of their nation. As a result of his experiences in Poland and his subsequent close association with the Poles, Gubbins took this commitment more seriously than most British officers; he considered it a personal debt of honour. Consequently, it was only with the greatest reluctance that he was forced to accept that the Polish problem was likely to prove insoluble.

It may be recalled that the Defence Committee had invited SOE in consultation with the Chiefs of Staff to make further recommendations about the control of resistance activities in Czechoslovakia and Poland. This invitation stemmed from a growing concern that continued British support for virtually autonomous secret armies in Central Europe would soon lead to friction with the Soviet authorities. There was little question that the Red Army would be greeted as liberators when they reached the borders of Czechoslovakia. Poland was obviously another matter. No one doubted that the arms and explosives and the very considerable sums of money which were being delivered to the Home Army from the UK would be used if need be by the Poles to prevent permanent occupation of their homeland by the Soviets. Moreover, the Foreign Office was justified in thinking that Gubbins and most of the Polish section of SOE sympathized with those Poles who maintained that, given Chamberlain's unsolicited pre-war guarantee to support the integrity of the defence of the pre-war Polish frontiers, the British were in honour bound to continue to the bitter end.

In any case, neither the Polish government-in-exile, nor the Polish section of SOE, were in a position to control the final destination of the money and supplies once these had been received by the Home Army. So far as HMG was concerned this was not a satisfactory situation but the Foreign Secretary was eventually persuaded that the attitude of the Polish Home Army was likely to be of considerable importance when Britain was confronted with the inevitable Soviet demand for the adjustment of Poland's Eastern frontier, and he had therefore obtained his colleagues' approval to raise both the frontier question and the support of Polish resistance with the Soviet Government during his forthcoming visit to Moscow in October, 1943. In the event the frontier was not discussed, and when Eden broached the question of continuing support of the Home Army Molotov had replied that he had no objection to supplies being dropped in Poland provided that they fell into safe hands. But, he had added reflectively, "In Poland who has safe hands?"

The CCS were embarrassed by the Polish approach and delayed their formal reply until 22 September. Their memorandum repeated that for geographical and logistic reasons it was impossible to meet the Poles' request to provide full-scale support for a general uprising of the Home Army, but they promised to increase supplies for sabotage operations. In order to leave no doubt in the Poles' minds, on 7 October the CIGS on behalf of the British Chiefs of Staff told the Poles that no additional aircraft could be provided and insisted that future approaches on the subject should in the first instance be made to SOE. This curt refusal even to discuss the Polish plan infuriated Sosnkowski. However, by the time he had recovered from the shock sufficiently to vent his fury on SOE, Gubbins was already on his way to Cairo. Nevertheless, to salve his conscience the latter made arrangements before he left to ensure that Sosnkowski's inevitable protest would be forwarded to the Prime Minister as soon as Selborne received it. In the covering memorandum which Gubbins drafted for Selborne, SOE supported the Poles' request for an airfield to be made available in Italy for future flights to Poland. This was a project which Gubbins had long had in mind and which Perkins had discussed at length with the VI Bureau. At the same time, Selborne promised the Prime Minister not to press for the additional aircraft demanded by the Poles until the New Year, by when the new airfield should be operational.

It is perhaps noteworthy that the language of Selborne's covering note to the Prime Minister is typical of the highly charged rhetoric that Gubbins was apt to employ when writing about Polish affairs. Although the Joint Staff Mission in Washington might fear that the Poles were living in a world of make-believe, their sufferings and sacrifices remained very real to Gubbins throughout the war. It was a subject on which he was personally vulnerable, and it is at least arguable that his sensitivity contributed to SOE's failure to face the Poles sufficiently brutally with the facts. Whereas in the early years of the war Britain had been willing, but unable, to send more than token supplies to Poland, now that circumstances had changed, they were unwilling for reasons of state to supply more than the minimum they considered necessary for current sabotage operations.

Nevertheless, the Chiefs of Staff had now left the Poles in no doubt how the land lay. Predictably for someone of Sosnkowski's temperament, and indeed for Poles in general, to receive directives from the British Chiefs of Staff that the activities of their Home Army should concentrate on petty sabotage of German communications and eschew grander strategic action for the liberation of Poland was intolerable. While agreeing with the logic of the Chiefs of Staff position, Gubbins shared the Poles' frustration and found their reproaches hard to bear; but it is unjustified to attribute to his continuing sympathy and encouragement the series of misunderstandings and miscalculations which culminated in that heroic and quintessentially Polish tragedy, the Warsaw Rising.

While Gubbins was immersed in Polish affairs, the threat to SOE Cairo's future existence was growing daily. Gubbins' firsthand knowledge of the Balkans was scant, and it will be recalled that when Nelson had reorganized Baker Street in November, 1941, he had been expressly excluded from Balkan affairs, at that time under the direction of George Taylor. By the summer of 1942, when Hambro appointed Gubbins as his Deputy for Operations, SOE Cairo, under the forceful leadership of Lord Glenconner and his ambitious chief of staff, Brigadier Keble, had come to consider themselves largely independent of Baker Street. All too often Hambro and Gubbins were called to account by the Foreign Office or the Chiefs of Staff for actions for which Baker Street's approval had been neither given nor sought. These misunderstandings had most frequently arisen because Baker Street received its directives from the Chiefs of Staff and the Foreign Office, while SOE Cairo was effectively under the orders of GHQ Middle East; and so long as active operations were being conducted in the Western Desert, military considerations were bound to prevail. During the first half of 1943, Hambro was accused by the Foreign Office on several occasions of allowing SOE Cairo, at the insistence of GHQ ME, to support left-wing paramilitary groups in Greece and Yugoslavia to an extent that was not acceptable to the Royalist government-in-exile with whom HMG was in diplomatic relations. So long as SOE Cairo took its orders (when it suited them) from GHQ ME rather than from Baker Street, apart from protesting to Glenconner there was little that Baker Street could do about these complaints.

Initially, Gubbins was not personally involved in these controversies (though his sympathies tended to be with the Foreign Office), but the priority given by the Chiefs of Staff in their 1943 directive to the support of resistance in the Balkans at the expense of France and the Low Countries directly affected his plans for North-West Europe. Consequently in drafting the various staff studies justifying SOE's apparently insatiable requirements for additional long-range aircraft, Gubbins had found himself obliged to examine the operations of SOE Cairo more critically than he had done hitherto. It must also be admitted that in many ways he found guerrilla warfare in the Balkans professionally more interesting and congenial than the clandestine operations in North-West Europe for which he was directly responsible, and which were proving so difficult.

Cairo's contumacy did not matter much until the beginning of 1943. But once the tide of war had turned in Russia's favour, political considerations began to bear heavily on resistance movements throughout Occupied Europe, and SOE's attitude towards the increasing influence of communist-dominated groups was scrutinized by the Chiefs of Staff and the Foreign Office more closely than previously. In this scrutiny Gubbins' personal political attitudes were often misconstrued. In the pre-war army he had had the reputation of being relatively 'progressive' in his political sympathies, and he was certainly well to the left of the Colonel Blimps depicted by the cartoonist David Low in the *Evening Standard*. But his detestation of the Soviet régime, his loathing of communism and his suspicions of Soviet motives were far better informed and far more deeply held than those of most of his colleagues. The exception was his Minister, Lord Selborne. As a devout churchman, Selborne exceeded Gubbins in his abhorrence of communism in all its forms. It may well have been that the anti-communist prejudices of Selborne and Gubbins helped to widen the split that was developing between Baker Street and Cairo on policy towards the highly politicized guerrilla movements in the Balkans. But this factor was not significant in the first half of 1943.

Gubbins had little firsthand knowledge of Greece. He had flown from Athens to Salonika on his way to Warsaw in September, 1939, and knew how the land lay, but little else. Yugoslavia on the other hand had been the scene of considerable clandestine activity in the early years of the war, involving MI(R) and the Mission to the Czechs and Poles, and Gubbins had taken a keen interest in the part played by SOE in the *coup* which had displaced Prince Paul in 1941. He had made the acquaintance of Monsieur Banac, a wealthy shipowner to whom he had been introduced by Edward Beddington-Behrens, who, like Banac, was a patron of the Yugoslav sculptor Mestrovic. Both Banac and Beddington-Behrens had friends in Royalist Yugoslav circles, whom Gubbins used occasionally to see in London, and who were strongly anti-Tito. Moreover his professional sympathies lay on the whole with General Mihailović, formerly an officer in the Royal Yugoslav

Army. Nevertheless, in the first half of 1943 Gubbins may be said to have had an open mind about guerrilla operations in both Yugoslavia and Greece.

Whatever the extent of Baker Street's alleged anti-communist consensus, it was certainly not shared by Brigadier Keble, who had been seconded to SOE as Glenconner's chief of staff by GHQ ME to ensure that SOE's paramilitary operations conformed with their requirements. There was nothing objectionable in theory about this arrangement, but Keble considered that he owed only nominal allegiance to Baker Street and looked for patronage to his military superiors in GHQ ME. It was not, however, only due to his influence that by the end of 1942 Cairo was advocating a change of policy towards Yugoslavia. Since 1942 it had no longer been SOE's policy that secret armies should remain passive until an opportunity arose for a general uprising. Instead they were required to keep up a continuous harassment so as to tie down as many enemy divisions as possible. Consequently it was now urged that unless Mihailović showed himself prepared to adopt an aggressive policy and fight the Germans rather than the Communists, SOE's support would be withdrawn from Royalist Četniks and transferred to Tito's Partisans. The desirability of such a change of policy on purely military grounds appeared self-evident in Baker Street. However, among more conservative circles in Berkeley Square and Downing Street, the proposal was not merely considered politically objectionable, but very close to insubordination. Cairo's recommendation was partly based on intercepted medium and low grade signal traffic including *Abwehr's* messages which, possibly through an administrative oversight, Keble continued to see long after his transfer from MI14 to SOE. However, owing to the stringent security precautions in Whitehall (and conceivably some malice on the part of SIS), this material, though available to selected senior officials in the Foreign Office, was denied to the country section officers dealing with Balkan affairs in Baker Street. Keble had no firsthand knowledge of SOE's headquarters in London, and in fairness it must be said that it may have never occurred to him that this top secret material was not being seen by those responsible for policy in Baker Street. He therefore concluded that the latter's persistent opposition and obstruction was the consequence not merely of perversity but of political prejudice – which up to a point it was. Keble had not been given the nickname 'Bolo' for nothing; and he resolved to short-circuit the resistance he was meeting in London.

When the Prime Minister was in Cairo in January, 1943, Keble had been required to brief him on guerrilla activity in the Balkans, and had been instructed to hand over a memorandum based on the German intercepted signal traffic which SOE Cairo had prepared for the Minister Resident. This memorandum set out the numbers of enemy divisions engaged with Tito's Partisans compared with the far smaller enemy forces contained by

Mihailović, and recommended that support should be given to Tito's Partisans. When he returned to London, the Prime Minister instructed the Chiefs of Staff to examine this memorandum. The latter's first reaction was neutral, but Selborne and Gubbins, neither of whom had seen either Keble's memorandum nor the secret intelligence on which it was based, argued strongly that any show of support for Tito would be an act of disloyalty to the Royalist government-in-exile which was not only recognized by HMG but included Mihailović, in *absentia*, as its Minister of War. SOE, conscious for once of the apparent orthodoxy of its attitude, expected Foreign Office support. However, the latter, which, unlike SOE, had access to the signals intelligence in question, proved surprisingly lukewarm.

In the event, it was the Chiefs of Staff who did their best to damp down the Prime Minister's enthusiasm, pointing out that the number of aircraft available for special operations in the Middle East was sufficient to support either Mihailović or Tito, but not both; that indiscriminate support for both rival factions would be more likely to lead to civil war than to joint action against the Germans; finally (and it was proved, erroneously), that under the Partisans chaos would ensue when the Axis forces were defeated. Churchill was not easily to be put off by these objections. He was attracted by the concept of an allied invasion of Italy, with revolts throughout the Balkans supported by SOE providing a major diversion. He returned to the charge and SOE Cairo was instructed to find out more about Tito. British liaison officers were duly despatched to Partisan HQ in Slovenia and Croatia, and it was through the latter that Cairo received word that Tito was ready to receive a British officer at his own headquarters. SOE Cairo selected Captain F. W. Deakin for this mission and duly despatched him at the end of May.

It was mainly on the basis of a report of Deakin's which was submitted to the Prime Minister that in June the Chiefs of Staff informed the Foreign Office that for military reasons it was desirable that GHQ ME should be instructed to supply arms and equipment to Tito's Partisans in Croatia. Although Selborne and Gubbins were even more unhappy than the Foreign Office about the prospect of having to support a communist régime, they seized the opportunity to ask for additional long-range aircraft for the Middle East, and Selborne sent a personal minute to the Prime Minister complaining that the present allocation was inadequate to comply with this new Chiefs of Staff directive. On 22 June, the Prime Minister forwarded Selborne's minute to the Chiefs of Staff, commenting that "this demand has priority even over the bombing of Germany". This *obiter dictum* seemed to SOE to be too good to be true, and as a result of the Prime Minister's intervention the number of long-range aircraft earmarked for SOE's Balkan operations was increased to thirty-six. At the same time, the decision to support Tito's Partisans as well as other Balkan guerrillas raised the question whether a clandestine and semi-civilian organization like SOE was competent to handle a paramilitary operation of the size apparently contemplated by the Prime Minister. Keble, with an eye to the main object, had no doubt about the matter; unfortunately for him, his luck was about to run out.

The lack of enthusiasm shown by Selborne and Gubbins for Tito and his Partisans may not have gone unnoticed by the Prime Minister. Churchill's imagination was fired by the signals now being received from Deakin. He saw in Tito and his Partisans romantic symbols of resistance which deserved his personal support. Although Baker Street had earmarked Lieutenant-Colonel Arthur Nicholls, Gubbins' GSO1, to replace Deakin, Churchill resolved to appoint a representative of his own choice to Tito's HQ. Partly on the recommendation of his son Randolph, but mainly on the recommendation of Rex Leeper, Ambassador to the Greek government in Cairo, he selected a Conservative Member of Parliament, Fitzroy Maclean, a former member of the Diplomatic Service and a Soviet expert.

Determined to see active service, Maclean had resigned from the Diplomatic Service ostensibly to stand for Parliament, had enlisted in his father's regiment, the Cameron Highlanders and was currently serving in the Western Desert as a captain in the First Special Air Service Regiment. Besides upsetting Baker Street, this appointment put Keble's nose badly out of joint, and Maclean's early experiences with SOE, both in London and in Cairo, which, it must be admitted, have lost nothing in the telling, showed up that organization in the worst possible light. From Selborne downwards, Maclean claimed to have met with nothing but discouragement and petty obstruction. It is, however, noteworthy that Gubbins who had previously known Maclean, at least by reputation, as a Soviet expert in the Foreign Office, always referred to him with respect and, once the decision to appoint him had been taken, did all he could to provide Maclean's mission with the necessary backing. It was in any case a confrontation which SOE could not have hoped to win and its unhelpful attitude towards Maclean's mission was seized on by its enemies, both at home and in the Middle East, and may well have contributed to the deep disfavour into which SOE generally, and its Cairo HQ in particular, was once again about to fall.

In the event it was not Baker Street's reluctance to support the Partisans, but what was rather unfairly held to be SOE Cairo's excessive enthusiasm for communist guerrillas in Greece which finally blew the fuse in August, 1943. SOE's dealings with Greek Resistance had long revealed a cognitive gap between Baker Street and SOE Cairo as wide in its way as that which existed over Yugoslavia.

However, it is necessary to go back to the autumn of 1942 in order to understand the crisis of August, 1943, in which a somewhat unscrupulous alliance between GHQ ME, the Foreign Office and the SIS all but succeeded in destroying SOE Cairo, secured the dismissal of both Glenconner and Keble, brought about Hambro's resignation as CD and the appointment of Gubbins as the third and last executive head of SOE and, while not terminating SOE's existence as an independent organization, caused fundamental changes in its chain of command.

In late November, 1942, a group of Greek patriots, drawn for the first and last time from both Royalist and Communist resistance movements, and led in person by British officers under the command of Colonel Eddy Myers, DSO, RE, had carried out a spectacular operation: the destruction of the Gorgopotamos bridge. This demolition (known as Operation HARLING) interrupted rail communications between Germany and Southern Greece for over six weeks at the time of the TORCH landings in North Africa. HARLING was welcomed by GHQ ME as an outstanding contribution but it was essentially a *coup de main* operation, executed by British officers with the indispensable assistance of Greek guerrillas.

It was the deception operation, ANIMALS as it was called, carried out at the request of GHQ ME, which brought home to the military authorities the additional possibilities of Greek resistance as an adjunct to allied strategy in the Central Mediterranean. Unfortunately, as in Yugoslavia, lasting cooperation between the rival resistance organizations in Greece proved impossible to achieve. Notwithstanding the unremitting efforts of a particularly distinguished body of British liaison officers, whom SOE Cairo had attached to resistance groups of all political complexions, by the spring of 1943 what amounted to open hostilities had broken out between EAM/ELAS, the communist resistance movement, and the minority resistance group, EDES, which, though Republican, was anti-Communist.

Whether or not they perceived the long-term consequences of their policy, SOE Cairo had a more realistic view than prevailed in Baker Street, or indeed in Whitehall, of the unlikelihood of a reconciliation between the two factions. Purely military considerations, particularly the role recently allotted to Greek resistance of providing strategic deception for the allied invasion of Sicily, favoured giving full support to EAM/ELAS. However, both the Royalist government-in-exile and the Foreign Office objected strongly, fearing that SOE's support of EAM would facilitate a Communist take-over in Greece after the Germans had left. Baker Street's attitude to Greek affairs was particularly wobbly. The head of the Balkan section, Lieutenant-Colonel J. Pearson, Royal Dragoons, had returned from a visit to Cairo much impressed by reports received from BLOs of the calibre of Myers and Woodhouse, then head of the mission in the Peloponnese. He had recommended full support of EAM/ELAS in flat contradiction of the views of his Minister, the staunchly monarchist Lord Selborne, whose dislike of EAM/ELAS was only slightly less intense than his antipathy for Marshal Tito's Partisans. Hambro was left in no doubt by the Foreign Office of their disapproval of SOE's attitude to EAM/ELAS.

However, with his numerous outside responsibilities, Gubbins, for his part, had greatly admired the efficient conduct of operations HARLING and ANIMALS whose success he rightly attributed to the professional leadership of Myers and Woodhouse. But having been excluded under Nelson's régime from Middle Eastern and Balkan affairs, he had not bothered much with Greece until the Chiefs of Staff directive of 20 March which, besides giving top priority to operations in the Balkans, required Baker Street's assessment of its ability to fulfil the directive.

Besides, in the spring of 1943 there seemed no immediate prospect of an agreed Anglo-American policy about Greece and SOE's task was complicated further by the inconsistency and the ambivalence of the Prime Minister's periodic directives to Cairo about the support of Greek resistance, an incursion at the highest level which added greatly to the general confusion. As early as March, 1943, both Hambro and Gubbins foresaw that a collision with the Foreign Office was almost inevitable and realized that if there was a fiasco over Greece, SOE would be blamed. But whatever their personal views, on the whole they favoured working with EAM/ELAS as well as with EDES, though Gubbins personally had no great confidence in Glenconner's military judgement or in his ability to control Keble, and would have preferred to have had someone with operational experience as head of the SOE Cairo now that its activities were becoming increasingly paramilitary in character.

On receiving the COS directive, Gubbins had felt a strong urge to go to Cairo to see the situation for himself, particularly in the light of the row developing between SOE and the Foreign Office over Greece, and the massive requirement for arms and aircraft now needed for the support of Tito's Partisans. But neither Selborne nor Hambro could spare him at a time when the COS discussion arising from the report from the *ad hoc* Committee for Equipment for Patriot Forces, and SOE's dispute with the Air Ministry about the provision of aircraft, were reaching a crucial stage.

In the event this veto may have proved beneficial because, not having been too closely involved in the hopes and fears of the various personalities dealing with special operations in Cairo, Gubbins was able to take a dispassionate view of SOE's future role in the Mediterranean and of the imminent redundancy of much of SOE's organization in Cairo.

Nevertheless, there were practical matters which had to be settled without delay. Accordingly, he sent Sweet-Escott, an expert on Greek affairs, and Wilkinson, who had been dealing with the Joint Planning Staff, to Algiers and Cairo. Their instructions were to seek AFHQ's agreement to set up a new air supply terminal in Tunisia from which Halifax aircraft could operate to Greece and parts of Yugoslavia, and to sound out SOE Cairo about transferring their operational base from Derna to this new establishment as soon as the latter was ready; secondly, to arrange for as much captured German and Italian arms and equipment as possible to be collected and handed over to SOE for delivery to Balkan guerrillas.

Gubbins' long-term objective, as Keble was quick to see, was to shift the control of Balkan operations, whose strategic importance he saw as primarily related to the forthcoming invasion of Sicily and Italy, from Cairo to AFHQ Algiers. In the circumstances it was hardly surprising that, although welcome at Algiers by AFHQ, Sweet-Escott and Wilkinson were treated with considerable suspicion in Cairo. It was argued with some justice that, despite the shortage of suitable aircraft and the vast distances involved, SOE Cairo was conducting remarkably efficient and smooth-running operations supplying dozens of British missions in the Balkans, whereas the capacity let alone the competence of the new establishment in Tunisia had yet to be proved. By the time Glenconner returned to London to argue Cairo's case in person, Gubbins had been fully briefed by Sweet-Escott and Wilkinson about the personalities involved and about the general situation in Cairo and in Greece which they confidently predicted would come to a head before the end of August. Wilkinson had also obtained Gubbins' somewhat reluctant agreement to undertake what proved to be a forlorn attempt to re-establish, with the help of Tito's Partisans, the overland courier lines between Yugoslavia and Central Europe, particularly Czechoslovakia, which had been in use until Hitler's invasion of the Balkans in 1941.

Sweet-Escott and Wilkinson were not alone in predicting an imminent crisis in the Middle East and, early in August, it was being put about in Whitehall — gleefully and not for the first time — that SOE had finally overstepped the limit and that the whole organization was about to be disbanded. On 10 August, in Glenconner's absence, Brigadier Myers had brought a delegation of Greek resistance leaders to Cairo, including four representatives of the now dominant communist organization ELAS. The latter had demanded an undertaking from the King that he would not return to Greece unless specifically invited to do so as the result of a national plebiscite. This ultimatum properly put the cat among the pigeons. The British Ambassador to the Greek government-in-exile, SOE's old enemy Rex Leeper, quickly disowned all knowledge of the delegation about whose visit he had in fact been kept fully informed. The Greek government-in-exile was aghast and King George of the Hellenes threatened to abdicate. The Prime Minister and the Foreign Secretary, seeing their plans for containing Soviet influence in the Eastern Mediterranean being put in jeopardy for what they took for excessive zeal, if not insubordination, on the part of obscure junior members of SOE Cairo, not surprisingly vented their wrath on Baker Street.

For the past two months, both Hambro and Gubbins had realized that the Greek situation was out of control — certainly so far as Baker Street was concerned — and that the Foreign Secretary and probably the Prime Minister were out for blood. However, there was not much that could be done to prevent these perennial crises in Cairo and experience had shown that they usually subsided with the end of the hot weather. It therefore came as a shock early in September to learn that the C-in-C Middle East, General Sir Maitland Wilson, had sent his DMO, Brigadier Davy, to London to convey in person to the Chiefs of Staff the recommendation of the Middle East Defence Committee that the responsibilities of SOE's Cairo office should be drastically curtailed and its activities placed directly under the control of GHQ ME. This proposition was recognized as a mortal challenge to SOE, and Selborne with the full support of Hambro and Gubbins went into action immediately both at the Ministerial and the official level.

During the second half of September, SOE's future independence looked seriously threatened, but its enemies, and they were both numerous and powerful, had underestimated the Prime Minister's confidence in his friend Lord Selborne — and, for that matter, in Gubbins in whose activities Churchill had always taken a personal interest. Further support came from an unexpected quarter. The Chiefs of Staff had learnt from experience the value of having SOE at hand to bear the brunt of the importunity of the allied governments-in-exile, in particular the Poles and Free French. In commenting on the Middle East Defence Committee's proposal they therefore opposed the latter's radical solution, the CIGS in particular arguing that dramatic change at the eleventh hour would militate against SOE's efficiency at the very time when the organization was required to play a prominent role.

The stakes were now very high and at a Meeting of Ministers on 30 September, presided over by the Prime Minister, discussion of the ME Defence Committee's memorandum inevitably led to consideration of SOE's future as an independent organization. The conclusions of the meeting were broadly that the Minister of Economic Warfare should continue to be responsible for SOE's activities, but that, although independent, SOE should be required to work more closely with the Foreign Office. In the Middle East a political guidance committee should be set up to advise the C-in-C, who would have the sole responsibility for the execution of SOE's policy towards Greece, Yugoslavia and Albania. This compromise, clearly a setback for SOE, was not acceptable to Hambro, and Selborne seems to have done little to try to dissuade him and Hanbury-Williams from resigning.

In any case, Selborne had felt for some time that SOE had reached the stage in its development when its executive head should be a professional soldier. He had no difficulty in obtaining the Prime Minister's approval for the appointment of Gubbins as CD in Hambro's place, with Sporborg, who had been serving as Selborne's personal adviser for SOE affairs, as DCD. Mockler-Ferryman had by now assumed full charge of special operations in North-West Europe and of the departments previously supervised by Hanbury-Williams; Venner remained Director of Finance, Boyle Director of Security and in charge of formal relations with the SIS and MI5, Davies Director of Production and Research. To instil some order into the administration which had been built up piecemeal over the years and was now patently inadequate for an organization of the size that SOE had become, Mr M. P. Murray, an Assistant Secretary, was seconded from the Air Ministry to act as an Establishment Officer. Finally, at Gubbins' request, the War Office agreed that Barry, as soon as he could be released, would return as Chief of Staff in charge of Operations.

Whatever Hambro's reservations, shared by several of the founder members of SO2 who saw the new arrangements as a military takeover, the principle endorsed by the Meeting of Ministers that SOE's operational activities should in future be under the direction of the appropriate theatre commander was entirely acceptable to Gubbins. Not only did it make obvious sense but it was precisely the solution which he and Holland had advocated in the MI(R) staff papers that they had prepared in the spring of 1939. An additional advantage was that it conformed closely with the United States' military doctrine which stressed the autonomy of the theatre commander; moreover an arrangement of this sort had already been tested in the Western Mediterranean where, for the previous nine months, Massingham had operated successfully under the direction of an Anglo/US staff section directly answerable to General Bedell Smith, Eisenhower's deputy.

13

SOE:1943/1944

Having learnt their lesson in the Middle East, the Chiefs of Staff saw to it that there was to be no ambiguity about the command structure in North-West Europe. On 5 October they directed that COSSAC, the Chief of Staff to the yet to be appointed Supreme Allied Commander for the invasion of North-West Europe, should exercise operational control over SOE's activities in his theatre, though not extending beyond the issue of broad general direction. Once again this delegation of responsibility was exactly what Gubbins intended. Nor was there any difficulty about delegating similar authority to the C-in-C of the new South-East Asia Command which had been agreed at the Quebec Conference in August and established in Delhi in October, 1943. SOE's activities in South-East Asia and the Far East had never been more than remotely controlled by Baker Street, and Lord Louis Mountbatten, the Supreme Allied Commander, had taken a keen and on the whole sympathetic interest in SOE's work ever since his time as Chief of Combined Operations.

Nevertheless whereas in South-East Asia and North-West Europe the limits of SOE's operational responsibilities could be clearly laid down by the Chiefs of Staff in a form which was acceptable to all concerned, the compromise agreed at the Meeting of Ministers seemed unlikely to be received with enthusiasm either in the Middle East section in Baker Street or in the Near Eastern (as opposed to the Balkan) section in SOE Cairo. Selborne had agreed that Lord Glenconner should not return to Cairo and that Brigadier Keble should be relieved as soon as an officer acceptable to GHQ ME could be found to succeed Glenconner. It had also been agreed that Glenconner's responsibility for propaganda and subversive broadcasting to the Near East, a hangover from SO1, should not devolve upon his successor but should come directly under the newly established Middle East Political Guidance Committee. This arrangement, too, was entirely acceptable to Gubbins who had little interest in propaganda. However, it was accepted by all concerned that for practical as well as for historical and personal reasons, SOE Cairo would retain for the time being

10. Gubbins in MI (R).

11. Jo Holland in 1939.

12. Dr Dalton, President Rackiewicz of Poland, General Sikorski and Gubbins in 1940.

a considerable measure of autonomy, if only because there was no immediate prospect of GHQ ME mounting any regular operations on a scale requiring coordinated support by patriot forces.

Hambro had been planning to visit Algiers and Cairo at the end of August, but on learning that Brigadier Davy was arriving in London Selborne had instructed him to delay his departure and had suggested that once Gubbins had drafted what the latter described as 'his counterblast' to General Wilson, he should go to Cairo in Hambro's place. It was clearly necessary for some senior officer to go there as soon as possible, but the Chiefs of Staff, at their meeting on 14 September, at which Gubbins was present, recommended that he too should postpone his departure until a decision had been reached about SOE. It was perhaps fortunate for Gubbins that he remained in London during the first half of September, when his own future as well as that of SOE was in the balance.

In the circumstances, it seems unlikely that Gubbins would have left for the Mediterranean within days of taking over from Hambro had his hand not been forced by OSS, and in particular by news of the imminent arrival of Colonel Donovan at AFHQ. Given the growing strategic importance of Balkan guerrilla operations now that the allies were fighting in Italy, OSS felt justifiably aggrieved at SOE Cairo's attempts to exclude them from South-East Europe. Moreover, the State Department was becoming increasingly suspicious of British political motives in the Balkans. While, therefore, it came as no surprise to Selborne and Gubbins that, hoping to profit from Baker Street's disarray, OSS were about to make a serious bid for primacy in this important area of special operations, it was disconcerting, not only to SOE but also to the Chiefs of Staff and the Foreign Office, when on 22 October Roosevelt suggested to Churchill that since there appeared to be so much confusion, Colonel Donovan should take control of all special operations in the Balkans.

Roosevelt's proposal was firmly rejected by the Prime Minister, who pointed out that SOE had already established some eighty British missions working with partisans and patriot forces over a wide area extending "some 900 by 300 miles". Meanwhile, on 11 October, Gubbins left for the Mediterranean, accompanied by Tommy Davies (in charge of supplies and technical development), Wing Commander Redding, the Air Liaison Officer (who incidentally was a protégé of Air Commodore Boyle's for whom he held a watching brief), Philip Rea, whom Gubbins had taken over from Hambro as his private secretary and personal staff officer and, as far as Algiers, by Robin Brook, the regional controller for North-West Europe with special responsibility for operations in France. According to SOE's war diary, the object of Gubbins' visit was to inspect SOE's establishments in the Mediterranean "in view of the need for reorganizing the SOE Cairo group in accordance with new procedures for its direction and control that had been laid down by the Prime Minister".

The party's first stop was at Algiers where it was clear from the moment of their arrival that SOE's stock stood high. Massingham had played an important part in the Italian surrender, having provided a secret radio link which proved crucial to the success of the negotiations, and SOE Cairo had undertaken at the Chiefs of Staff's request the deception operation (ANIMALS) in Greece at the time of the invasion of Sicily.

Gubbins found the warmth of his reception all the more gratifying after the bruising which SOE had recently received in London, and thanks to Douglas Dodds-Parker all doors were open. Gubbins had put Dodds-Parker in charge of Massingham during his visit to Algiers the previous spring to repair the damage left by Munn. He was one of the original members of MI(R) who had joined the Polish Mission in April, 1940. He had not only an extraordinarily wide acquaintance but his manipulation of the old boy network was exceptional even in SOE. He had visited the United States during the Depression and got on well with the Americans, but it was his friendship at Oxford with Colonel Charles Saltzman, a senior member of Eisenhower's staff, that assured his acceptance by the US element at AFHQ. Dodds-Parker was no less fortunate in having served in Cairo in 1940 under General Jock Whiteley, now the senior British officer at GHQ; while Dick Barry, until recently his immediate superior in Baker Street, was a member of the AFHQ Operations staff. Equally assured was Dodds-Parker's entrée to the office of the British Minister-Resident, Mr Harold Macmillan, since the latter's assistant was Roger Makins, whose clothes-fag Dodds-Parker had been when at school together at Winchester.

Even without Dodds-Parker's assistance, Gubbins' visit to AFHQ would have been a success. The least supercilious of men, Americans found Gubbins easier to deal with than most British officers, and he for his part found their enthusiasm and their ingenuousness both attractive and inspiring and a welcome change from the war-weariness and cynicism of Whitehall. Besides it was nice for him to be treated with the respect due to the head of SOE, even nicer for once not to have to explain away his organization's shortcomings. The régime enforced by Dodds-Parker was somewhat reminiscent of a bracing north Oxford preparatory school but there was no doubt of Massingham's efficiency, nor of the loyalty and zeal of its officers, many of whom had been personally selected by Gubbins and were his friends.

Among the immediate tasks which Gubbins and Brook had to undertake in Algiers was the reorientation of the French section. For the first six months of its existence, this had been headed by Jacques de Guelis, a genial and gallant anglophile Frenchman, who had been educated at Oxford and in his British uniform looked indistinguishable from the other members of

Massingham. Of F section, de Guelis had been one of the first to be parachuted into France and had not joined the Free French organization. Now that de Gaulle had moved the *Bureau Central de Renseignements et d'Action* (BCRA) from London to Algiers, and the French Committee of National Liberation (CLN) had been formally recognized by the US and British governments on 26 August, the Free French influence was increasing daily and de Guelis' previous reluctance to rally to de Gaulle and his association with F Section threatened to become a liability. Gubbins therefore decided that he should be replaced by Brooks Richards, a lieutenant in the RNVR, who had recently been awarded a Bar to his DSC for conspicuous gallantry when serving with SOE's detachment in Tunisia. This reorientation had the approval of the Minister-Resident's office, but in the autumn of 1943 the US authorities were still suspicious of the Free French, and Gubbins was well aware of the political implications of relegating de Guelis, who was later to return to the field and play a distinguished role at the time of Operation ANVIL.

Brooks Richards' appointment was not the only organizational change which Gubbins made during his stopover at Algiers. After consulting AFHQ, he agreed to Dodds-Parker's proposal that the day-to-day running of Massingham should be entrusted to Colonel John Anstey, a pre-war director of W. H. Wills, leaving Dodds-Parker with a roving commission to liaise with AFHQ and its advance headquarters in Italy and to keep them in touch with Massingham's by now extended outstations. He also confirmed Gerry Holdsworth's appointment to command SOE's advance headquarters near Brindisi, which had fallen to the 8th Indian Division some three weeks previously. However, Gubbins' main object in visiting AFHQ was to consider the future organization of SOE in the Mediterranean.

Now that SOE's operations were to come under the direction of individual theatre commanders, it was essential in planning SOE's future deployment for Gubbins to anticipate the reorganization of Mediterranean commands which seemed bound, sooner or later, to follow the Italian surrender and the invasion of the Italian mainland. It was also imperative to take immediate advantage of the occupation of the heel of Italy as a future base for supplying resistance movements in the Balkans.

Gubbins was unfortunately unable to see Mr Macmillan, who was indisposed, but he gave a presentation of his plans to General Eisenhower and his Deputy, General Bedell Smith. He had no difficulty in obtaining AFHQ's agreement that the air and supply facilities which had been established at Protville in Tunisia as recently as July should be relocated and enlarged as soon as possible on a site to be chosen on the Adriatic coast. This establishment could then serve as the collecting point for captured enemy arms and equipment which were being assembled for onward transport by every means available to guerrilla forces in Yugoslavia, Greece and Albania. To have secured AFHQ's approval of these plans was an essential preliminary to his forthcoming visit to Cairo, since the Balkan operations which this future Italian air base was intended to support were still, in October, 1943, the operational responsibility of GHQ ME. Moreover, in the words of SOE's war diary, "the most pressing military problem, and the one which had undoubtedly influenced C-in-C ME in putting forward his proposals, was that the support of guerrilla operations in the Balkans was now assuming such magnitude as to leave doubt as to whether SOE could effectively handle it." By the evening of 14 October he had completed his business at Massingham, and the following day, leaving Robin Brook behind in Algiers to tidy up the French connection, Gubbins and his party took off for Cairo.

Gubbins spent his first week in Cairo paying courtesy calls and inspecting SOE establishments. However, it was a matter of urgency to find a replacement for Glenconner and this was the principal subject discussed when he called on the C-in-C ME. General Wilson's candidate was Brigadier William Stawell, MC, whom Gubbins had known when Stawell had been DDMI at the War Office in 1940. On the face of it, it seemed an admirable choice. Stawell, who was currently BGS Home Forces, had served in Macedonia, Serbia, Bulgaria and Turkey in the aftermath of the First World War and, on learning that he could be made available without delay, Gubbins readily endorsed General Wilson's recommendation.

Apart from Stawell's appointment, no decisions were taken at the first meeting between Gubbins and the C-in-C. Although he had only just arrived in Cairo, Gubbins realized that the moment could hardly have been less propitious for broaching the relocation of SOE's Mediterranean headquarters. GHQ was smarting from the collapse of its plan to take the Dodecanese Islands and capture Rhodes — a failure which they attributed to the precipitate transfer to 15th Army Group of the military units and landing craft earmarked for this operation. Moreover, the situation was exacerbated by AFHQ's refusal to detach, even temporarily, the naval and air forces now urgently needed to extricate the troops already committed to this ill-fated operation. The resulting anti-Americanism was fuelled by the fact that Cairo had become a military backwater and many of the establishments which had played so crucial a role during the first three years of the war were now largely redundant. An exception was SOE's headquarters located at Rustum Buildings and locally known as MO4. In these circumstances, it seemed to Gubbins virtually inconceivable that GHQ ME would agree to relinquish to AFHQ their operational direction of guerrilla warfare in the Balkans, which Ministers had specifically delegated to them as recently as 30 September as a direct result of General Wilson's representations, unless they received a new directive from the Chiefs of Staff.

With an energy which had not yet been impaired by the debilitating local climate — the autumn of 1943 in Cairo was exceptionally hot and sticky — Gubbins set about familiarizing himself with some at least of the multifarious activities which stemmed from Rustum Buildings. The Cairo headquarters had been built up piecemeal; in its early days, it had been predominantly civilian in character, the nucleus of its Balkan organization having been created by George Taylor when he was still a member of Section D. Over the years, GHQ ME had made numerous attempts to take over the organization, and several able and distinguished regular officers had served briefly on its strength. But the latter had all decided sooner rather than later that the road to promotion was a cul-de-sac and had left either when offered more active employment or once their temporary rank had been confirmed.

Brigadier Keble, the present chief of staff, had until then had an undistinguished war. However, he soon exhibited his determination to make the most of his new appointment, and his ambition was facilitated by the fact that Glenconner's interest in special operations was largely confined to matters of higher policy, leaving the day-to-day running of Rustum Buildings to Keble — an arrangement with which, to begin with, both GHQ ME and, for that matter, Baker Street, were quite content. So was Keble, who found no difficulty in getting his own way. It is some measure of the influence of this hitherto unknown officer that, less than a year after his appointment, he had been largely responsible for reorientating British policy towards Yugoslavia; had caused King George of the Hellenes to threaten abdication; and his own dismissal had been demanded not only by the Foreign Secretary but by the Prime Minister himself.

It was characteristic of Gubbins that at their first meeting he should have left Keble in no doubt that he was to be returned to duty as soon as a military successor to Glenconner could be found, or that, meanwhile, he proposed to install Wilkinson in Keble's outer office to monitor the various messages which SOE Cairo was exchanging with its numerous missions in the field. It must be said to Keble's credit that he not only accepted this arrangement with remarkable good grace, but during the six weeks that he remained in charge, he showed Gubbins no disloyalty and continued to direct SOE's affairs with exemplary zeal before he vanished into the military obscurity from which he had emerged.

Gubbins' first impressions of this controversial figure were considerably more favourable than he had expected. Despite inordinate ambition and a certain uncouthness of manner, Keble struck him as an extremely efficient officer with a remarkable grasp of detail. Unscrupulous he might have been

– he was reputed to have resorted to measures little short of blackmail on occasions – nevertheless he was indisputably the mainspring of the Cairo organization. Ministers had demanded his immediate removal, but it could not be denied that it was largely thanks to his energy and initiative that SOE Cairo at this time was controlling no less than eighty separate British missions in the Balkans. Moreover, several of these missions included individuals of exceptional ability, with many months of experience in guerrilla fighting: men like Deakin, Bailey and Hudson in Yugoslavia; Myers, Woodhouse, Stevens and Harington in Greece; Dunbabin and Leigh Fermor in Crete; and Maclean and Smiley in Albania were already legendary figures in their respective territories.

Nevertheless it was obvious that, despite, or possibly because of, Keble's brilliant improvisations, many of the administrative arrangements were proving increasingly inadequate to meet the growing operational pressure. Radio operators and, above all, cypher personnel were being grossly overworked; and the backlog of operational messages – some of them weeks old – was altogether unacceptable. Gubbins immediately telegraphed to London adding his authority to Keble's repeated requests for signals reinforcements. Lack of communications personnel was an administrative shortcoming which Keble had inherited, and which had considerably aggravated the Greek crisis in August, 1943, by when there was such a backlog of undecyphered telegrams that only flash signals dealing with imminent air operations were being dealt with within twenty-four hours. The decyphering of the longer reports on which politico-military judgements could be made might be delayed for weeks. This fate had overtaken a series of telegrams addressed to SOE's former critic, Rex Leeper, by David Wallace, whom the Ambassador had arranged to be attached to Brigadier Myers as his political adviser. This incident, though not deliberately malicious, as Leeper maintained, was to say the least an unfortunate prelude to the crisis surrounding the visit of the Greek resistance leaders already described.

Nor was Keble responsible for the siting of the SOE training and parachute schools in Palestine or for the fact that air operations to the Balkans had to be flown from an airfield near Derna. Nevertheless, the dispersal of these two establishments raised almost insuperable administrative problems and accounted for much of the apparent inefficiency for which the staff of Rustum Buildings was frequently blamed by outsiders.

Although Gubbins remained convinced of the need to transfer many, if not all, the current activities of SOE Middle East to new locations in Italy, after his first few days in Cairo he realized that he had seriously underrated the local administrative difficulties, the strength of the personalities involved and, above all, the natural inertia with which he had to contend. Nor could he deny that there were cogent arguments in favour of retaining the *status quo ante*. The removal of SOE's training establishments from Palestine, the radio station from Heliopolis, and the packing and despatch stations from Derna, and relocating these essential facilities on virgin sites somewhere in Southern Italy was not an undertaking to be embarked on lightly, particularly as arrangements had to be made for carrying out an ever increasing number of operations during the transitional period. Moreover, the Middle East Defence Committee and its offshoot, the Policy Committee, with all their prejudices so far as SOE was concerned, had by now acquired considerable experience of the politico-military problems inherent in Balkan resistance movements; certainly, no comparable institutions were available in Italy, or likely to be set up in the foreseeable future. Finally, the presence in Egypt of King George of the Hellenes, King Peter of Yugoslavia and the Greek and Yugoslav Royalist contingents provided additional and, it must be admitted, compelling reasons for keeping the direction of Greek and Yugoslav resistance in Cairo for at least as long as SOE was dependent for its political directives on the Minister of State and the British Ambassadors accredited to the governments in question, while for its military directives regarding guerrilla operations in the Balkans, SOE looked to GHQ ME. These were not arguments that could be brushed aside as the excuses of staff officers who were thoroughly well dug in and had no wish to change their domestic arrangements. Nevertheless, the latter argument, although unspoken, was perhaps the most powerful with which Gubbins had to contend.

For his part, he was convinced that the logic of the situation made it almost certain that whatever the outcome of the visit of the Prime Minister and the Chiefs of Staff to Cairo, and of the subsequent Tripartite Conference at Teheran, there were bound to be changes, and probably substantial changes, in the Mediterranean Command. Meanwhile, as the C-in-C ME himself was the first to agree, nothing was to be gained by forcing the issue of the reorganization of SOE Cairo; and, before coming to a final decision, it was obviously prudent for Gubbins to see for himself how things stood in Italy and, in particular, how arrangements were proceeding for the collection of captured enemy arms.

Fitzroy Maclean's first reports from Tito's headquarters in Bosnia had made it clear that the Partisans' immediate requirements for arms and equipment were on a scale never contemplated by SOE ME, and fully justified the C-in-C in questioning whether a clandestine organization like SOE could handle an operation of this size. However, for the time being there was no alternative to the use of SOE's existing facilities. Moreover, Gubbins had little doubt that Maclean would appeal to the C-in-C ME and, if necessary, to the Prime Minister, if he found that his requirements were not being met, and that all concerned would put it down to SOE's inefficiency. One thing was certain: the only chance of meeting Tito's insistent demands for supplies lay in collecting the enemy arms and equipment captured at the time of the Italian surrender and transporting this *matériel* by every possible means across the Adriatic.

Maclean had already made a personal reconnaissance of the islands of Korcula and Vis, both of which were still in Partisan hands. While he was on Korcula, a consignment of arms had been delivered by a motor launch of the Royal Navy. However, he knew from personal experience that the Germans were rapidly consolidating their hold on the Adriatic coast, and that if this supply route was to be exploited, no time was to be lost. Gubbins had no need to be reminded of the urgency of the situation. On learning that Maclean had left Tito's headquarters bringing with him a detailed list of the Partisans' immediate requirements, he took off for Brindisi accompanied by Davies, Redding and some other officers. His object, in the words of the SOE war diary, consisted of "visiting authorities and making arrangements for the establishment of the first elements of the advanced headquarters which was to be set up there".

It is impossible to pinpoint the exact date of Gubbins' departure for Italy, but early on 5 November Baker Street received a telegram from Cairo reporting that Gubbins had just returned from his reconnaissance in Italy, having postponed his departure for thirty-six hours to "meet and bring along Tito". The telegram continues: "Fitz arrived Bari 0900 hours 3rd ... we left midday for Malta after full discussions with Harcourt and naval authorities re immediate measures to help hard-pressed Partisans in Dalmatian Islands areas. Huot and OSS present." Maclean has noted in *Eastern Approaches* that at Malta the Governor, Lord Gort, invited them to have a drink with him to hear about Yugoslavia, and that the following day they took off for Cairo.

Both Maclean and Gubbins agreed to return to Italy within the week, but on reaching Cairo they parted. Maclean dined that night at the Mohamed Ali Club with Sir Alexander Cadogan, William Strang and Oliver Harvey, Anthony Eden's private secretary, all of whom had accompanied the Foreign Secretary to Moscow and were on their way home. The following morning Maclean saw Mr Eden himself. This was an important meeting at which he not only gave Eden a written report on the situation in Yugoslavia, but sought to convince him that, whether we gave assistance or not, Tito and his followers would, as he put it, "exercise decisive influence in Yugoslavia after the liberation".

During these days Gubbins moved in less exalted circles but was no less active than Maclean. His immediate task was to enlist the help of GHQ ME in finding someone with previous administrative experience to put in charge of SOE's future supply and despatch depot at Brindisi. Within the week he had recruited Colonel H. C. P. (Bonzo) Miles, who joined SOE on 9 November, though the official announcement that he had been "selected for appointment as Commander Advanced Base Force 133" and promoted Acting Brigadier was delayed until 27 November when Stawell, promoted Acting Major-General, took charge of SOE's Cairo office. When Gubbins returned to Italy about 11 November, Miles was included in his party. So too was Donald Hamilton-Hill, formerly of Auxiliary Units, who had recently been in charge of the despatch station at Protville and who had also been responsible for collecting the equipment abandoned by the Germans and Italians in Tunisia.

Once Maclean had agreed that Hamilton-Hill should be responsible for collecting the captured equipment, the next question that arose was its onward transport. The tonnage that could be parachuted to the Partisans was obviously inadequate and, until the situation permitted secure airfields to be constructed in Yugoslavia, the only alternative was to send the stores in by sea. Already 650 tons of arms, equipment and general supplies had been delivered to the Dalmatian Islands in October, and a further 1950 were successfully delivered in November before the Germans put a stop to this traffic. Some of this material had been delivered by Royal Naval coastal vessels operating under the direct orders of Flag Officer, Taranto. However, the bulk had been transported under arrangements made by SOE's Advance HQ under Gerry Holdsworth.

At this time, SOE's fleet based on Brindisi consisted of the motor launches of the Naval section and a squadron of Italian MTBs which the Duke of Aosta had been persuaded by Dodds-Parker to put temporarily at the disposal of SOE. Dodds-Parker had also secured Donovan's agreement that OSS with its ample funds should charter a fleet of caiques and fishing vessels. All these auxiliaries sailed under the orders of Commander Holdsworth and Commander Morgan Giles, RN.

Meanwhile, however, the situation on the Dalmatian coast was rapidly deteriorating and Gubbins shared Maclean's views that it was of paramount importance for the allies at least to defend Vis and establish there both a small naval base and, if possible, an airfield. On 11 November Gubbins submitted a formal request for an Infantry Brigade to defend Hvar and Vis and to reinforce the Partisan Brigade which at that time was the sole garrison of these islands. To the disappointment of all concerned − and not least of Brigadier Miles, who saw the possibilities of enlarging his command − Gubbins' request was turned down both by GHQ ME and by 15th Army Group. Once again, Maclean had found SOE a broken reed.

Besides dealing with the problems concerning Yugoslavia, Gubbins also had to sort out a muddle over the handling of operations in Italy. Until 1943, activities in Italy had been minimal, many of the courier lines established laboriously from Switzerland proving to be under Italian control. Early in 1943, however, an advance detachment of the Italian section led by Malcolm Munthe was put under Dodds-Parker's command at Massingham. When Dodds-Parker had appointed Holdsworth to command Massingham's advance headquarters in Italy (Maryland), he had assumed that he would also be in charge of Italian operations. An SOE detachment had taken part in the Salerno landings and Munthe and Michael Gubbins had rescued the Italian philosopher, Benedetto Croce, from the Sorrento peninsula. Munthe, with Michael Gubbins as his second-in-command, was now chiefly concerned with establishing escape lines from Rome. Gubbins had visited the advance headquarters at Naples and satisfied himself that Munthe's relations with HQ Fifth Army were functioning satisfactorily.

Meanwhile, however, the head of the Italian section in London, Major Roseberry, had been sent out to Maryland. He not only had contacts with Italian security but he also controlled the links with Switzerland. Not for the first time, differences arose between Baker Street and a subordinate headquarters, in this case Maryland, over the control of operations in the field. Dodds-Parker had already been sent for and a meeting was held shortly after Gubbins' arrival. Roseberry had deployed the usual argument that, so long as SOE depended for political guidance on the Foreign Office, operations in Italy must be subject to Baker Street's overall direction. Gubbins, however, had supported Dodds-Parker in the view that military factors were paramount; in any case, in accordance with the recent directive received from the Prime Minister, SOE's activities in the Italian theatre must come under the control of 15th Army Group even though the latter was an integrated Anglo-US headquarters. Henceforward Baker Street's influence on operations in Italy was remote and its involvement mainly confined to logistics. It was a pattern that was to be repeated elsewhere.

By 16 November Gubbins was back in Cairo. Taking Miles and Davies with him, he called on General Gammell, an old friend from the Norwegian campaign, and now General Wilson's Chief of Staff, to report progress in setting up the headquarters in Italy — which appropriately enough had been given the code name JUNGLE. Gammell, who had never shown much interest in SOE and whose mind at this moment was on the fall of Leros, took note that Brigadier Miles would be returning to Italy as soon as Stawell arrived in Cairo, and that meanwhile Lord Harcourt was in charge of the advance headquarters.

The following day Gubbins held a full-scale meeting with General Donovan and eight members of OSS to discuss the latters' many grievances about the way in which they had been excluded from participating in Balkan guerrilla operations. Gubbins on this occasion was accompanied by Keble,

Guinness, Miles, Rea and Wilkinson. He reported on his meeting with Huot and other OSS representatives in Bari, and expressed his appreciation of the contribution which OSS had made in chartering local fishing boats to ferry arms and supplies across the Adriatic. Unfortunately, after one very successful shipment, OSS had been forbidden further participation owing to differences at the highest level about the conditions for American support of communist resistance movements. Gubbins seems to have mollified Donovan for the time being; on 22 November the latter wrote: "Thank you again for all your help and I hope we shall soon meet in America."

However, members of the OSS office in Cairo continued to share the State Department's suspicions that British motives in trying to keep OSS out of the Balkans were as much political as military. Resentful though he may have been over SOE's attitude and over the firmness with which the Prime Minister had rebuffed his personal initiative to take charge of Balkan operations, Donovan had by no means abandoned the struggle. He drew fresh encouragement from a discussion he had had with General Wilson, never an admirer of SOE, who had intimated that he would be quite happy if responsibility for supplying the Balkans were handed over to OSS. In short the possibility of OSS being put in charge was a threat which Gubbins had every reason to take seriously, but clearly no decisions of substance were likely to be reached before the Prime Minister and President Roosevelt had had the chance to discuss Balkan affairs with Marshal Stalin at Teheran. Meanwhile Gubbins' immediate task was to install Stawell as head of SOE Cairo. On 21 November he issued a directive on the new organization (shortly to be redesignated Force 133) which was to take effect "from 8.30 am on Wednesday, 24 November". On the same day a telegram came from Sporborg saying that Selborne thought it a mistake for Gubbins to leave Cairo at least until the Prime Minister had left for Teheran.

So far as Gubbins was concerned, although he remained in Cairo, the SEXTANT Conference (21 to 27 November) was, to say the least, a dispiriting experience. In a war diary synopsis of his subsequent report to Selborne it is recorded that "at no time was he called on officially to attend the discussions ... in regard to US and Greek affairs .... CD, however, did meet General Ismay, Admiral Willis (C-in-C Levant), Air Chief Marshal Tedder, General Eisenhower and Field-Marshal Dill. But only Tedder and Willis required CD's definite views on Balkan problems. CD also had two meetings with Mr Macmillan ... and one with the Prime Minister.... Mr Churchill spoke encouragingly to CD of SOE's operations in general, though he jokingly referred to the 'vipers' which SOE had stirred up in Greece."

Gubbins had been counting on the support of the Chiefs of Staff to overcome the opposition which he expected GHQ ME would offer to his plan to move Stawell to Italy. But only Mr Macmillan, who mentions in his diary that he saw Gubbins on 26 November, showed any interest in SOE's reorganization in the Mediterranean. Understandably, the Chiefs of Staff had more important matters on their mind. Nevertheless, Gubbins' exclusion even from the British briefing meetings on the support of guerrilla activity in the Balkans, which was on both the bipartite and tripartite agenda, seems hard to justify and Gubbins felt the humiliation keenly.

Nor was Stawell settling in as easily as had been hoped. On 27 November he took up his appointment as Commander Force 133. But Gubbins found him entirely bewildered by the complexities of the various activities which, over the years, had come to be directed from Rustum Buildings. Besides, Stawell seemed temperamentally unsuited to the intrigues and jostling which characterized the *demi-monde* of special operations in the Middle East. Realizing that, once Wilkinson had left for Yugoslavia, there would be no one in Cairo with sufficient experience of Baker Street to act as Stawell's adviser, he sent for Sweet-Escott, one of SOE's most experienced officers, now temporarily in charge of the Free French section in London while convalescing from malaria. It was the most he could do to help Stawell.

Although it had been agreed that Maclean should report directly to the C-in-C ME, MACMIS, as his mission was now called, was still for the time being entirely dependent on SOE's supply and signals organization. Rightly or wrongly, Maclean's high-handed behaviour had become a byword in Rustum Buildings and MACMIS's demands weighed heavily on Stawell. Moreover, the latter also had under command Brigadier Armstrong with Mihailović's Ĉetniks, and Brigadier 'Trotsky' Davies as head of SOE's latest mission to Albania. It might be argued that both these missions were wasting assets, but so far as Stawell was concerned they were an administrative responsibility and a continual worry. Besides, there were SOE's activities in Greece and Roumania, and the active operations in Crete and Bulgaria, which were also under GHQ's operational direction and the direct responsibility of Force 133. The conclusion was inescapable: however desirable it might be on general grounds to move Stawell to Italy, it was clearly going to be impracticable to wind up SOE Cairo for the time being. While this was a source of intense frustration to Gubbins, Stawell found the idea of indefinitely remaining in Cairo and the prospect of setting up a new organization in Italy equally daunting.

Gubbins had an additional worry. During the first week in December he had received a series of extremely disquieting telegrams from Baker Street. Sporborg reported that the Air Ministry had alleged that SOE's operations in the Netherlands had been controlled by the Germans since 1942 and that consequently Bomber Command had suspended all SOE flights to Europe until further notice. This was a major crisis which might have been thought to demand Gubbins' instant return. It is indicative both of his own *sang froid* and of his confidence in Sporborg that he decided to remain in Cairo at least until the Prime Minister returned from Teheran. He did not underrate the seriousness of the crisis in London, but he rightly concluded that the previous six weeks' work would be entirely wasted if he left for England before finalizing SOE's Mediterranean organization.

Meanwhile Gubbins was getting the measure of the Cairo headquarters. Some of the old guard at Rustum Buildings, particularly those officers concerned with Near Eastern affairs, remained suspicious of him; but he soon won the confidence of the younger members of the country sections, and particularly of the young liaison officers (BLOs) who staffed SOE's Balkan missions. Many of the latter maintained a somewhat flamboyant style of living at the various private establishments in Zamalek which they maintained for their periods of 'rest and recreation'. Gubbins spent as much time as he could in their company; he found it gratifying to be accepted by these intelligent and dashing young men, not only as their commanding officer but as a battle-scarred member of their own tribe. Some of these friendships, which he particularly valued, lasted for the rest of his life.

It seemed certain that when Churchill returned to Cairo on 2 December Yugoslav affairs would be high on the agenda. The previous month, on learning that Maclean had decided to report back to Cairo, Tito had asked whether he would like to take with him two Partisan officers as emissaries of good will. Maclean had realized that this proposal was unlikely to find favour with the Royal Yugoslav government, which would probably react as strongly as had the Greek government in rather similar circumstances earlier that summer. Delay was inevitable while the matter was thrashed out. As he had foreseen, by the time a decision had been reached at GHQ ME in favour of the proposal, the Germans had reoccupied the Dalmatian coastal strip. The saga of these two emissaries and the British officers who accompanied them has been told elsewhere. It culminated in a German air attack in which, sadly, two British officers and one of the Yugoslav emissaries were killed and the other Yugoslav severely wounded. However, on 3 December Maclean at last succeeded in making a daylight landing on an improvised airstrip near Glamoc and the following day the party arrived in Cairo. With him Maclean had brought Major Deakin and, in place of Ivo Ribar who had died in the air attack, Vlatko Velebit, an officer of equal distinction who, for the next half century, was to play a role of the highest importance both on the international scene and in the affairs of his own country.

During the following days the Prime Minister, who was still in Cairo, summoned separately Maclean and Deakin to seek their impressions of events in Yugoslavia. Moreover, in view of the decision so recently reached at the Tripartite meeting to give all-out military support to Tito's Partisans, it was necessary that King Peter should also be made aware of the new situation. It was arranged that both Deakin and Maclean should have separate meetings with him.

Now that Yugoslav affairs were being decided at the highest level, Gubbins accepted that events were moving too fast for him. However, on the strength of the information which SOE Cairo's Balkan section had already received from Mihailović's headquarters and the account which Maclean had given him of the extent of Partisan operations and of the alleged Četnik collaboration, he had telegraphed to Baker Street on 19 November recommending that the SOE mission to Mihailović should be withdrawn as soon as practicable. He realized that, even if his recommendation was accepted, the evacuation of Armstrong and his officers promised to be exceptionally difficult, and there was a serious risk that they might become the first victims of Churchill's *renversement d'alliances*.

On 10 December Gubbins was invited to a luncheon party given by the Minister-Resident, Mr Casey, to review the situation. Among those present were the Prime Minister, the Foreign Secretary, the Chiefs of Staff, General Ismay and the C-in-C ME; so too were Maclean, Deakin and Vlatko Velebit. Gubbins was not asked for his opinion. Such was the Prime Minister's enthusiasm for Tito's Partisans that none of the guests felt inclined to speak up for Mihailović. Although no final decision was taken at this luncheon, it was abundantly clear to Gubbins that the Četnik cause was lost.

The need to provide support for Tito's Partisans had highlighted, as nothing else, shortcomings in the coordination of support for Balkan guerrillas as a whole. In November, while en route to Alexandria in HMS *Renown*, Churchill had minuted:

"The campaign in Italy has taken an unsatisfactory course. Side by side with this the allies have also failed to give any real measure of support to the Partisans in Yugoslavia and Albania. These forces are containing as many divisions as the British and Americans put together ... yet no ships with supplies have entered the ports taken by the Partisans ... complete neglect to do anything effective in this extremely important Balkan theatre .... We shall certainly be accused of shortsightedness or even worse in this affair."

He continued:

"The 'débâcle' had occurred because of the imaginary line drawn down the Mediterranean which relieves General Eisenhower's armies of responsibility for or interest in the Dalmatian coast and the Balkans. These were assigned to the Middle Eastern command under General

Wilson but he did not possess the necessary forces; that one command has the forces but not the responsibilities and the other the responsibilities but not the forces is certainly a very bad arrangement and reflects severely on our conduct of the war."

Gubbins would have been greatly encouraged had he known of the existence of this minute. The rationalization of the arrangements for supporting Balkan guerrillas was, after all, the prime reason for his presence in the Mediterranean. So far, no decision had been taken and he made no secret of his frustration. Harold Macmillan noted in his diary of 5 December: "We had General Gubbins (SOE) and a lot of talk about the future organization of the Mediterranean Command. I think that undoubtedly it will be decided to unite the Mediterranean Command under one allied commander − that is, Cairo and Algiers will be amalgamated. Who this Commander will be is not so clear − whether Eisenhower or Alexander."

Gubbins had not long to wait before the first pieces of the puzzle were put into place. On 6 December, before Roosevelt left Cairo for the United States, he had obtained Churchill's agreement to the appointment of General Eisenhower as Supreme Allied Commander in North-West Europe. At the same time, it was agreed that a British officer should replace General Eisenhower as Supreme Allied Commander in the Mediterranean. Although for Congressional reasons President Roosevelt had asked that these appointments should remain confidential for the time being, Gubbins was informed of them on 10 December, and the following day he telegraphed to Baker Street giving his preliminary reactions.

However, the crucial question for SOE, the identity of Eisenhower's successor, was still under active discussion, and it was not until 14 December that Macmillan noted in his diary that General Wilson had arrived in Tunis and that "he is definitely to get the Mediterranean Command (*not* Alex, which I deplore)".

By the time a public announcement was made, Gubbins had returned to London where his presence was urgently required to deal with the Dutch crisis. He took off for Massingham on 11 December and, after a short stop in Algiers where he had meetings with Giraud and Soustelle, arrived home on 16 December.

Although Gubbins had been kept informed by telegram of the situation in London, which during the first two weeks of December had been built up into a major crisis, he had not realized the extent to which the affair had been engineered by the Air Ministry acting in consort with the SIS. On 30 November the C-in-C, Bomber Command, without consulting SOE, and with a reckless disregard for the effects of his action on European resistance, abruptly countermanded all SOE sorties to Western Europe. The following day, at Attlee's staff conference and in the absence of Portal, who was with the Prime Minister in Teheran, Air Marshal Bottomley, the Vice Chief of the Air Staff, alleged that SOE's operations in the Netherlands had been controlled by the Germans since 1942; in consequence the C-in-C Bomber Command had suspended all flights supporting SOE's operations in Europe until further notice. This allegation was immediately reviewed by Ministers and, in Churchill's absence, Attlee remitted the matter for examination by the JIC and summoned a meeting which was attended by the Secretary of State for Air, Selborne and Gubbins' Deputy, Harry Sporborg. SOE was charged, among other things, with having ignored previous warnings from the SIS that their Dutch organization was penetrated. This charge was demonstrably untrue. It had been suspected for months that all was not well with SOE's Dutch operation. Nobody in Baker Street, least of all Gubbins, denied that the 1942 'Plan for Holland', concocted by the Dutch authorities in consultation with SOE, had proved a disaster, resulting in forty-three of the fifty-six agents parachuted into Holland falling straight into enemy hands. But, in making his grand remonstrance, what Bottomley chose to overlook was that Baker Street had become suspicious at the beginning of the summer, 1943, and *at the end of June all flights to Holland had been suspended*. Subsequently, after close consultation with the SIS, and with the full knowledge and agreement of the Air Ministry, two (but only two) trial sorties to Holland were made in the autumn of 1943. Both had failed, and *from mid-November onwards*, on SOE's recommendation, further flights to Holland had been suspended.

There had therefore been no possibility, at the time Bottomley made his protest on 1 December, of any RAF aircraft or crews being put at hazard on account of SOE's current operations to Holland. Selborne did not deny that German penetration might have occurred, but he pointed out that even if the VCAS's allegations were true, the penetration was limited to Holland. This statement was disputed by the Secretary of State for Air who claimed that SOE's organizations in Denmark and Poland were also insecure. Selborne agreed that an enquiry on Denmark and Poland should be held and that if penetration was proved in these two countries, the scope of the enquiry should be extended to cover all the resistance groups patronized by SOE throughout Europe. Meanwhile air deliveries to Poland and Denmark as well as to Holland should be suspended. Denmark was almost immediately cleared and special flights to that country resumed. (This dispensation, the cynics suggested, may have been partly due to the fact that much of the Danish secret intelligence which reached the SIS derived from resistance sources working under the aegis of SOE.)

Meanwhile the JIC had broadened the scope of its enquiry into German penetration on the lines proposed by Selborne at the Meeting of Ministers, and had embarked on a general review of SOE's activities not excluding Baker Street's higher direction and organization. This was conducted in no very friendly spirit. Some new evidence on insecurity was produced, including Free French operations in France. Baker Street was only too well aware of the dangers presented by the Free French system of centralization, which violated all the established rules and about which they had frequently protested. Moreover the fact that they had already cancelled future flights to Holland showed the extent of their suspicions of the Dutch organization. However, the JIC report damned SOE's activities with faint praise, and recommended fundamental changes in its direction and organization which not only went beyond the enquiry's terms of reference but which would have meant in effect SOE's virtual abolition as an independent service.

On Selborne's instructions, Gubbins prepared a *pièce justicative*. This memorandum not only contained a detailed refutation of the JIC's main charges but pointed out that many of the recommendations about SOE's higher direction had been considered and rejected at the Ministerial Meeting presided over by the Prime Minister on 30 September, barely three months previously. The Chiefs of Staff also forwarded comments on the JIC report. These endorsed the need for closer integration of SOE with the SIS either under the Minister of Defence or under the Foreign Secretary, a prospect which the Foreign Office at any rate viewed with little enthusiasm. The Defence Committee met on 14 January, 1944, and under the shadow of a telegram from the Prime Minister to Lord Selborne − "We will certainly go into this on my return" − Attlee deferred consideration of the future of SOE. However, in the interim, the Committee approved the resumption of flights to Holland and invited the Chiefs of Staff to consider urgently SOE's request for additional aircraft. Further consideration was also to be given to means of controlling operations in Poland and Czechoslovakia which had become a potential embarrassment to Anglo-Soviet relations now that the Red Army had crossed the pre-1939 Polish frontier. Though inconclusive, this meeting was held to be a victory for SOE.

The whole matter was duly submitted to Churchill shortly after his return from Marrakesh. He ruled that SOE should continue with its existing constitution, and a general blessing was given to the development by which the control of special operations was progressively passing from Baker Street to the headquarters of the Commanders-in-Chief concerned. This decision justified Selborne's confidence in his personal influence with the Prime Minister. From then onwards, until SOE was finally disbanded at the beginning of 1946, no further serious attempt was made to interfere with its constitution or with its higher direction.

1943 had been a turbulent year for SOE, but the pattern which had finally emerged was not merely satisfactory, so far as Gubbins was concerned, but remarkably similar to the model that he and Holland had originally conceived for the conduct of irregular operations. Simplistic this model may have been, largely ignoring the political dimension which continued to cast such a long shadow on SOE's activities, but in purely military terms the organization was sound and Gubbins was confident, now that he was its head, that he could make it work. Much of his confidence derived from his certainty that he could count on the support of his Minister, Lord Selborne, whom he consulted daily, and from whom he had no secrets. Indeed, now that the extent of Baker Street's incompetence in dealing with the German penetration in Holland had been acknowledged, and to some extent repaired, Gubbins was not aware of any other skeletons likely to be discovered. But although the auspices for the coming year seemed to be set fair so far as SOE was concerned, he was about to meet with a personal disaster in 1944 which only those who have experienced a similar loss can fully apprehend.

14

SOE: 1944

Whatever Whitehall's reservations about the integrity and effectiveness of SOE, the strategic desirability of supporting guerrilla operations in the Balkans was no longer in question, having now received the specific endorsement of the three heads of government at Teheran.

Thanks largely to Gubbins' personal exertions during the previous autumn, OSS had been presented with a *fait accompli* in Southern Italy and, while in Cairo, President Roosevelt had agreed to the appointment of a British major-general to coordinate the arrangements for the supply of Balkan resistance under the direction of the Supreme Allied Commander Mediterranean. But while SOE had successfully pre-empted responsibility for supplying the guerrillas, the organization for directing operations had yet to be decided. From discussions which Gubbins had had with General Gammell in London, he understood that General Wilson's intention was to establish a separate branch in his new headquarters in Algiers to control SOE/OSS activities. Moreover, to balance Stawell's appointment, Wilson had it in mind to appoint a United States officer as head of the staff section controlling special operations. This prospect was not altogether welcome to SOE which considered itself the senior partner, particularly in the Eastern Mediterranean.

General Wilson's Memorandum on the *Organization of Special Operations in the Mediterranean* was taken by the Chiefs of Staff on 4 January. Its principal features were that the special operations should be divided into four theatres; that their local direction should be delegated to the respective theatre commanders; and that overall control and coordination should be entrusted to a joint SOE/OSS staff at AFHQ, with a director of special operations who would be immediately responsible to SACMED. The Foreign Office's immediate reaction to this essentially military solution was that it took insufficient account of the fact that subversive warfare and politics were interrelated. Moreover, the proposed organization appeared to ignore the lessons so painfully learnt in Cairo, where months of futile disagreement between the Foreign Office and SOE had only been resolved by the appointment of a standing committee in which divergencies between political and military objectives could be ironed out. Nothing of this sort existed at AFHQ, nor was there much likelihood of reconciling Anglo-US Balkan policy even if a joint coordinating committee were set up. Besides, it was difficult for Foreign Office views on Balkan affairs to be represented properly at AFHQ so long as the Yugoslav and Greek governments and the respective British embassies were located in Cairo.

An even more serious objection was raised by SOE's Communications section; signal traffic from the Balkans would have to be handled by SOE's radio station in Cairo for the foreseeable future since it would be several months before suitable arrangements could be made for communication with Italy. It might take even longer before new signal plans and crystals could be delivered by secure means to the scores of British liaison missions now operating in the field. These considerations were familiar to all who had been dealing with the matter in recent months and the irony of General Wilson's *volte face* now that he had been appointed SACMED was not lost on members of SOE. While Gubbins could not deny the short term advantages of the *status quo*, he was convinced that if guerrilla operations in the Balkans were to play any significant strategic role either in providing diversionary support for the Italian campaign or as part of the OVERLORD deception plan (BODYGUARD), SOE's Balkan activities must, in the long term, come directly under SACMED's control, just as the aircraft allotted for their support must come under the orders of Mediterranean Air Command, a decision which the Chiefs of Staff had taken as long ago as 29 July, 1943, "to ensure flexibility and economy". After a preliminary discussion, the Chiefs of Staff agreed to defer further consideration of SACMED's proposals until the Foreign Office had had an opportunity to examine their political implications. Later that afternoon Gubbins reported to Selborne that SACMED's Memorandum seemed generally acceptable so far as SOE was concerned, once the technical radio problem had been overcome.

General Wilson's Memorandum was doubtless one of the main subjects when, on 5 January, Gubbins called on General Paget, the new C-in-C ME. Gubbins had a high regard for him as a professional soldier. However, there was no knowing how he might react to the complexities of the Balkan politics which governed so many of the activities of Force 133, or to the general atmosphere of intrigue which characterized the Cairo scene and Rustum Buildings in particular. Reports reaching Baker Street indicated that Stawell was showing increasing reluctance to leave Cairo for Italy, and much depended on whether Paget would prove any keener than his predecessor to relinquish control of SOE's operations in the Balkans.

There was, however, a joker in the pack. While these discussions were proceeding in London during the first week in January, the Prime Minister was rapidly recovering his strength at Marrakesh. Stimulated by his son Randolph, who was shortly to become a member of Fitzroy Maclean's mission, he was renewing his interest in Yugoslav affairs. "Next to SHINGLE [the Anzio landing] and landing craft, the Yugoslav problem with its intricacies about abandoning Mihailović and reconciling King Peter to Tito, has been our chief interest out here," wrote Jock Colville (*Fringes of Power*, 7 January). The occasion was a major briefing conference a fortnight before the Anzio landing. Maclean was also present, having arrived in General Wilson's aircraft, though he took no part in the Anzio discussions.

When the generals, admirals and air marshals departed the following day, leaving Maclean and Randolph at Marrakesh, the Prime Minister once again returned to the Yugoslav question. Jajce, where Tito had had his headquarters, had recently fallen to the Germans and, feeling that the Marshal needed some encouragement, the Prime Minister wrote him a personal letter which he instructed Maclean to hand to Tito himself. In this letter Churchill not only promised "all aid in human power" but formally undertook that the British government would give no further military support to Mihailović.

This is not the place to discuss the wider implications of disowning Mihailović, which were considerable, but the practical consequences for SOE promised to be scarcely less far-reaching. There was the immediate problem of withdrawing the military mission headed by Brigadier Armstrong which was attached to Mihailović's headquarters in Serbia. That this withdrawal was successfully accomplished some four months later was largely due to the magnanimity of Mihailović and his Četniks who, despite their disappointment, did everything possible to assist the evacuation of the British mission. The fate of Armstrong and his mission was not to be Gubbins' only preoccupation; he was deeply troubled by the proposal to abandon a former ally, a professional officer with whose policy he felt considerable sympathy. On the positive side, the decision to disown Mihailović meant that once Armstrong and his mission had been rescued, SOE need have no further direct involvement in Yugoslav politics, thus removing a continual source of friction between Baker Street and the Foreign Office. Secondly, a decision to cease giving military support to the Četniks greatly simplified the supply arrangements both by air and sea. Thirdly, the presence of King Peter and the Royal Yugoslav government in Egypt could less convincingly be advanced as a reason for delaying Stawell's move to Italy. It was to be some time before news of the Prime Minister's dramatic communication to Marshal Tito reached the ears of Baker Street.

Meanwhile Stawell had returned to Cairo from his first tour of inspection of Force 133 establishments at Bari convinced of the need for his headquarters to remain in Cairo for the time being, and it came as no surprise to Gubbins that General Paget appeared to be of the same opinion. Matters were brought to a head by General Wilson summoning both Gubbins and Stawell to Algiers for discussions. On 15 January Stawell telegraphed to Baker Street that he was leaving that day for Algiers with a brief approved by General Paget and that he was sending Sweet-Escott back to London 'fastair' to report. On 16 January Gubbins replied to Stawell at Algiers, "hoping to see you earliest at Massingham but will await Escott's arrival here".

Gubbins' readiness to leave for Algiers at such short notice indicates the importance which he attached to settling SOE's Mediterranean organization, for in the middle of January he had other things on his mind. It will be recalled that, on 14 January, he and Selborne had attended a meeting of the Defence Committee under Attlee's chairmanship to discuss the situation in Holland. Selborne had made a spirited defence of the part played by Baker Street, and once again the decision about SOE's future had been deferred until the Prime Minister's return. However, Selborne had seized the opportunity of one of his rare attendances at a Defence Committee to reiterate SOE's increasing need for long-range aircraft and for once his appeal had been supported by the Foreign Secretary. As a result of his discussion, Ministers had instructed the Chiefs of Staff to reconsider the allocation of aircraft for special operations and the latter were due to take this item on 19 January.

Gubbins had every confidence in Sporborg's ability to present SOE's case, but would obviously have preferred to have attended himself when a matter so vital to SOE was discussed. Besides, the form of SOE's higher direction and its future as an independent organization had still to be decided. The omens looked favourable, but until the Prime Minister had given his ruling, no one could be sure, and Mr Churchill was not due back from Marrakesh until 18 January. Nor at the time of his departure for Algiers had Gubbins even the benefit of knowing the Chiefs of Staff's definitive views on Wilson's Memorandum; the Foreign Office's written comments were not forwarded to the COS Secretariat until 18 January and this letter and another about SOE's activities in Greece were due to be taken by the Chiefs of Staff on 21 January. The arguments against delaying his departure were almost equally compelling. Stawell had not consulted Baker Street about the brief "approved by Paget" which he was taking to Algiers. Moreover, news had been received that General Donovan had left Cairo for Italy *en route* for Algiers, and it was clear that SACMED was in no mood to wait much longer. In the event, by awaiting Sweet-Escott's return to London, Gubbins missed the first meeting "to discuss the future of OSS/SOE in the Mediterranean" which was held at AFHQ on 17 January. With General Gammell in the chair, it was attended by Mr Macmillan, his assistant Christopher Steel, Donovan, Stawell and several staff officers from AFHQ.

By the time Gubbins arrived on 19 January the 'bigwigs' had already left Algiers for Italy. He was shown the record of the meeting, which he thought vague and inconclusive, and he was able to have talks the same afternoon with General Whiteley, Gammell's British deputy, and with Roger Makins, who was Macmillan's deputy. So he was fairly well briefed by the time he left for Italy on 22 January "in pursuit of the bigwigs" and accompanied by Stawell, Miles and Dodds-Parker. He finally caught up with Wilson at his advanced headquarters at Naples on 25 January, when SACMED held an 'exploratory' conference. This meeting was attended by Devers (USAAF), Slessor (Mediterranean Air Command), Strong (G2) and Rookes (Deputy Chief of Staff). Donovan and Stawell were also in attendance.

The following day Gubbins called on Macmillan. The lobbying was intense and Gubbins duly reported that Donovan had emerged from a meeting with SACMED on 28 January "looking like a cat who has stolen the butter". However, no final decisions were taken, and on 29 January Gubbins and Dodds-Parker returned to Algiers with General Wilson in SACMED's aircraft. Stawell flew straight back to Cairo with instructions to start moving Force 133 in stages to the Naples area, the move to be completed by the end of March.

SOE's responsibility, for the time being, for providing logistic support for Tito's Partisans was meanwhile taken for granted, and while in Italy Gubbins had paid a flying visit to Bari. Here he was approached by a Soviet General Sudakov. Sudakov was on the staff of Andrei Vyshinsky, who was now the Soviet member on the Advisory Council for Italy, and he wished to discuss arrangements for the local accommodation and the onward passage of a Soviet mission to Marshal Tito which was due shortly to arrive from Cairo. Gubbins and Stawell had a conversation with Sudakov lasting an hour, and recommended him to make arrangements direct with Tito's representative at Bari, General Vlatko Velebit. At the same time Gubbins urged Sudakov to keep the mission in Cairo until the necessary administrative arrangements had been completed. However, on 29 January, while waiting to take off from Naples in SACMED's aircraft, Gubbins "saw a Soviet plane alongside full of Russian officers and routed for Bari". He drew General Wilson's attention to them, but the latter was disinclined to get involved.

While all this was going on, the Chiefs of Staff were holding their own deliberations in London. On 28 January instructions were sent to SACMED which added considerably to the confusion: a special operations committee similar to that which existed in Cairo was to be instituted at AFHQ; Tito and Mihailović must be dealt with from the same centre; and this centre should receive advice both from the Foreign Office representatives in Cairo and from Mr Macmillan in Algiers. However, until the present delicate situation between Tito and Mihailović had been clarified, the Chiefs of Staff directed that operations should be controlled from Cairo, though "for the shortest possible time".

The Chiefs of Staff and the Foreign Office also considered that SOE and OSS must be integrated, and that the Chiefs of Staff must retain control of all operations in Poland from bases in Southern Italy. This directive appeared to overlook the fact that three weeks previously the Prime Minister had personally promised Tito to withdraw all further British military support from Mihailović; General Wilson wisely decided to treat the Chiefs of Staff communication as a general directive and to sort the matter out himself.

On 30 January Gammell held another meeting which included Slessor and representatives of the Royal Navy, SOE, OSS, OWI (US Office of War Information) and other interested parties, when, according to Gubbins, it was decided to recommend to SACMED "the creation of a section of AFHQ on the General Staff side to control and direct special operations."

The following day Gubbins and Dodds-Parker had a private meeting with Gammell. Inevitably all these conflicting recommendations resulted in delay and the waters were still further muddied by a complaint from Macmillan to the Prime Minister that SACMED was not receiving any of the reports which Maclean was telegraphing to Cairo; and by General Donovan's unwillingness to allow OSS officers at Tito's headquarters to come under Maclean's orders so long as Maclean was not under the orders of the Combined Chiefs of Staff.

On 2 February Gubbins wrote to Miles, "still in Algiers trying to get concrete decisions on our new set-up and the establishment of the SO Section in AFHQ which is to direct our operations generally in the Mediterranean theatre .... I hope they will soon make up their minds." Later on the same day he telegraphed to Selborne that he was hoping to leave for London on 4 or 5 February, but "was still awaiting final decisions on the SO Section at AFHQ and nomination of officers for posts". In the event he left for home on 3 February, having agreed with Gammell a draft AFHQ directive for Stawell as "Commander SOE in the Mediterranean Theatre". The following day the new Special Operations section at AFHQ was officially constituted and a US officer, Brigadier Caffey, was appointed to head it.

If Gubbins thought that this was the end of the matter he was soon to be disillusioned. On receiving SACMED's directive, General Paget immediately flew to AFHQ to protest; on 5 February SACMED, in a telegram to the Chiefs of Staff, conceded that, while control of operations in support of the Partisans would pass to AFHQ, the operations themselves would continue to be controlled by GHQ ME subject to higher policy and general direction from AFHQ, this decentralization being necessary because of the need to deal with the Balkans as a whole, and on account of the complicated radio arrangements which were centred in Cairo. Four days later Stawell reported from Cairo; "Commander in Chief (Paget) just back from AFHQ informs me that (a) move AFHQ to Caserta now postponed indefinitely (b) Supreme Commander does not require me at AFHQ (c) responsibility for Balkans has been delegated to Mideast." However, for the moment Gubbins no longer cared about the outcome. By the time Stawell's telegram was received in Baker Street he had heard that his elder son, Michael, had been killed in action.

Soon after leaving Cheltenham College, Michael had received a commission in the Cameron Highlanders. In September, 1941, Gubbins arranged to have him seconded to SOE and posted as an instructor at the paramilitary training school at Arisaig. He proved a good fieldcraft and demolition instructor, and when Massingham was established in North Africa in November, 1942, Michael was promoted to Acting Captain and sent out to Algiers to help set up the training section. The first students consisted of seventy members of the *Corps Franc*, which incidentally included Lieutenant Fernand Bonnier de la Chapelle who was to assassinate Admiral Darlan.

Once the training section was running smoothly, Michael sought more active employment. As a first step he succeeded in getting himself transferred to the naval section commanded by Holdsworth, who put him in charge of naval training at Sidi Ferruch. At the end of July he persuaded Holdsworth to let him hand over his training duties to Andrew Croft and take part in active operations with the naval section, which, at this time, consisted mainly of landing stores in Corsica from the French submarine *Casablanca*. Michael subsequently played an active part in the liberation of the island and, in a letter from Massingham dated 5 August, 1943, Wilkinson wrote to Gubbins: "As you will have heard, unofficial reports say that Michael did awfully well on SCALP II and should be in the running for a gong. He has won golden opinions here for his conscientiousness.... [He] is really a very good officer and taking things by and large he hasn't had much fun since he has been here and has acquired much merit for his uncomplaining attitude."

Besides the landing of the SOE-trained *bataillon de choc* at Ajaccio (which was incidentally the last 'Giraudist' operation in which SOE was involved) in August and September, Michael also took part in several hazardous, but generally fruitless, attempts to make contact with British prisoners-of-war known to be in hiding near the east coast of Italy. Late in September, at Holdsworth's request, Michael was posted to SOE's advance headquarters in the heel of Italy, now known as No 1 Special Force.

Among the components of No 1 Special Force was the advanced detachment of SOE's Italian section which had landed at the Salerno beachhead. This detachment was commanded by Malcolm Munthe and, when Naples was taken, the SOE party set up its headquarters in the Villino Salve and established a training base on the island of Ischia. (It seems likely that it was in Naples that Gubbins during his visit to Italy had a last meeting with his son.)

While examining the possibility of using small boats to land agents behind the German lines, Munthe learnt of the imminent allied landing at Anzio. He was quick to appreciate the significance of this operation and succeeded in obtaining approval for the inclusion in the assault group of a small SOE detachment consisting of himself, Michael Gubbins and Max Salvadori, a British officer of Italian origin recently awarded an MC for his part at the Garigliano crossing. In the Anzio bridgehead Munthe set up his wireless station at the Torre San Lorenzo on the sea shore near Nettuno. He describes how dangerous it was to light a fire lest the smoke gave their position away and how they spent the freezing winter nights huddling round a shielded brazier in the depths of a disused stable. He also describes a minor incident which might serve as Michael's epitaph. The tower, where Munthe had established his headquarters, was used by the US army as an observation post. One night, when Michael had climbed up to the rafters to sleep, one of the US servicemen who manned the observation post remarked to Munthe "that must be the son of an English gentleman and a very sweet mother".

Radio communication between Rome and No 1 Special Force was only intermittent, and early in February it became imperative to send a messenger to Rome to report on the situation. By the time a reliable Italian had been found and his *bona fides* checked, the Germans had intensified their counter-attacks and it was not until 6 February that a lull set in. However, in order to straighten the British line, some of the forward positions had had to be abandoned; to reach the cave where the Irish Guards had arranged to hold the newly recruited courier, it was therefore necessary to cross an exposed stretch of no-man's-land. The courier spoke no English and, since Salvadori had had to be evacuated with jaundice, Munthe was the only member of the party who spoke sufficiently good Italian to brief him. Michael, eager for excitement, and arguing that only he knew the detailed route that the courier was to take, insisted on accompanying Munthe to the rendezvous.

Munthe describes how at about four o'clock in the afternoon of 6 February, as dusk was falling, he and Michael had set out. To begin with they were in dead ground, sheltered by an embankment. However, their road led to a roundabout with a cross in the middle, which even in the half-light was covered by mortars and machine guns firing on fixed lines.

Emerging from the shelter of a roadside ditch, Munthe and Michael immediately came under fire. Both took cover in a slit trench but Munthe was seriously wounded in the head and chest and Michael was killed instantly. Munthe was rescued under fire by stretcher bearers of the Irish Guards, but what was left of Michael had to be abandoned.

The Director on weekend duty at Baker Street was Air Vice Marshal A. P. Ritchie who had recently taken over from Grierson and who barely knew Gubbins since the latter had returned from the Mediterranean only three days previously. For a senior RAF officer, 'killed in action' had by this stage in the war become all too commonplace. On receiving the signal reporting Michael's death, he marked it 'deepest sympathy' and placed it in Gubbins' in-tray on top of the pile of operational telegrams. That Monday morning Gubbins came in early intending to work quietly on his briefs for the Chiefs of Staff meeting that afternoon when both Greece and SOE's Mediterranean organization were to be discussed. Consequently neither his military assistant, Philip Rea (he later became Malcolm Munthe's father-in-law) nor his personal secretary, Margaret Jackson, was in time to intercept the signal and soften the blow. Overwhelmed by grief and remorse, he steeled himself to attend the Chiefs of Staff meeting, where the proceedings were naturally overshadowed by his personal tragedy; his contribution to the discussion of the proposed organization of special operations in the Mediterranean could only have been perfunctory. The hectic activity of the last three weeks now seemed pointless and he did not demur when the Chiefs of Staff adopted General Wilson's latest proposals which differed substantially from the organization which he had agreed with Gammell only a few days previously at their final meeting in Algiers. Michael was dead, and it was as Gubbins was later to remark to Wilkinson, "a totally useless death".

The organization for directing special operations in the Mediterranean was not the only item concerning SOE which was taken by the Chiefs of Staff at their meeting on 7 February. They also reverted to the question of guerrilla activity in Greece which they had previously discussed in Gubbins' absence at their meetings on 21 and 25 January. Whereas the long-term political objective was to secure Greece as an area of British influence in the Eastern Mediterranean, at that time the primary interest of the Chiefs of Staff in supporting Balkan guerrilla movements was to contain as many as possible of the German divisions which might otherwise be deployed against the Red Army in the East, or as reinforcements in North-West Europe or Northern Italy. Apart from this diversionary value, of which intercepted enemy radio traffic provided some proof, the possibility existed of using the guerrilla movements as an adjunct to the general plan for strategic deception

(BODYGUARD) in preparation for OVERLORD, by keeping alive the threat of an allied landing in Greece or of an amphibious operation in the Adriatic. A side effect of these deception plans was the increasing number of secret reports suggesting that certain satellite countries might, "if all went well" be detached from their allegiance to the Axis powers. Unfortunately, however, the patriots concerned in these schemes were more often than not themselves the victims of British deception and their peace overtures were prompted by the erroneous belief that an allied invasion of the Balkans was actually about to take place.

It will be recalled that the diversionary potential of the Balkans, let alone the possibility of establishing there some form of secondary front, had long excited the fertile imagination of the Prime Minister. However, the communist EAM/ELAS, which both General Wilson and the Chiefs of Staff considered "by far the most effective resistance movement in Greece" he anathematized as "bandits" and "a mere scourge on the population" while bombarding at the same time the Chiefs of Staff and Lord Selborne with his suggestions for involving Britain more deeply in Greek affairs. The Prime Minister's enthusiasm for Greek guerrillas was not shared by Sir Orme Sargent, the Deputy Under-Secretary at the Foreign Office. In a minute to the Chiefs of Staff dated 19 January he had written, "The truth of course is that the whole guerrilla movement in Greece has been largely fiction created by SOE in order to justify a vast expenditure of men and raw material in that country". The Chiefs of Staff, remembering the destruction of the Gorgopotamos bridge at the time of the Battle of Alamein and the use of Greek guerrillas to deceive the enemy about the allied landing in Sicily, took a less jaundiced view of SOE's achievements in Greece. Nevertheless, it must be admitted that as an appreciation of the current and future value of Greek resistance, Sargent's minute, though it infuriated Gubbins at the time, proved to be not far wide of the mark.

Now that the allied victory was at last in sight, Balkan guerrilla movements, not even excluding some at least of Tito's Partisans, tended to view killing Germans as of secondary importance compared with the task of securing a dominating position after the war for the particular political faction that each represented. This was an attitude which Mr Churchill found impossible to accept, and the reluctance of the Greek guerrillas of all political complexions to incur what they now considered to be unnecessary losses of men and *matériel* was better understood in Rustum Buildings, where regular reports were received from BLOs in the field, than in Baker Street or Whitehall where wider horizons were contemplated.

The specific issue before the Chiefs of Staff Committee at its meetings on 7 and 14 February was a strategic plan nicknamed NOAH'S ARK which had been prepared by SOE Cairo at the instigation of GHQ ME. The plan's objective, with which Gubbins was both familiar and in general agreement, was to ensure that when the time came for the Germans to withdraw their occupying forces from Greece, their withdrawal should be so harassed by Greek guerrillas that these units would be totally unfit for deployment elsewhere until they had been entirely re-formed and re-equipped. However, in order to conserve their strength for a large-scale operation of this kind, it was essential that during the remaining winter months the Greek resistance groups should avoid active operations and consolidate their positions. In Gubbins' view NOAH'S ARK was just the sort of operation to be entrusted to guerrilla forces. Moreover, it took account of the physical exhaustion of the Greek resistance groups, which in any case lacked the arms and ammunition to undertake a sustained offensive against the Germans, at least until SOE obtained sufficient long-range aircraft to replenish their resources. Besides, time was needed for the various BLOs to attempt to reconcile political differences and produce an agreed and coordinated plan of operations. It therefore came as disagreeable news to Gubbins that a project in which, for once, every effort had been made by SOE Cairo to reconcile both political and military directives, and which was certainly more realistically conceived than many of SOE's initiatives, should for different reasons have been rejected out of hand by both the Foreign Office and the Chiefs of Staff. The principal Foreign Office objection was that if the British military authorities appeared to advocate a policy of passive inactivity at a time when communist resistance movements world-wide were being called on by Moscow to do all they could to relieve pressure on the Red Army, it would give the Soviet Union justifiable grounds for complaint and might even provide an excuse for Soviet intervention in Greek affairs, which it was British policy at all costs to prevent. More cynically, the Foreign Office argued that unless the various Greek resistance groups could be induced to fight the Germans, they would certainly use the arms and equipment supplied by SOE to fight each other. Indirectly, therefore, SOE's proposal ran counter to British policy towards Greece which, as the Foreign Secretary had made clear in his statement on 3 January, was to reconcile the two principal warring factions: EAM and EDES.

The Chiefs of Staff objected to NOAH'S ARK on strategic grounds. To suspend active operations in Greece until the Germans started to withdraw would run clean counter to the deception plan (BODYGUARD/ZEPPELIN) of which the object was to persuade the enemy that the allies were preparing a substantial amphibious landing in the Balkans during the summer of 1944. A more dubious argument advanced by the CIGS was that a policy of inaction was bad for guerrilla morale. He therefore advocated resuming air supplies to EAM/ELAS, which SOE had been ordered to suspend, in a hopeless attempt to redress the balance between ELAS and EDES, the former having secured the bulk of the arms and equipment surrendered by the Italians in 1943. The Chiefs of Staff even went so far as to support Cairo's earlier recommendation that Brigadier Myers, the hero of Gorgopotamos, should be sent back to Greece to stir up action. These proposals put the cat properly among the pigeons. Both the Prime Minister and the Foreign Secretary strongly opposed supplying arms to EAM/ELAS and even more strongly objected to the return of Myers, which was finally vetoed by the Prime Minister on 25 February.

Gubbins was present at several, but not all, of the discussions on Greece, both in the War Cabinet and in the Chiefs of Staff Committee, and his engagement book also records meetings with Myers, Orme Sargent and General Ismay. He was left in no doubt that for the time being Greece had become a major preoccupation. On the other hand he felt no personal commitment to Greek resistance groups; he was naturally suspicious of EAM and had little confidence that they would be influenced one way or the other by considerations of British foreign policy or higher strategy if these requirements conflicted at all with their own political and military aims. He was therefore opposed to a suggestion by the Vice Chiefs of Staff, later supported by the Foreign Office at the official level, that in an attempt to reconcile the rival factions SOE should appoint a joint commander of all the resistance movements in Greece. He was equally opposed to breaking relations with EAM, and withdrawing BLOs, a course of action now advocated by Eden and to a lesser extent by the Prime Minister. He considered unrealistic the Chiefs of Staff concept of Greek resistance being capable of maintaining a sustained offensive against the Germans under winter conditions, and could not bring himself to accept the logic of the Foreign Office's prediction that from now onwards Greek resistance activities would be almost exclusively political and their military value a wasting asset.

The immediate deadlock was broken by Colonel Woodhouse, now the senior BLO in Greece. On 28 February he succeeded against all odds in negotiating an armistice between EAM and EDES. This contained a secret clause which he ensured was immediately leaked to the Germans, committing the Greek resistance to facilitate the entry of allied forces into Greece before the end of the Occupation. Woodhouse's brilliant diplomacy both satisfied the Foreign Office's desire that the warring factions should be reconciled and at the same time met the Chiefs of Staff requirement that Greek resistance should play a significant role in the BODYGUARD deception plan.

It was by no means the end of the Greek tragedy, but at least for the time being Gubbins, besides grieving for Michael, was able to attend to the other and equally pressing matters which had accumulated during his absence.

It will be recalled that, immediately following Gubbins's appointment as CD, the Chiefs of Staff had directed that the future control of special operations in Northern and North-West Europe should be exercised by COSSAC. Liaison with the COSSAC headquarters at Norfolk House had therefore been entrusted to a new directorate which had been set up in Baker Street under Brigadier Mockler-Ferryman. Initially the COSSAC planners had considered resistance too unreliable a factor for inclusion in their detailed operational plans. However, in due course they had accepted that at the time of invasion there would be spontaneous risings and that they would have to use SOE to deal with them. Accordingly, after consultation with Baker Street, COSSAC issued a general directive indicating four roles in which they considered that resistance groups might usefully be employed; guerrilla operations by the Maquis were not included.

First, the directive laid down that during the run-up to D-Day SOE should concentrate on the creation of clandestine networks for general sabotage and subversion with targets that comprised strategic industries, power supplies and rail and canal communications. Secondly, these clandestine networks should include special groups to go into action at the time of the landings, attacking vulnerable points and communications and preventing the Germans sending reinforcements to the beachheads. Thirdly, there was the need to take control of, supply and coordinate any spontaneous patriot risings. Finally, Baker Street was invited to examine ways in which resistance organizations, under strict control from London, might participate in the strategic deception plan (BODYGUARD).

Ever since Operation ROUND-UP had first been mooted in 1943, Gubbins, with his experience of the lead times involved in organizing effective resistance, had been haunted by the fear that the allied invasion would find SOE unprepared and, indeed, that this unpreparedness might not be confined to the organization in the field. It was obvious that misunderstandings might arise between, on the one hand, SOE's country sections, still mainly staffed with civilians unversed in (and in some cases hostile to) military procedures, and, on the other, the professional planners at COSSAC, composed for the most part of staff officers ignorant of the characteristics of resistance and impatient with its many imponderables. Moreover, besides whipping the country sections in Baker Street into shape, described by a well qualified observer (Lieutenant-Colonel Hugh Saunders, RA) as possibly Gubbins' most remarkable achievement when he took over as CD, he also had to hand-pick and train the Staff College graduates who were to form Mockler-Ferryman's staff and, when the invasion took place, man the special force sections attached to higher formations of the invasion force. As far as possible, Gubbins undertook this latter task himself, for he had learnt from his experiences in the Middle East the crucial importance of securing the personal loyalty of seconded army officers both to SOE and to himself.

By this stage in the war, research and development, and the supply of technical equipment now being produced on a considerable scale, were in the extremely competent hands of Colonel Tommy Davies, and Gubbins had no cause to worry on this score. Similarly, Group Captain Venner, who had remained in charge of SOE's finances, could be relied on to obtain the necessary Treasury backing. Even though vast sums of money were sometimes involved, his rigorous supervision ensured that there was never the faintest suspicion of irregularity at the Baker Street headquarters throughout the war. On the other hand, Nicholls' demands for signals personnel and radio equipment were often contested by the Service Ministries and required Gubbins' personal intervention at the highest level to ensure they were met. Even so SOE's communications proved only just adequate on D-Day, when over two million groups were transmitted and received by its radio stations. As a professional soldier, Gubbins gave more personal attention to the administrative and logistic side of SOE when he took over as CD than had either of his two predecessors. Visits to specialist establishments and outstations took up what might have appeared to outsiders as a disproportionate amount of his time.

COSSAC's requirement that SOE should equip and, as far as possible, control the spontaneous resistance which might erupt at the time of the invasion was one of the aspects of SOE's preparations for OVERLORD in which Gubbins took a personal interest. As already noted, this problem had been examined exhaustively by SOE's Planning section in the autumn of 1942, the favoured solution being the formation of small highly trained groups, each consisting of an organizer, a demolitions officer and a radio operator, who were to be dropped blind at no great distance behind the lines, and who were to operate, at least initially, in uniform. It was intended that these groups, later to be known as Jedburghs, should provide direct radio communication between Corps HQ and any indigenous resistance groups active in the Corps sector. Moreover, the organization of the Jedburgh missions provided a welcome opportunity for including members of OSS in the plans for OVERLORD.

Gubbins' relations with David Bruce, the head of OSS in London, had always been excellent, and the latter had shown praiseworthy restraint in not attempting to compete with Baker Street by organizing independent and duplicate clandestine networks for special operations in North West Europe. In January, 1944, a fully integrated SOE/OSS headquarters had been established in London for coordinating special operations in France and the Low Countries in connection with OVERLORD, but by mutual consent SOE had remained the senior partner. By contrast, the Jedburgh missions

13. With Tulla and Gerd Cottell (in head scarf) at Lacey Green.

14. Colin with David Keswick, Isle of Harris, 1970.

15. At luncheon in Stornoway on 23 January, 1976, Colin holds his commission as Deputy-Lieutenant of the Islands Area, Western Isles.

were planned from the outset as a joint Anglo-US venture, with which the French were later to be associated. Gubbins consequently attached more than usual importance to the Jedburghs, devoting what some of the older hands in Baker Street considered to be excessive attention to the recruitment and training of what was essentially a paramilitary force.

Whenever possible, Gubbins made a point of seeing organizers, both before they set out for and on their return from their missions to the field. In handling these interviews, he was at his best. He briefed himself fully beforehand, showed an instinctive understanding of the problems facing the individuals concerned and took infinite trouble to remedy even the most trivial complaints. Within strict limits of security, he also explained general policy and the wider aspects of the operation in question and its particular importance in the general strategic plan. Gubbins had the gift of inspiring confidence, and in many cases a loyalty amounting to devotion. But each interview was a virtuoso performance, and he found this intense personal leadership emotionally exhausting. Michael's death had been a tragic reminder of how blindly war destroys its victims, and many of the people who were now leaving for the field were his personal friends.

It had recently been arranged that CD should see the agenda of the Chiefs of Staff meetings in advance so that he could ask to attend the discussion of any item of special interest to SOE. The frequency of these attendances varied but on average they occurred once a fortnight. In addition, when in England, Gubbins made a point of calling on General Ismay once or twice a month. He had a short daily meeting with Selborne, and on the comparatively rare occasions when the latter attended the War Cabinet, he sometimes took Gubbins or Sporborg with him. Besides his informal briefings from Ismay, Gubbins called once a fortnight on Orme Sargent at the Foreign Office, and on the Chief of the SIS, Sir Stewart Menzies. Meetings with David Bruce were frequent and mostly informal, the two men having become close personal friends. At the working level, Gubbins' visits to the Service Ministries, particularly the War Office, were generally concerned with obtaining additional personnel or supplies. He was very rarely invited to attend meetings of the Joint Intelligence Committee, on which SOE had no permanent representative, and it was the task of Air Commodore Boyle to keep in touch with the intelligence community and especially with the security service.

In Baker Street, Gubbins had revived the SOE Council, which had fallen into disuse under Hambro, using it to keep his Directors informed of general policy, but many important decisions were reached at small office meetings. Though by this time he had surrounded himself with an extremely competent personal staff to whom he was never afraid to delegate responsibility, Gubbins was an accomplished draftsman and, whenever time permitted, he liked to prepare his own memoranda and submissions.

In the spring of 1944 his work load was heavy, but by no means intolerable. Nevertheless, he was responsible for the lives and fortunes of hundreds, and at times of thousands, of persons in the field, and since, by their nature, SOE's operations often had political as well as military implications, Gubbins frequently found himself acting at a higher level than most military officers of his age and rank. On the whole, he enjoyed his contacts with politicians, generally finding Ministers easier to deal with than senior military officers who had a tendency to try to put him in his place. He looked forward to his regular meetings with the heads of state and leading members of the various allied governments-in-exile, though with none of them was he able to establish the close relations he had had with General Sikorski.

To the disappointment of its enemies in Whitehall, SOE had survived virtually intact the *Englandspiel* disaster. The Dutch had rationalized their organization and were as anxious as SOE to repair the damage with the least delay. On 2 March Gubbins accompanied Selborne to a luncheon party at the Savoy with Prince Bernhard of the Netherlands, the titular head of Dutch Resistance. It was agreed that while Prince Bernhard, as head of the Dutch Force of the Interior, would report directly to the Supreme Allied Commander, at the official and technical level his staff would be virtually integrated with the Dutch section of SOE. Although anomalous, this was to prove an entirely satisfactory arrangement.

The shortage of long-range aircraft available for special operations — notably Halifaxes and Liberators — continued to limit the development of European resistance, and the competing claims of SOE and SIS, not to mention Bomber and Coastal Commands, led over the years to inter-departmental warfare of exceptional ferocity. So long as SOE's future as an independent organization had remained in doubt, the Air Ministry were able to put off allocating additional aircraft; indeed, some cynics in Baker Street alleged that it was largely to justify such a deferment that the Air Ministry had made their accusations in December, 1943, of German penetration of European resistance movements. Now that the tide of war had turned in the allies' favour, resistance, not only in Occupied Europe but also in South-East Asia, was no longer a mere hypothesis but an increasingly active condition.

The rapid advance of the Red Army was compelling the Foreign Office to turn its attention to the post-war role of Britain in Europe, and the importance of supporting resistance movements was by now clearly perceived in political as well as military terms. Thus it was that at a meeting of the

War Cabinet on 3 January, which Selborne had been invited to attend, he had secured Eden's support for the general proposition that, during the next six months, resistance movements had a vital role to play in the defeat of Germany, and once again the Chiefs of Staff had been instructed to undertake a detailed study of the number of aircraft which could be made available for their support.

The Prime Minister's return from Marrakesh in mid-January and his decision to reprieve SOE had brought matters to a head. At their meeting on 19 January, which Gubbins was unable to attend owing to General Wilson's summons, the Chiefs of Staff had not disputed that more long-range aircraft were needed for special operations. However, overriding priority had traditionally been given to intelligence-gathering, and Coastal Command urgently required additional long-range aircraft for anti-submarine surveillance at a time when the US armed forces were being ferried across the Atlantic in preparation for OVERLORD. Besides these commitments and Churchill's promise to Tito of virtually unlimited support, the Prime Minister had personally ordered the intensification of bombing attacks on German cities as a gesture of support for the Soviet Army. It was obvious that there could not be enough to go round.

The allocation of aircraft for special operations had last been reviewed in July, 1943, when fifty-two long-range aircraft had been earmarked; however, the majority had been designated for the support of Balkan guerrillas and were not available (and in some cases not suitable) for operations in Central and Eastern Europe. SOE had protested at the time that this modest provision was inadequate even to meet the tasks given it by the Chiefs of Staff in their 1943 directive, and in the meantime several additional commitments had arisen as a result of the Cairo and Teheran Conferences.

At Teheran the Heads of Government had agreed to give massive support to Tito's Partisans who could now only be supplied by air, while the Chiefs of Staff were instructing SOE to give high priority to organizing resistance in the Italian theatre, AFHQ were demanding supplies for the French Maquis in the South of France; and the plans which Baker Street had drawn up in consultation with COSSAC for the support of OVERLORD required the delivery of some 350 tons a month of arms and explosives to North-West Europe.

Nor was this all. In his new-found enthusiasm for the French Maquis, which he envisaged replicating the exploits of Tito's Partisans "between the Rhone and the Italian frontier and between the Lake of Geneva and the Mediterranean" the Prime Minister had given a personal undertaking to de Gaulle and to d'Astier de la Vigerie, the French Commissioner for the Interior, to step up supplies to Southern France, since he understood that the French Consultative Committee in Algiers were accusing the British and

US authorities of keeping the French Resistance short of arms and supplies for political reasons.

Moreover, deeply embarassed as he was by his enforced abandonment of the London Poles, no sooner had the Prime Minister returned from Marrakesh than in response to an appeal from Mikolajczyk he had promised to treble airborne supplies to Poland. Both d'Astier and Mikolajczyk had hastened to tell Gubbins that their direct approaches to Churchill had been immediately successful where SOE had failed so dismally over the years to meet their requests. However, their jubilation was short-lived. The prospect of having to divert to special operations up to 300 aircraft from the strategic bombing offensive in the run-up to D-Day was altogether too much for Portal and the Air Staff, though they dared not totally ignore the views of the Defence Committee and the Prime Minister's personal undertakings. Grudgingly they agreed to make available for special operations an additional sixty sorties a month. As always there was the caveat that the intelligence requirements of SIS were to have overriding priority. Sporborg's opinion that the "outcome could be regarded as satisfactory" was not shared by Gubbins who foresaw that the Prime Minister's enthusiasm for arming the French Maquis in order to provide a diversion from the Italian campaign would absorb most, if not all, of the additional aircraft promised for special operations in France.

Moreover, the failure to provide adequate additional support for operations in Greece, Albania and Bulgaria had caused SOE Cairo to protest in February that its "operational programme had been reduced to near chaos". On receipt of the Cairo telegram, Gubbins had undertaken an immediate review of the situation. There was little more that SOE could do, but he instructed the Planning section to continue producing a steady flow of memoranda, analyzing resources and estimating requirements, which he personally scrutinized and frequently amended before they were submitted to the Air Ministry or the JPS. It was a time-consuming and frustrating process, but, as his engagement diary shows, even more demanding were the incessant representations of the various allied authorities registering disappointment and dissatisfaction with SOE and with the provision of aircraft for the support of their patriot forces. With liberation in sight, this support was becoming a matter of vital political importance to the emigré governments in London. Among the most importunate were the French and, with more justification, the London Poles whose authority was now being mortally challenged by the advancing Russians and their Polish communist protégés.

Gubbins felt the hopeless position of the Poles particularly keenly. Their Home Army, for so long the paragon of patriot forces on which so many of his early hopes had rested, was no longer of strategic interest to the Western allies. Indeed it had become a liability, increasingly regarded in Whitehall as a major impediment to the establishment of cordial post-war Anglo-Soviet relations.

In December, 1943, when making his grand remonstrance, Air Marshal Bottomley, the VCAS, had included the Polish Home Army among resistance organizations alleged to have been penetrated by the enemy. This slander was easily rebutted, and the resumption of flights to Poland authorized without delay, though, equally, without much success; throughout the winter of 1943/44, weather conditions were exceptionally bad and over a period of four months there were only two successful sorties to Poland from the UK.

So far as relations between the Polish VI Bureau and SOE were concerned, more lasting damage was caused by the enquiry which followed Bottomley's allegations. This drew attention to certain anomalies, in particular to the privilege, hitherto enjoyed without question by the Poles (and shared, for that matter, by the Czechs and even to some extent the Free French) of sending uncensored messages to their home forces in their own cyphers without informing SOE, or any other British agency, of their contents. Moreover, it could not be denied that SOE had no means of ascertaining, other than from Polish sources, to what extent the Chiefs of Staff directives, duly conveyed by SOE to the VI Bureau, were carried out by the Polish Home Army. Nor was it known what became of the very large sums of money which the Polish secret couriers took with them for 'military and political purposes' and which were provided by SOE without further question and for accounting purposes debited to the Anglo-Polish debt. At least $35,000,000 in gold and currency were despatched to Poland between February, 1941, and October, 1944. In the past, none of this appeared to matter very much. However, now that the Red Army was approaching the pre-war Polish frontier, Soviet suspicions of the Home Army, which were warmly reciprocated, demanded that Baker Street's relations with the Poles should at least be re-examined, however unwelcome this examination might be to either or both of the parties concerned.

It will be recalled that, on the Prime Minister's instructions, Eden had sent for the Polish Prime Minister, Mikolajczyk, and acquainted him with the outcome of Churchill's discussions with Stalin and their agreement about Poland's Eastern frontiers. This meeting, at which Mikolajczyk rejected the proposed solution as totally unacceptable both to the Polish government-in-exile and to the clandestine administration inside Poland, took place on 3 January. In the circumstances, it is not surprising that, on 4 January, Mikolajczyk summoned Gubbins for an informal exchange of views on Soviet-Polish relations and the urgent need for increasing supplies for Poland. While Gubbins urged the Poles to pin their hopes on the establishment of SOE's new operational base in Southern Italy, he was well aware that the major limiting factor was the shortage of long-range aircraft, and the relatively low priority given to Polish operations compared with the support prescribed at the highest level for Tito's Partisans, Italian patriots and, after the Prime Minister's return from Marrakesh, for arming the *Maquis* in Southern France. It did not help that, in order to sweeten his discussions with Mikolajczyk on Poland's Eastern frontiers, the Prime Minister had promised that airborne supplies to Poland would be trebled during the next three months. It was a gesture that not only displeased Eden but was equally unwelcome in Baker Street where it was obvious that fulfilment was impossible with existing resources.

The Polish question bore particularly heavily on Gubbins at a time when he was deeply distressed by Michael's death. His engagement diary shows how frequently his help and advice were sought by individual Poles. On 19 February he lunched with Colonel Gano, the head of Polish Intelligence. With his strong sense of obligation to the Poles he must have found his luncheon a particularly painful occasion. On 28 February he had a further meeting with Mikolajczyk and, on 9 March a formal interview with General Sosnkowski, the Polish C-in-C, and General Kopanski, his Chief of Staff.

It would be interesting to know whether the Polish question was discussed when, on 20 February, Gubbins entertained Chichayev, the London representative of the NKVD, to a quiet supper in his flat. Unfortunately no record is available.

In March, 1944, Gubbins decided that a visit to India was overdue; neither Nelson nor Hambro had found time to do this. In any case, he needed to return to Cairo now that the *Directive of Special Operations in the Mediterranean* (MEDCOS 66) was about to be finalized. Before leaving, however, on 7 March he attended an investiture at Buckingham Palace to receive the CMG to which he had been appointed in the New Year's Honours, and was deeply touched when HM The King, not aware of Michael's death, enquired after the boy whom he remembered when Michael had been on guard at Balmoral.

Gubbins left the United Kingdom by air on 14 March to find that the final discussion of MEDCOS 66 had been postponed. On 20 March he sent a telegram to Lord Selborne reporting that "it has now been definitely decided that Brigadier Stawell and his staff should move there [Caserta] by the first week in April and that the country sections for Yugoslavia and Albania should be installed in Bari by the middle of the month". In the event, by the time MEDCOS 66 was finally considered on 22 March, Gubbins had already left for India.

In the circumstances his precipitate departure is hard to explain considering that this important meeting was attended, among others, by the Minister-Resident in Algiers, Mr Macmillan, the Supreme Allied Commander Mediterranean, General Wilson, the C-in-C Middle East, General Paget, and the AOC-in-C Middle East, Air Marshal Slessor. It was formally agreed that HQ SOM should be established at Mola di Bari, a small fishing port half way between Bari and Monopoli, the headquarters of No 1 Special Force. Meanwhile it was agreed that Brigadier Barker Benfield, who was about to arrive from England, should take charge of the rump of SOE Cairo's organization which remained responsible for paramilitary operations in Greece and Crete, for the Levant fishing fleet, for the sabotage, subversion and covert propaganda which SOE continued to conduct (though on a reduced scale) in the Near and Middle East and, last but not least, for covert operations in Roumania, which were later in the year to become the subject of one more blazing row between SOE and the Foreign Office, during which the Prime Minister, not for the first time, threatened to shut down SOE for good, commenting "It does seem to me that SOE barges in an ignorant manner to all sorts of delicate situations.... It is a very dangerous thing that the relations of two mighty forces like the British Empire and the USSR should be disturbed by obscure persons playing the fool far below the surface."

Gubbins had never felt altogether comfortable in Cairo. "As you probably know, or at least must have suspected," he wrote to Wilkinson thirty years later, "there was not much support in the top echelon of SOE for any idea that I should go out to Cairo and try to put things right – not in 1941 nor more so perhaps in 1943 until I took over from Charles Hambro when of course it was the first major personal investigation I had to make. I suppose those concerned felt that I might upset our local bigwigs – Pollock, Terence Maxwell, Glenconner, Keble etc." Gubbins was shocked to find that even in 1943 the head of SOE was not accepted unreservedly by the military establishment.

Nor could he count entirely on the loyalty of his staff in Rustum Buildings. In May, 1974, replying to another letter of Wilkinson's, Gubbins wrote, "Yes, Cairo was a sink of iniquity with an evil atmosphere which permeated every service there. I remember vividly the look of horror on the faces of the Rustum troglodytes when I announced that they were almost all to be shifted to Italy in the very near future. This was in October or November, 1943, after I took over from Charles Hambro and knew that my first priority was to sort out Cairo. You may remember that one of the first things I did after my arrival was to lay down that you were to be provided with a copy of every telegram and paper that left the offices – much to Keble's wrath. I did not know who to trust, if anyone! But I really was astonished at the reaction to the Italy move. I thought they would all be keen to get nearer the war, where things mattered: not a bit of it! Apart from a few worthy exceptions they were all as sick as mud; God knows what they thought they were achieving in Cairo."

Considering that Gubbins had spent most of the previous six months trying to bring about the move of SOE's Mediterranean headquarters to Italy, he might have been expected to wait four more days for approval of MEDCOS 66 by the Supreme Allied Commander. However, he himself might have felt that, having now satisfied himself that Stawell's move to Italy was assured, there was no reason to linger in Cairo merely to see the decision formally endorsed by the Commanders-in-Chief; nor did he need to be reminded that the future direction of special operations in the Mediterranean, and indeed elsewhere, was to be exercised by the theatre commander. But, quite apart from his characteristic impatience with formality, Gubbins never felt altogether at ease with the 'Bigwigs' as he used to term them. He found General Wilson snubbing and was understandably reluctant to attend meetings where he was not only outranked but often found himself forced on to the defensive where SOE was concerned. On the other hand, it must be said that busy Ministers and senior officers who were involved, sometimes unwillingly, in SOE's affairs were resentful when Gubbins found excuses for absenting himself from their discussions; and critics of SOE − quite wrongly − attributed his offhand behaviour to a swollen head.

15

SOE: 1944/1945

The explanation of Gubbins' apparent discourtesy may have been that, while in Cairo, he had received an urgent invitation to lunch with Admiral Mountbatten at the new South-East Asia Command Headquarters at Kandy, and future prospects in South-East Asia would certainly have seemed more alluring than celebrating SOE's virtual demise in the Eastern Mediterranean.

Gubbins had been very impressed with Colin Mackenzie, the civilian head of SOE India, when the latter had been recalled to London to account for his apparent disregard of orders over an operation in Goa (LONGSHANKS). On becoming CD, one of Gubbins' first tasks had been to find a replacement for Mackenzie's military deputy. He persuaded his old friend Guinness to accept this appointment. Guinness, after taking part in the North African landings, had returned to regular duty and was understandably reluctant to jeopardize his career once again by involving himself with SOE.

Gubbins briefed Guinness early in October, 1943, and the latter's recollection of this briefing provides a unique insight into Gubbins' conception of SOE's future role in South-East Asia. The basic assumption was that, with Mountbatten's appointment as Supreme Allied Commander, operations in the area were likely to move from the defensive to the offensive and it was therefore necessary to expand SOE's establishment and coordinate its plans with military requirements. Owing to the shortage of time he had decided to go for guerrilla forces rather than for the establishment of networks of secret agents. While every effort should be made to support the half-dozen SOE parties already in the field — for example in Burma — there was little hope of reinforcement in the time available. It took far longer to train secret agents than to train guerrilla leaders. Above all, Guinness was to ensure that the activities of Force 136, as the India mission was to be known in future, should conform with the theatre commander's plans and meet the military requirements of local army commanders. Political matters were to be handled by Mackenzie.

Colin Mackenzie, who was later to become one of Gubbins' few close friends, was the sort of all-rounder that he most admired. He had been a classical scholar at Eton, and at Cambridge, besides obtaining a first class degree in economics, had been awarded the Chancellor's Medal for English Verse. In 1918, while serving with the 1st Bn Scots Guards in France, he had been severely wounded, losing a leg which was amputated at the hip. This wound left him painfully crippled but had in no way diminished his enthusiasm for field sports. Between the wars Mackenzie had been a director of J. & P. Coats, the cotton textile manufacturers, and had rapidly earned a reputation for progressiveness and far-sightedness. He had been recommended to SOE by Lord Linlithgow, the Viceroy, also a pre-war director of J. & P. Coats. Mackenzie, although by nature somewhat private and reclusive, had become the friend and confidant of successive viceroys and commanders-in-chief. His friendship with Gubbins lasted until the latter's death.

Now that he was CD, Gubbins could at least be assured of the highest air priority. Even so, in the spring of 1944, it took him three days to fly from Cairo to Delhi, giving him ample time to reflect on the future role of SOE in South-East Asia and the Far East. Overshadowing all these plans was the anxiety that, when the moment came for active cooperation, SOE would not be in a position to provide the support which he had promised Mountbatten and Pownall the previous autumn.

In March, 1942, responsibility for India and the Far East had been given to George Taylor and, like SOE Cairo, it was Taylor's hallmark that the so-called India Mission bore. Like Cairo, it had been conceived essentially as a clandestine rather than a paramilitary organization. There were other superficial similarities: both missions had originally had civilian heads; both organizations had been built up piecemeal at a time when the regular forces were in retreat; moreover, the India Mission had even less idea than SOE Cairo of its future role once the tide turned. As in the Middle East, vast distances separated the headquarters of Force 136 from its various training, logistic and operational outstations. In the case of India these ranged from the North-West Frontier to Trincomalee with the headquarters at Meerut, some forty miles north-west of Delhi. In many cases the sole communication between these far-flung units was by civilian telephone line which was already heavily overloaded with priority military traffic. Moreover, Mackenzie with his artificial leg could only travel with difficulty and in great discomfort, and in fact rarely left his office at Meerut.

Guinness later remarked that when he had arrived in Delhi in the autumn of 1943 he had found the India Mission "reminiscent of the state of Baker Street when I had first joined SOE in 1941". One thing, however, was certain: with Mountbatten's appointment and the offensive plans of the Combined Chiefs of Staff, SOE's future tasks would be entirely different from the defensive role consisting of stay-behind parties and scortch-earth preparations which had hitherto been the India Mission's first priority.

Gubbins arrived in Delhi on 21 March, and his first report, a manuscript letter to Selborne dated 27 March (from which extracts relating to the Middle East have already been quoted) was distinctly optimistic:

"What a contrast between my welcome here and my reception in Cairo last October, in spite of the fact that there was some unease, (as I discovered later) that I had come to carry out 'reforms' as in Cairo, and possibly to 'militarize' the Far Eastern group. I took an early opportunity, on a lead from Mackenzie, to clear away those suspicions.

"The internal spirit here is excellent, due obviously to the influence of Mackenzie himself. There is a feeling of mutual confidence and loyalty which does one good to see — it is a happy show, and yet there is discipline and hard work. Similarly relations with the services and the outside world are very good. I have seen both Mountbatten and Auchinleck, and both have expressed their full confidence in Mackenzie and in SOE, so that we are set on a good course and have all the backing we require. Mackenzie has done a very good job of work. While he remains the head of our Far Eastern group (which I hope will be until the end of the war) you need have no fear of another 'Cairo' and you can be confident that the name of SOE will stand high. Both Mountbatten and Auchinleck are ready and willing to receive him at any time — they told me so themselves. Mackenzie has a wonderful grasp of the details of his work, which are as complicated as those of the Mediterranean, particularly on the Chinese side, and those in authority realize it. The result is that he gets what he wants and I have found little left for me to take up personally with the higher commanders, a very good sign indeed.... His general demands for personnel are not as large as I had expected, but they are adequate. As you know, he tends towards underbuilding, and purposely, but in going through his organization and establishment I have pointed out the vital necessity of building up a properly qualified and trained staff in advance of active operations, even though they may appear temporarily top heavy, and I have amended his plans accordingly.... I leave for Australia tomorrow."

In fact Gubbins had scarcely had time to get his bearings in Delhi before taking off for his luncheon engagement with Mountbatten on 25 March at the new HQ SEAC at Kandy. The only other person present was General Wildman Lushington, RM, whom Mountbatten had brought with him from

HQ Combined Operations as his personal staff officer and, from the written report which Gubbins subsequently gave Mackenzie, there seems to have been a wide-ranging discussion of Force 136's future role and requirements. Although saying that he made it a rule never to interfere in matters of staff duties, Mountbatten characteristically discussed in detail Force 136's staff organization, in particular the arrangements for liaison with his own headquarters which he thought excellent, and "the general set-up satisfactory and working smoothly". Gubbins was able to agree since the set-up was based on the paper which he himself had submitted to General Pownall six months previously with the object of bringing the arrangements for coordinating special operations in SEAC into line with the organization in Western Europe and the Mediterranean.

On several occasions Mountbatten expressed his complete confidence in Mackenzie and his staff. Nevertheless, towards the end of the meeting he raised the question of the move of HQ Force 136 from Delhi to Kandy. According to Gubbins' report, "It was clear that the matter had been in the forefront of his mind the whole time," though he realized that "it was entirely an internal matter.... with which he should not interfere". Whatever personal reservations Gubbins may have had, knowing Mackenzie's extreme reluctance to leave Meerut, he decided to temporize by saying that he thought the presence of a senior representative of SOE at the Kandy HQ would serve Mountbatten's purpose. But he promised that the position would be reviewed in six months or so. In the event it was to prove every bit as difficult to move HQ Force 136 to Kandy as it had been to move HQ Force 133 to Italy. Gubbins concluded his report by saying that before leaving he had taken the opportunity to point out to Mountbatten that "although it was the direct relationship between our operations and his main military operations which bulked largest in people's minds, yet there were many other ways in which we could serve him, i.e. long-range penetration in French Indo-China, Siam, etc. and this you were doing".

It had been altogether an encouraging exchange of views and, on 28 March, he set out for Australia.

Special Operations (Australia)(SOA) had been set up in April, 1942, at the request of the Commander-in-Chief of the Australian Military Forces. But SOA was not directly subordinate to SOE and Gubbins was well aware that Baker Street's influence on operations in the South-West Pacific area (SWPA) was more than usually remote. He wrote:

"The whole military situation in Australia is very involved and there is a maze of cross-currents which are very difficult to chart and to navigate unless one proceeds with the greatest precaution (sic) and with a good background of understanding. In the first place is the fact that SWPA is an American theatre with an American Commander-in-Chief, who, however, has his headquarters on Australian territory ... thus in practice the Americans have complete command and control, and are in no way diffident of showing that that is the position."

Nevertheless, although SOA was not an SOE mission, its relationship with the regular headquarters in the theatre, though for local reasons exceptionally complicated, followed the general pattern established by SOE elsewhere. As far as operations in the SWPA were concerned, SOA was operationally responsible to GHQ SWPA. However, the channel of command was tortuous and, as Gubbins was to report, "SOA has not only to fight its battle with GHQ but has to put up with certain stupidities on the part of Australian staff officers as well."

General MacArthur, the Supreme Allied Commander, SWPA, was the ultimate authority for operations in his theatre, but for administration the head of SOA, Lieutenant-Colonel John Chapman-Walker, was responsible solely to General Blamey, the Australian Commander-in-Chief. As for operations outside the SWPA, but where Australia remained the base, Chapman-Walker was responsible to Mountbatten for activities targeted within SEAC. The position regarding special operations in either command was obscure, but Gubbins assumed that in practice SOA would not undertake these without the approval of Baker Street.

Gubbins arrived at the SOA HQ in Melbourne on 3 April. He formed a good impression of Chapman-Walker, who "had established excellent relations with General Blamey and with General Willoughby, MacArthur's Director of Intelligence," and had successfully fought off various attempts by the Australian and US military authorities to take over his organization. He thought that Chapman-Walker was correct in having SOE HQ at Melbourne, near the centre of Australian military life, and not at MacArthur's HQ at Brisbane. Submarine operations took place from Perth and air operations from the Darwin area and both these locations were more easily reached from Melbourne than from Brisbane. Nevertheless, there was a lot of lobbying to be done at GHQ Brisbane and there was no officer except Chapman-Walker who could deal at the top level. He could only compete with the situation by flying frequently to Brisbane (1000 miles) to see that all was well and make his contacts.

In his report, Gubbins pointed out:

"The fundamental difference between SO work in Europe and SWPA was that in the latter there were few areas where the inhabitants had any real desire or heart to take action against the occupying power, even if stimulated by the arrival of allied forces. There might be two exceptions i.e. in Portuguese Timor where the natives had quite considerable initiative (Dutch Timor was worse than hopeless) and in Borneo, particularly North Borneo, and possibly Sarawak. In North Borneo it was rather the Chinese than the Malays, but even in those more favourable areas it was unlikely for anything like real guerrilla warfare to be carried out without the closest and strongest regular support. Therefore the work of SOE must tend towards *coup de main* operations against selected targets, general anti-shipping action and action by small parties put in for rather general purposes of information, a small base either for information or as a relay station etc. In all cases, white officers and other ranks must form possibly sixty or seventy per cent of each party put in."

These conclusions are substantially different from his pre-conceived notions when briefing Guinness.

Gubbins had timed his arrival in Melbourne to enable him to see General Blamey before the latter left on 5 April on a visit to London with Mr Curtin, the Prime Minister, and he then flew across to Brisbane to make his number with Generals Sutherland, Willoughby and Lumsden, and other senior members of General MacArthur's staff. Gubbins' general impression of GHQ was that "the mass of officers do not even try to hide the fact that they consider the campaign in SWPA a purely American affair, and that applies particularly to Sutherland and Willoughby, whereas MacArthur himself does, I think, take a wider view, if one could get personal access to him which is not at all easy, with so many Cyclops and Cerberus on guard [*sic*]. I am sure that many matters, particularly those concerning SOA are dealt with by Sutherland in MacArthur's name without any reference to him whatsoever."

Gubbins had an hour's discussion with General MacArthur "who did most of the talking". He reported that in general "MacArthur had expressed his interest in and appreciation of SOE activities, and stressed that he was not opposed in any way.... I think MacArthur was genuine when he told me he was out to support activities of the type that SOA is carrying out and realized their place in his general strategy ... but was quite unable to bring Admiral Kincaid to the same point of view and get him to allot the submarine craft necessary for full support." Gubbins concluded his report on a rather more elevated note:

"On the operational side Chapman-Walker must just keep pegging away at GHQ like the importunate widow until he gets a fair chance to show the capabilities of SOA, but in this connection I think it most

188

important that while Mr Curtin and General Blamey are at home they should have impressed upon them the importance of the contribution which SOA can make towards maintaining the Australian part in the Pacific war. I am sure that Blamey particularly will appreciate this point. It is essential for the Empire's prestige that Australia should play a wide part and should have a properly developed weapon in SOA which can influence events after the war far more widely than its small expense would seem to suggest."

Gubbins returned to India from Australia by way of Ceylon, arriving at Colombo on 13 April and remaining apparently until 17 April for discussions with HQ SEAC. From Colombo he flew to Poona to inspect the new supply and development centre which was still under construction. He next visited SOE's operational complex in and about Calcutta where he arrived on 20 April before returning to Meerut on the 25th. There was still a great deal to discuss with Mackenzie, particularly the outcome of his meeting with Mountbatten, SOE's future operational plans in South-East Asia and the chronic administrative staff shortages "which could not stand up to increased activity".

He left Delhi on his return trip on 1 May. There is no record of his movements until 10 May when he was due in Algiers. The journey would have accounted for three or four of these days, and he may have seized the opportunity to fly privately to Italy in order to visit the Anzio bridgehead where Michael had been killed, and where his friend Gerald Templer was now commanding a division. Holdsworth has left a poignant description of a subsequent visit to HQ No 1 Special Force:

"Colin Gubbins later came to Monopoli and in the efficient way service people have, Michael's kit was laid out on the floor of his room — sailors would never do such a thing. They never found a trace of Michael. Colin Gubbins had spent a day looking at graves, looking for a trace."

Colin's cousin, Mary McVean, was serving as a FANY in No 1 Special Force and remembers that "Gerry [Holdsworth] was very distressed by Colin's grief, but there was nothing he could do except to fetch a carefully hoarded bottle of Black Label whisky which the two men drank together". Another FANY remembers Gubbins walking backwards and forwards among the sand dunes at Massingham murmuring "so useless, so useless".

With OVERLORD now less than a month away, Gubbins was increasingly anxious to get back to Baker Street. However, he had promised Mountbatten that while in Algiers he would do what he could to clarify policy regarding special operations in Indo-China. This territory was still under Vichy administration, but, with its large expatriate French community, offered considerable scope for special operations. However, this potential could only be exploited properly with the cooperation of the Free French. Owing to the opposition of the United States to de Gaulle assuming control of former French colonies, Mountbatten was unable to accept Free French officers in his integrated headquarters for operations in Indo-China. When, therefore, in July, 1943, a Free French officer called de Langlade had been sent out to India, instead of being attached to Mountbatten's headquarters, he had been taken on by Colin Mackenzie as a liaison officer and head of the Indo-China section of SOE India. The following October a small number of Free French officers and Annamite troops were mustered in Algiers. The intention was to send them to India for training by Force 136 and for subsequent employment in French Indo-China. Unfortunately, in December, 1943, President Roosevelt publicly declared his opposition to the restoration of French authority in Indo-China. This declaration effectively torpedoed SOE's plans.

Moreover, although disagreeing with the President's attitude and notwithstanding the views expressed by the Chiefs of Staff in several appeals by Admiral Mountbatten and Lord Selborne, the Prime Minister refused to urge the President to adopt a less uncompromising position. The immediate matter which Mountbatten had asked Gubbins to look into, the proposed appointment of a French military mission to HQ SEAC, now had to be postponed indefinitely. The Free French had, therefore, suggested that General Blaizot, a four-star General, recently rallied to de Gaulle, who was the leader-designate of the French mission to SEAC, should now pay Mountbatten an informal and unofficial visit. At a luncheon which Blaizot gave Gubbins, at which he was gratified to have been received with full military honours, he urged his host to arrange his informal visit direct with Mountbatten and not through military or diplomatic channels. Meanwhile, he recommended that wide powers should be delegated to de Langlade so that operational planning could start without delay. In due course the Prime Minister was prevailed upon to approach the Joint Chiefs of Staff about the Blaizot mission. However, Roosevelt remained adamantly opposed and, in the event, it was the British who unilaterally authorized the General to pay his 'informal' visit; and in October Churchill agreed that the visit might be extended indefinitely.

Nevertheless, Indo-China remained a political minefield which proved the undoing of Bobby Guinness. The following November he was dismissed at Mountbatten's insistence in order to placate members of the U.S. Staff. The latter had been outraged to discover that, on a secret mission to Indo-China, de Langlade had carried with him a letter of introduction from General de

Gaulle. Guinness was not the only victim. Early in 1945 Gubbins himself was reprimanded by Sir Orme Sargent for having taken Foreign Office approval for granted in agreeing to a French plan to bring from North Africa a paramilitary force, the so-called *Corps Léger d'Intervention*, for use in Indo-China. Sir Orme pointed out that this project was a clear breach of the directive that no French ground forces should go to the Far East.

As regards OVERLORD, Gubbins was reassured to find that Massingham's plans for interrupting road and rail communications at the time of the assault were as far advanced as they could be in the circumstances. At this stage planning and control was divided between SOE and OSS, on the one hand representing AFHQ (and later the planning staff for Operation DRAGOON, the landing in the South of France), and the French political and military authorities on the other. Periodical clashes of interest were inevitable, but once he had introduced Dodds-Parker to General de Lattre de Tassigny, the new French commander, Gubbins saw nothing on the French account to detain him in Algiers.

There remained, however, one other matter which required his concurrence before he returned to England. Macmillan noted in his diary for Sunday, 14 May: "Motored back [from Tipasa] in time for lunch. General Gubbins (SOE) to luncheon.... After luncheon Gubbins and I (with Dorothy) motored over to Dodds-Parker's place. Here we found Slessor, Gammell and General Caffey (US). Dorothy bathed and we conferred. The chief subject was the organization of an Adriatic command (for work in Dalmatia and with Tito). We agreed the paper, for Wilson to send to London."*

The decision to establish the Balkan Air Force (BAF) set the seal on a process which had been evident ever since Maclean arrived in Yugoslavia. From then on SOE's role in the Balkans had steadily diminished until, on 1 June, the Balkan Air Force took charge not only of all air operations in the Balkans but also the coordination of planning and execution of all special operations across the Adriatic. Stawell's HQ, now at last set up in Bari and known as Force 266, became formally subordinated to the regular military. SOE in fact now no longer bore any responsibility for operational policy governing supplies to the Partisans, although SOE channels continued to be used for this purpose.

Gubbins had never been engaged in Yugoslav affairs to the extent that he had been involved with the Poles and Czechs, and this fairly abrupt termination of SOE's long-standing commitment to and interest in Yugoslav resistance was therefore less wounding than might have been expected.

* Keswick and Dodds-Parker were also present at this meeting.

However, besides extinguishing SOE's operational role across the Adriatic, the takeover by BAF promised to be disastrous for other SOE activities dependent on air support from Southern Italy. Clandestine operations of this sort could not be properly supported by regular air transport and bomber personnel who it was proposed should now take over the majority of the tasks previously performed by the special air crews sent out from England. CLOWDER (a project to penetrate Austria) was not the only SOE mission to lose irreplaceable agents and material as a direct result of the inexperience of BAF's untrained air crews. There is no evidence that this factor had been properly evaluated in Baker Street where, in the late spring of 1944, attention was almost exclusively focused on preparations for OVERLORD. But even if Gubbins had not been absent from London during the crucial two months when the concept of the BAF was under discussion in Whitehall, it is unlikely that SOE would have been able to influence the course of events. The Prime Minister as well as the Chiefs of Staff had long felt, with some justification, that the scale of guerrilla operations in the Balkans had grown both too large and too important for SOE to handle. A no less weighty consideration was that the formation of the BAF provided an opportunity for an RAF headquarters to conduct inter-service operations in an independent role. This had been the declared aim of ambitious RAF planners like Slessor and Elliot.

Any regrets which Gubbins may have had about SOE's vanishing role in the Balkans were amply compensated by the almost unlimited possibilities for special operations in the South East Asian theatre particularly since these plans had the enthusiastic support of the theatre commander. He returned to London on 17 May confident that, no matter what had taken place in the Balkans, SOE still had an important role to play.

By the early summer of 1944 SOE was in the final stages of gearing itself into the gigantic military machine now poised for the invasion of North-West Europe. The Baker Street headquarters had been transformed from a community of individual enthusiasts into a military bureaucracy. This administrative transformation, not always entirely beneficial, had been largely brought about through the efforts of Murray, who, it will be recalled, had joined the organization soon after Gubbins' appointment as CD to act as his Administrative Deputy and "tidy up the mess in Baker Street". Hitherto unsuspected hierarchic channels were charted and spheres of responsibility delineated and displayed in the euphemistically described 'Conference Room' for the edification of visiting VIPs. Besides the display of staff duties, a top secret exhibition of weapons and devices, the latter known colloquially as 'gadgets' was on private view in one of the dissecting rooms of the Natural History Museum in South Kensington. Among the distinguished visitors to this sanguinary display was HM King George VI.

Meanwhile an ever increasing volume of minutes and memoranda (from which SOE had hitherto been reasonably free) put an effective brake on the unorthodox initiatives with which SOE had long been identified in Whitehall.

Happily this rationalization came too late to do much damage for by the time Gubbins returned to London in the second half of May Baker Street's direct operational responsibilities were confined to Germany and Austria (the latter soon to be transferred to AFHQ), the promotion of sabotage (but not the support of secret armies) in Poland and Czechoslovakia and certain secret evacuation lines. However, although the actual operational responsibility for resistance in France had now devolved on SACEUR and was shortly to be delegated to General Koenig, the day-to-day management of the agent networks, the logistic support and the arrangements for the delivery to the field of personnel and supplies remained mainly the responsibility of Baker Street. So did the maintenance of the indispensable radio communications which were now SOE's most valuable contribution to resistance in North-West Europe. Seen from Baker Street, there was no doubt that SOE's contribution to OVERLORD, the consummation of four years' work, was bound to be the achievement by which the organization, and Gubbins personally, would in the last resort be judged. It was to prove in his own words "a howling success".

SOE's role in the Normandy landings has been described by numerous historians, notably by M. R. D. Foot in *SOE in France*, and the details of these activities are outside the scope of this narrative. Nevertheless Gubbins' part in transforming vision into reality and above all in establishing a highly effective dialogue between an originally civilian organization like SOE and the military staffs directing OVERLORD were indispensable factors in the achievement of such a spectacular success. It is a matter of record that, in conjunction with massive air operations, SOE's plans for sabotaging communications and preventing German formations from reaching the beachhead resulted in at least three thousand confirmed rail cuts between 6 and 27 June. On average two or three days' delay was imposed on the German reinforcements. Individual resistance groups produced some other striking successes; for example, the legendary exploit of the two French schoolgirls belonging to F Section's PIMENTO network who, by sabotaging the axle boxes of the transporter cars, delayed the departure of the Second SS Panzer Division (*Das Reich*) from Montauban by a whole week. This unfortunate division, harassed by the guerrillas of George Starr's WHEELWRIGHT circuit, did not in fact reach Normandy until D+17. The civilian population often paid a heavy price for this delay, for it should not be forgotten that it was the Second

SS Panzer Division, its nerves tried beyond endurance by the guerrilla sniping on its way north, which perpetrated the infamous massacre at Oradour.

While the interruption of enemy road and rail communications with the beachhead was, perhaps, SOE's most tangible contribution to the allied landing, the success of the French resistance groups in putting the overland telephone and telegraph system out of action forced the Germans increasingly to rely on radio communications which were susceptible to interception. Moreover, although not a true function of SOE, the value of the tactical intelligence supplied by resistance groups to local military commanders was specifically mentioned by Eisenhower in his report to the Combined Chiefs of Staff.

Of more abstract strategic importance was SOE's contribution to BODYGUARD/FORTITUDE, the strategic deception plan designed to mislead the Germans into thinking that the main allied landing would take place in the Pas de Calais. In Selborne's words, "The dispersal of many troops and their concentration in areas removed from the bridgehead became one of the most important tasks demanded of SOE." In this and in much else the work of the resistance far exceeded expectations.

In one area, however, SOE's performance fell short of its prospectus. Spontaneous French resistance proved beyond the power of SOE or OSS to control. Nevertheless, one should not underestimate the part played by SOE in harnessing the action of the French maquis to the general strategic plan and in supplying and supporting these highly autonomous groups of *résistants*.

"Here also we are in good heart," wrote Gubbins to Wilkinson shortly after the invasion, "and here also we do not any longer have to cheat and crawl and we have had the highest unsolicited testimonies (*sic*) from the Chiefs of Staff, SHAEF and Monty." Even the sceptical Desmond Morton, in a minute dated 17 June, reported to the Prime Minister that "the resistance has so far done a better job than I expected they would". It was this report which prompted Churchill on 20 June to urge Selborne to support the maquis in open guerrilla warfare: "Every effort must be made to supply the maquis at once with rifles, Bren guns, piat guns, mortars and bazookas with ammunition .... Pray tell me if I can help you to accelerate action." Selborne needed no such encouragement and circulated to colleagues a report on SOE's contribution to OVERLORD. He was, however, unwise enough to include a recommendation that Brigadier Myers, "of Greek guerrilla fame" should be appointed to advise General Koenig on maquis matters. This suggestion predictably infuriated Churchill. Selborne also included a proposal (can it have been Gubbins' suggestion?) that additional support should be provided to the maquis over and above the figure allotted by

SHAEF. The Chiefs of Staff endorsed SHAEF's rejection of this proposal on the ground that "it would involve a dispersal of effort which would have no operational value". Moreover, when Churchill's minute was discussed by the Chiefs of Staff on 24 June, Gubbins, who was present, seized the opportunity to criticize the supply arrangements to North-East France. He was, in the words of David Stafford, "put firmly in his place by the CIGS, Sir Alan Brooke, who said forcibly that he had no doubt that SHAEF knew what they were doing and that in any case SOE should confine discussion of such problems to within SHAEF". Brooke could not have made it clearer that, although SOE might still have a role to play in France, special operations in that country were now of subsidiary interest to the war leadership, and that the Chiefs of Staff were content to delegate matters to Eisenhower. The reproof was deserved, but it was, perhaps, ungenerous of Brooke to have snubbed Gubbins in his hour of triumph.

Whatever role SOE still aspired to play in France, it was now gravely threatened from another quarter. Memories of French indiscretions over the ill-fated Dakar expedition and continuing uncertainty about the security of the French ciphers meant that de Gaulle's headquarters was kept in ignorance until 3 June of the exact date and place of the invasion. This constraint made it difficult for members of SOE to work out joint plans with their French opposite numbers. Since early 1943, COSSAC had periodically issued agreed directives to Baker Street about the tasks which they wished the French resistance to undertake at the time of the invasion. However, detailed plans for the direct support of the initial operations were not made until a week before the invasion and it was only possible to agree on the operational details with French headquarters on the very eve of the landing.

SOE's apparent lack of confidence upset de Gaulle who understandably considered it of the highest importance that his Committee of National Liberation, which he claimed as the provisional French government, should be acknowledged as the supreme authority directing the Free French Forces of the Interior. Anglo-American recognition of a French provisional government was withheld until October, but de Gaulle's claim to direct French resistance was accepted as reasonable by both the British and United States governments and by Eisenhower. The implementation of this policy involved a major reorganization at the height of the battle. Although potentially disastrous from a purely military point of view, the political pressure was such that Gubbins could only accept the *fait accompli* and devote his energies to damage limitation.

Under the arrangements proposed by the French authorities, all SOE sections working into France (with the exception of the section dealing with the Polish *emigrés* in the Pas de Calais) were to be joined with the *Bureau de Récherche et d'Action à Londres*. The joint organization was to be placed under the command of General Koenig, the hero of Bir Hachim, who had recently arrived in London from Algiers. Koenig's joint staff, designated *L'État Majeur des Forces Françaises de l'Interieur*, comprised both trained professionals like Buckmaster and Barry, whom Gubbins had hastily seconded to act as Chief of Operations, and the experienced members of the former *Bureau Centrale de Renseignements et d'Action* on the one hand, and on the other the influx of politically ambitious French senior officers who arrived from Algiers with little if any experience of the technicalities of special operations.

There was no time to establish a working relationship and the general atmosphere of incompetence, mutual suspicion and political intrigue was soon apparent to British officers working in the field. "London's pulse was beating feebly," complained Hutchison, the former head of RF Section who, after plastic surgery to alter his appearance, was personally conducting operations behind the lines.

For Gubbins it must have been deeply distressing to see the organization to which so much effort had been devoted put at risk at the last moment by the inexperience of a scratch headquarters staff over whom he personally had no control. On 30 July he wrote to Wilkinson in Italy, "The taking over of French resistance by General Koenig has led to a first class battle here lasting six weeks. I have got most of my own way through sheer force of the logic of events, but I feel that Koenig will make an awful mess of the whole thing as he is now operationally responsible." The comments of Ronald Thornley, the sceptical head of SOE's German section, were more pungent: "On matters affecting Gaul the paramilitary boys have paid the penalty in full and the entire outfit is now in the process of being taken right out of the hands of this organization. Maurice [Buckmaster] is asking me plaintively whether I think our section could house him at a later date."

These French intrigues on top of the news of the abortive Warsaw Rising were almost too much for Gubbins to bear and he thankfully escaped from Baker Street on 10 August. It was his first trip to France since the invasion and he planned to visit HQ 21 Army Group and First Canadian Corps to inspect the special force detachments with these formations and "among other things to explain where they stood *vis-à-vis* General Koenig and the EMFFI". However, by the time he arrived in France the battle had moved on and General Koenig himself was about to become the Military Governor of Paris.

Gubbins returned to London with his morale fully restored.

"I have recently visited Mike Rowlandson," he wrote to Wilkinson, "and his detachments [Jedburghs]. Our whole French business has been a howling success thanks largely to Mike [Rowlandson] and Robin

[Brook] and Nick [Nicholls], the last named's work [radio communications] has been exceptional, and his communications with the field, particularly with Jedburghs, have been almost faultless. I have had a very difficult six weeks on the '*Affaire* Koenig' both with him and SHAEF, but he would insist on trying to bust up SOE so the only thing to do was to counter-attack strongly and we are nicely settled again now, but it has not been easy. SHAEF have behaved like rabbits. My present position is that I have written off France now and want to leave it entirely to the French and Americans and gather our resources together for the main effort which is Germany. I have pulled Thornley away from Mockler-Ferryman and have got Dick [Barry] back and am now running Germany essentially under myself."

However, before Gubbins had any hope of giving Germany his undivided attention, there was much unfinished business to be tidied up in London.

There had been grudging acknowledgement in Downing Street that SOE's performance in France had been better than expected. Moreover, since the turn of the year SOE's relations with the Foreign Office had markedly improved, due possibly to the fact that Sir Orme Sargent, the Deputy Under Secretary, found it easier to deal with Sporborg than to deal with Gubbins, and because there was a growing awareness among the middle-ranking officials that SOE's relationships with European resistance groups might well prove of political value when it came to the reconstruction of liberated Europe. However, the SIS was jealous of Selborne's reputed influence with Churchill and saw to it that any failings on the part of SOE were brought to the attention of the Foreign Office as well as of No 10 Downing Street. Above all, the SIS was determined that SOE's Charter should not be prolonged beyond the end of hostilities. This view was shared by Sargent who remained unhappy about SOE's intimacy with the exiled governments in London and genuinely nervous that accidents by inexperienced SOE officers might jeopardize Anglo-Soviet relations whose improvement was, after the defeat of Germany and Japan, the principle objective of British foreign policy. The Foreign Office was particularly anxious about SOE's activities in Eastern Europe. In the case of Roumania, where an SOE mission had recently been arrested, their anxieties, as we have seen, were shared by the Prime Minister.

In these circumstances it was unfortunate that immediately after his return from India Gubbins should have let himself become involved in a confrontation with the Foreign Office over a matter in which SOE was only marginally concerned. In its desperate search for means of striking directly against Germany, SOE had evolved a vague plan of recruiting Soviet citizens taken prisoner while serving in the German armed forces and infiltrating them, with the help of the maquis, to subvert their fellow countrymen similarly employed in South-Eastern France. Incredibly, no less than thirty-six Russians were persuaded to volunteer.

It was while discussing plans for this operation that Selborne became aware that it was proposed to repatriate all Soviet citizens taken prisoner while serving with the German armed forces. Appalled at this prospect, he wrote to the Foreign Secretary on 21 June, saying that these Russians had been "forced by barbarous methods to work for the Germans and most of them had only joined the German ranks under incredible duress." Selborne sent a copy of his letter to Desmond Morton who showed it to the Prime Minister. Churchill was anyhow having second thoughts and, after seeing Selborne's letter, he wrote to Eden: "I think we dealt rather summarily with this at Cabinet and the point put by the Minister of Economic Warfare should certainly be reconsidered. Even if we are somewhat compromised, all the apparatus of delay must be used. I think these men were tried beyond their strength." Eden, irritated by Selborne's intervention, replied rather tartly that if we did not send these men back to Russia what were we to do with them? "We certainly don't want them here."*

As for SOE's plan for using the Russian prisoners-of-war with the maquis, the Foreign Office, after cautiously welcoming the proposal, decided that prior Soviet agreement must be obtained before any Soviet citizens were despatched to the field under SOE's auspices. The Soviet reaction was predictably hostile and it was agreed that Chichayev should interview four individuals whom SOE had trained and who were ready for despatch. In due course, the following October, Chichayev informed Gubbins that the Soviet government did not agree with the project and protested vigorously at British 'disloyalty' in proceeding without their consent. By this time the proposal had been overtaken by the allied advance and the plan was quietly dropped. There had never been any suggestion that, in return for their service, these men should be granted asylum in the United Kingdom. All thirty-six were in due course returned to the USSR and it is sad to relate that one of them tried unsuccessfully to commit suicide, while two others asked to be shot in England rather than that their families in the USSR should be persecuted by the Soviet authorities on account of their apostasy. There is no doubt about the damage which this project caused to SOE's relations with the NKVD nor of the resentment of the Foreign Office over SOE's interference.

---

* This problem was to arise in more acute form ten months later in Carinthia when General Keightley, commanding the British Fifth Corps, found himself having to dispose of forty thousand surrendered Cossacks whom he was instructed to repatriate in circumstances that remain controversial nearly fifty years later.

Indeed, there was general feeling in Whitehall that since its successes in France SOE was getting rather above itself.

On his way back from India in May, 1944, Gubbins had had a long and, from SOE's point of view, satisfactory discussion with General Gammell, SACMED's Chief of Staff, about the responsibility for special operations in the Mediterranean. However, the establishment of HQ BAF, under the forceful command of Air Vice-Marshal Elliot, upset these arrangements. The idea of establishing BAF as a theatre command, with Elliot in charge and Fitzroy Maclean its representative at Tito's headquarters, appealed to Slessor and had the tacit support of the Chiefs of Staff and in particular of General Ismay. Of more practical importance, BAF controlled the limited resources of aircraft allotted to special operations in the Mediterranean and had been made responsible for deciding the priorities between the requirements of Maclean's mission and SO(M). Consequently Elliot was in a position to exercise excessive influence on policy affecting territories such as North Italy and Central Europe, which were outside the BAF theatre. Conflicts of interest were inevitable, and Stawell was clearly no match for Elliot.

During July numerous complaints reached Baker Street from the SO(M) country sections. Matters came to a head with the promulgation of the new SO(M) war establishment in which the country sections dealing with clandestine as opposed to paramilitary activities were savagely pruned.

Having personally negotiated the terms of reference of the Commander SO(M) on what he thought were very favourable terms, Gubbins was incensed by Stawell's apparent passivity and wrote to him in no uncertain terms:

"I am appalled by the views in AFHQ's wire to the War Office regarding war establishments for the special operations section, in which apparently policy is taken out of your hands....More particularly as another paragraph in the wire limited your functions to administrative duties in provisioning etc. To what level have we sunk! In my talks with Gammell early this year he agreed entirely that your position entailed the right and duty to advise SACMED on subversive and clandestine warfare i.e. it is for you to say whether the resources of SOE (including, if you like, those of delivery of stores) can best be used, at what time and in what place.

"In the present situation we seem to have got to the point where RAF are pinching everything for their own territory (what we rather feared when it was set up), whereas in truth Italian resistance is paying a far better and more immediate dividend, which is what is required now, than Tito's very half-hearted efforts in Yugoslavia .... It is, however, up to you to point out to SACMED what your views are, and in conversation with me you agreed that Tito was having us for a sucker....

"There is another point: BAF seem to be dictating what our operations and policies should be in Hungary. That is not their job. Hungary is only in the initial stages now when only SOE, i.e. yourself, can plan how to bring it along. It is only when it reaches the point where there is overt action ready or in operation that BAF should step in and direct it through Force 266. They cannot have any conception of how to commence underground warfare in practically virgin territory.

"The war is drawing to a close and Germany is breaking up. I want you now to concentrate on the next moves which I hope will be Austria and Hungary and the North-East corner of Italy, which is the crucial point in your theatre. We should be building up there now among Italian and Slovene resistance in preparation for active operations when Alex reaches there.... I do hope you will assert your position *vis-à-vis* Caffey who should be, as I see it, the staff section dealing with staff duties in connection with your work, but not the planners or policy makers for SOE....

"We will do everything we can to support you here as I feel that, from a subversive warfare point of view, the Western front is becoming a French/American field entirely owing to the efforts of SHAEF and General Koenig, and the sooner we step out gracefully (to reappear in due season when the bedfellows have quarrelled) the better."

It is at least arguable that by this stage in the war there was no longer time to build up "in practically virgin territories" resistance movements which would be of significant military value, and that in purely military terms BAF may have been right in preferring to employ the limited resources of aircraft in support of Tito's Partisans rather than dispersing their effort on SOE's peripheral missions such as CLOWDER. Italian resistance was unquestionably a force to be reckoned with and deserving full support, but in strategic terms concentrating on building up Tito's Partisans accorded better with the allied strategic policy of tying down as many German divisions as possible in the Balkans.

In answer to one of Wilkinson's protests that he was finding it very uphill work trying to obtain high-level support for CLOWDER from AFHQ, RAF and indeed SO(M), Gubbins wrote, "I have just written very strongly to [Stawell] regarding BAF's assumption that they run Albania and Hungary operationally and that SO(M) is merely a 'Harrods'..... I have stirred Selborne into taking a very strong line with SO(M) on the maintenance of

SOE's integrity and I think that will also help.... I do watch the whole Mediterranean situation and your own carefully, as does David [Keswick]."

Both Selborne and Gubbins were agreed that it was time to relieve Stawell, but it was proving difficult to find someone with SOE experience and of sufficient standing to take his place. Barry, the original candidate, was fully occupied with France. Louis Franck, who was Keswick's choice, (Keswick had been a member of the highly successful 'Franck Mission' in West Africa in 1941) had the necessary SOE experience, but doubts had been expressed whether he would be accepted by the senior military officers with whom he would have to deal – he had a very pronounced Belgian accent. "I know you do not like the idea of Louis," Gubbins wrote to Wilkinson, "but I and David are getting quite desperate trying to prop up SO(M) and there is simply no one else.... I am certain that Louis will do well and not tread on other people's corns." Gubbins confidence was fully justified: Louis Franck proved to be one of his most successful appointments, remaining Commander of SO(M), which he later transferred to Siena, until the end of the war.

For the time being, however, the demands of the revolt in Slovakia and the Warsaw Rising demonstrated, to Gubbins' dismay, how futile it was for Baker Street even to contemplate providing effective support for mass risings in Central and Eastern Europe, relying on BAF's limited allocation of long-range aircraft. Nevertheless, the Poles and Czechs were more than usually heavily on Gubbins' conscience during the summer of 1944. It was their secret armies which had provided almost the only tangible assets which SOE could show during the first two years of its existence: the first connection with European resistance had been the flight to Poland in February, 1941, which at a crucial moment in SOE's development had done so much to reassure the Chiefs of Staff that European resistance was worth cultivating. Besides, Gubbins had always felt a strong sense of obligation to both the Czechs and the Poles. Frequently consulted on a wide range of matters, Gubbins had shared the hopes and fears of both governments throughout the war, making many friends in the process. Loyalty to his friends was one of Gubbins' strongest characteristics and he feared above all that in the interests of *rapprochement* with the Soviet Union, about which he personally entertained grave doubts, SOE's obligations to the Czech and Polish Underground would be conveniently forgotten. While accepting the supreme military importance of the Red Army's advance, Gubbins saw more clearly than most people in England at that time the probable consequences for the small nations of Central and Eastern Europe, and shared to the full the anxieties of his Czech and Polish friends.

In these circumstances it was no surprise that one of his first visitors after his return from India was the Czech General Miroslav who, while expressing regret that Britain had refused to conclude a civil affairs agreement with the Czech government, enquired anxiously whether SOE's support for the Czech Secret Army would continue as before. Gubbins was in no position to give such a general assurance. The Chiefs of Staff had specifically limited SOE's involvement in Czechoslovakia to the support of sabotage actions (as opposed to the support of the general rising which the Czechs both at home and in London considered to be the ultimate role of their Resistance). Confirming that supply drops on the existing modest scale would continue for as long as possible, Gubbins urged Miroslav to concentrate his attack on sabotage of German communications and war industries, and warned him to avoid at all costs a general revolt. This warning went unheeded and the following August guerrilla warfare broke out in Western Slovakia in the neighbourhood of Banska Bystrica. The Czech government's urgent requests for bomber support and supply drops were initially turned down by the Chiefs of Staff, and by the Foreign Office anxious as ever first to ascertain the views of the Soviet government. When General Ingr returned to the charge in late September, Gubbins, out of loyalty to an old friend, wrote a covering minute strongly recommending that favourable consideration be given to the Czech request. Ingr's *démarche* was rejected by the Chiefs of Staff on the ground that their directive of 20 October, 1943, had specified that the Czech Resistance should confine its activities to sabotage and should not indulge in open guerrilla warfare. At the same time the Chiefs of Staff told Gubbins that SOE's covering minute in support of Ingr's request indicated that Baker Street had "considerably exceeded these instructions" and had in fact led resistance groups in Czechoslovakia to believe that they might expect British assistance for a full-scale rising. Although this charge was strenuously denied by Gubbins, there remained in Whitehall a suspicion of ambiguity in SOE's relations with both Czechs and Poles. Accordingly the Chiefs of Staff ordered a review of their directives to SOE which covered the latter's activities in countries "where subversive operations were still taking place". Although the Foreign Office subsequently reversed its ruling about supporting the Slovak rising, nevertheless the general impression remained that SOE, and Gubbins in particular, had been guilty of raising false hopes of large-scale RAF support for paramilitary operations in Slovakia.

Although it was the Slovak rising that prompted the Chiefs of Staff to admonish SOE, their strictures applied more obviously to SOE's relations with the Poles. The truth was that without a considerable measure of encouragement for their national aspirations, and the ambitions of their Underground forces, SOE could hardly have expected to have retained the confidence of the various allied authorities in London or of their people in the field.

Gubbins himself was punctilious in following the Chiefs of Staff's directives in any formal communications with the Czechs and Poles, but these were few in number and the situation was not as simple as it appeared. There was what can only be called a deliberate misunderstanding between the British Chiefs of Staff and the Czech and Polish Resistance, and there was also an organizational weakness in Baker Street. When the Chiefs of Staff's directives were received by CD, security demanded that their distribution should be severely restricted and their contents bowdlerized. No particular importance seems to have been attached to ensuring that these directives were brought to the notice of country section heads with the force of an imperative. Rather, they had often been treated as little more than general guidance. It was, to say the least, unrealistic to imagine that the Czech and Polish, or any other, Underground would accept directives from the British Chiefs of Staff when they frequently ignored instructions from their own governments if these did not suit them. It was natural that resistance organizations working in extreme danger under enemy occupation should consider that they were the only judges of the operations they should undertake and that it was merely up to their headquarters in London to supply the means. It was a responsibility which governments-in-exile knew that they neglected at their peril. In the early days SOE was far too dependent on the Czechs and Poles to question this relationship. Later it seemed natural that where the Home Armies were concerned the Czech and Polish sections in Baker Street should consider themselves their servants rather than their masters. Besides, it was obvious that there was no way of ascertaining whether the Chiefs of Staff's directives were being followed − or even if they had been transmitted to the field accurately, or at all. SOE had no independent sources of intelligence to check this. In fact, from 1943 onwards, Polish headquarters at least had made a serious and sustained effort to inform their Home Army of the severe limitations of air supply. But neither SOE's Polish section nor the VI Bureau had it in them to tell the Home Army that, owing to the impossibility of providing adequate air support, their plans were plain rubbish.

1944 had been an unhappy year for the London Poles. The betterment of Anglo-Soviet relations had now become a main objective of British policy and the Soviet authorities had made no secret of their suspicions about the activities of the Polish Home Army. The recent JIC enquiry had focused unwelcome attention on the autonomy enjoyed by the VI Bureau in directing Polish resistance. Awkward questions had been asked and Baker Street forced to admit how little control it was able to exercise. The anti-Soviet complexion of the Provisional Administration was scarcely in doubt. But the discontinuance of SOE's support would have caused untold hardship and dealt a mortal blow to the Polish Underground, which Gubbins was determined to prevent.

On the same day that Eden had informed Mikolajczyk, the Polish Premier, of the outcome of Churchill's discussion with Stalin during the former's December visit to Moscow, and their agreement about the realignment of the Polish Eastern frontier, Gubbins accompanied Lord Selborne to a meeting under Attlee's chairmanship. This meeting considered a Foreign Office memorandum recommending a fundamental change in SOE's relationship with the Polish General Staff and in particular the withdrawal of the Poles' privilege of sending uncensored messages to their Home Army. Fortunately SOE was not alone in thinking that the Foreign Office's proposals went too far, and the Polish question was remitted to the JIC for further examination. The JIC recommended that the Poles should at least be required to deposit copies of their ciphers with the British authorities. This was an absurd suggestion since the Poles' messages were re-enciphered using random numbers, and was anyhow scarcely less objectionable than Eden's original proposal of censorship. Fortunately, on Selborne's insistence, this recommendation was overruled by the Prime Minister on the latter's return from Marrakesh, though Churchill stipulated that copies of the Poles' secret signals should be handed over *en clair* to SOE. This compromise failed to satisfy Eden who renewed his complaints that SOE had far less control over the Polish Underground than it had over other European resistance groups. However, he was finally persuaded by Selborne that pursuing this matter might prove counter-productive at a time when Mikolajczyk was dependent on these secret channels for his attempts to induce the Home Army to accept the new frontiers. It is a tribute to Selborne's persuasiveness that Eden not only relented but even supported SOE's request for additional arms to be sent to Poland on condition that these were for the purpose of sabotage (as opposed to the preparations for guerrilla warfare favoured by the Home Army).

Subjected by Churchill to almost intolerable pressure to accept the Teheran decision about their Eastern territories, the Poles were in no doubt about the precariousness of their position. Nevertheless, they continued to express to SOE their dissatisfaction with the limited quantity of supplies that were reaching Poland. During the winter 1943/1944 weather conditions had been exceptionally bad and over a period of four months there had only been two successful sorties from the United Kingdom. The establishment of the Polish Special Flight at Brindisi and three successful two-way operations to landing grounds in Occupied Poland during the spring and early summer of 1944 raised new hopes inside Poland that sufficient stores might yet be received in time to support a general rising. These hopes were encouraged by General Stanislaw Tatar, known as 'Tabor' who had been the Director of Operations at Home Army headquarters and who was among those brought out of Poland in the first so-called 'Bridge' operation on 15/16

April, 1944. Sosnkowski had immediately appointed him Deputy Chief of Staff at Polish GHQ with special responsibilities for the Home Army.

Although at this stage in the war the Chiefs of Staff attached little military value to the Polish Home Army, on 20 May, 1944, one of its detachments had captured virtually intact a German V-2 rocket which had fallen into a swamp some eighty miles east of Warsaw and failed to explode. With the imminence of the German rocket attacks on London, this exploit caused considerable excitement in Whitehall and SOE was instructed to examine urgently whether it would be possible to pick up the key components and bring them back to England for technical inspection. This projected operation, which was successfully accomplished on 25/26 July, may well have been one of the subjects which Gubbins discussed with General Tabor when he lunched with him on 20 June. Another was SOE's proposal that the mission in Moscow should be used to establish contact between the Polish Home Army and the advancing Soviet forces so that their operations could be coordinated. At a meeting at Downing Street at the end of May, attended by Eden, O'Malley, the British Ambassador to the Polish government-in-exile, Romer, the Polish Foreign Minister, and Raczynski, the Polish ambassador, Churchill had rejected this proposal, although it was favoured by the Foreign Office and had only been proposed by SOE as a last resort, since the first contacts between the Home Army and the Red Army had so far been disastrous.

Finally, now that most, if not all, of Poland would be in Soviet hands in a matter of weeks, the question for the Home Army was no longer whether but when to go into action. This was a decision which Gubbins felt strongly must be left to the people on the spot. Nor dared he have given Tabor any reason to think that in the event of a general rising the Chiefs of Staff would relent and provide any of the substantial support from the United Kingdom on which the Home Army was still relying, despite the serious and protracted efforts of couriers from the VI Bureau to disillusion them.

However, considered plans were rapidly being overtaken by events. General Sosnkowski, apparently against his personal judgement, had allowed instructions to be issued to the underground authorities that they should come into the open and declare themselves if about to be overrun by the Red Army; in practice, such disclosure had proved almost invariably fatal. On 7 July Sosnkowski sent a further signal to the Home Commander directing that if it should prove possible at the last stage of the German retreat and before the entry of the Red Army, units should try to gain possession, even for a brief time, of Wilno, Lwow, any other large centre of population or any clearly defined territory. "We should do so and thus appear in the role of undisputed owner." It was not a realistic scenario and the signal was one of the causes of the Warsaw Rising which the government delegates in

Warsaw decided to initiate when, on 25 July, they received authority to "take any decisions necessary".

The following day a telegram was received in London from General Bor, Commander of the Home Army, asking for the Polish Parachute Brigade to be sent to Warsaw and for neighbouring airfields to be bombed. In handing Eden a copy of this telegram, Raczynski informed him that the Polish government wished to send to Warsaw four squadrons of Polish Air Force bombers escorted by a fighter squadron to land on airfields captured by the Home Army. It did not need Gubbins to tell the Poles that the British authorities were unlikely to accede to this request. Nevertheless SOE supported the despatch of the Parachute Brigade and proposed sending its own mission to Warsaw, an operation which it had been planning for some time.

News of the Warsaw Rising was received in London on 1 August. The Polish Ambassador immediately asked for drops of arms and ammunition. Raczynski's representations were followed by approaches at all levels. HM King George VI and President Roosevelt received telegrams from President Raczkiewicz; Sir Alexander Cadogan, General Ismay, the individual Chiefs of Staff, General Wilson and Air Marshal Slessor were all approached in turn. Inevitably, as his engagement book shows, Gubbins received more than his share of these representations, both official and unofficial and, knowing their futility, found them intensely painful.

The details of the Warsaw Rising have passed into legend. The reckless gallantry of the Polish Resistance, cynically dismissed by Stalin as "the group of criminals who have embarked on the Warsaw adventure in order to seize power"; the matchless heroism of Polish, British and South African air crews; the cold-blooded refusal of the Soviet authorities either to come to the Poles' aid or to offer facilities for allied aircraft, dropping supplies at extreme range, to land and refuel; and the countless individual acts of bravery have been recounted many times over. On 10 August, realizing that there was nothing more that he could do in London to help the Poles, Gubbins paid a flying visit to the Normandy beachhead to inspect the SOE detachments at the headquarters of higher formations. He had never made any secret of his partiality for the Poles, and his detractors lost no time in criticizing his role in the Warsaw Rising. On the one hand, in some liberal circles he was identified with the small group of Polish officers who were in favour of keeping the Home Army intact for eventual use against the Russians. On the other, he was accused by the British Intelligence community of having encouraged the Poles for personal ambition to embark on this desperate adventure which ran clean counter to the directives SOE had received from the Chiefs of Staff. Both charges were absurd. Had he been consulted, Gubbins might have urged caution, but he would have left the final decision to the man on the spot. Anyhow, neither he nor anyone else in London could have dissuaded the leaders of the Warsaw Underground once they had the bit between their teeth. These were desperate men, very nearly at the end of their tether, who saw in the Warsaw Rising a faint hope of liberating, at least temporarily, the capital of their homeland.

It was also true that, for the first two years of the war, SOE, with the tacit approval of the Chiefs of Staff, had encouraged the Poles to plan for a general rising when Germany appeared to be on the point of collapse. However, this scenario had long since been overtaken by events and abandoned. In London, at least, plans for a general rising were admitted by Polish headquarters, as well as by SOE, to be unrealistic. Inside Poland the situation looked different; and Sosnkowski's order to seize centres of population as a token of national independence, sent at Tabor's instigation, at least gave the Home Army something to fight for and justify the years of danger and sacrifice. In these desperate circumstances, Sosnkowski was not alone in thinking that false hopes were probably better than none and it was, anyhow, not in his nature to intervene.

Another reason for the contradictory instructions emanating from London at this critical juncture was that both the Polish Prime Minister and the Commander-in-Chief were absent from London: Mikolajczyk, urged by Churchill, had flown to Moscow to make his own accommodation with Stalin, while Sosnkowski and his Chief of Staff had left on 10 July on a visit to Italy to steady the morale of the Polish Corps which had been shaken by the news of the rapid advance of the Red Army and the overrunning of Poland's Eastern territories. In the circumstances it is understandable that, while in Italy, Sosnkowski sent a series of ill-considered telegrams to the Home Army first of all advocating a limited rising and then pouring cold water on the idea. This indecisiveness on the part of their Commander-in-Chief encouraged the Home Army to make their own decisions. The reasons for the failure of the Warsaw Rising were numerous and controversial, but the part played by Gubbins and SOE was not one of them.

Even SOE's most vindictive enemies among the intelligence community had come to recognize the value of the European Resistance as a collateral source of military intelligence. Information about the development of the German unmanned missiles, the so-called V-1 and V-2, had been kept under careful review since 1943 by a Cabinet Committee presided over by the Prime Minister. Most of this intelligence derived from top secret radio intercepts and aerial photographs. However, in the first half of 1944 valuable supplementary information was often obtained from resistance sources.

Of unique importance was the V-2 rocket already referred to. This had been duly dismantled and brought to London with the help of SOE in August, 1944. However, SOE's contribution was already of sufficient importance for Gubbins to have been appointed to the so-called CROSSBOW committee when this was reorganized on 22 June and placed under the chairmanship of Mr Duncan Sandys MP, the Parliamentary Under-Secretary at the Ministry of Supply. This committee reported directly to the Prime Minister, the Secretary of State for Air and the Chiefs of Staff; its members included SOE's old enemy, Air Marshal Bottomley, the Deputy Chief of Air Staff, the Air Officer Commanding Defence of Great Britain and General Pile, GOC Anti-aircraft Command. Gubbins' inclusion on this Ministerial committee gave him lively satisfaction. He attended his first meeting on 14 July and the CROSSBOW committee subsequently took priority over his other engagements when he was in England until it was dissolved after the last of the V-2 sites had been overrun by the allied advance.

Meanwhile, as we have seen, Gubbins had decided to focus his attention on Germany. The 20 July plot and Count Stauffenberg's attempt on Hitler's life had revealed the existence of an extensive conspiracy inside Germany and had raised questions about SOE's complicity. In fact SOE took a considerably more cynical view than the bulk of British informed opinion about the nature of this conspiracy. The extent of this cynicism is apparent in the following extract from a letter from Thornley to Wilkinson dated 1 August, a bare ten days after Stauffenberg's attempt to assassinate the Führer.

"As you know, members of this famous right wing group, such ones as von T[rott] and von M[oltke] had been circulating throughout neutral countries with remarkable freedom during the past three years making contact (very clandestinely, of course) with agents of such expert and security-minded organizations as OSS etc. and it was not surprising to me to get a report the other day stating that Colonel Stauffenberg's liaison with the Wilhelmstrasse etc. was effected through von T. I have no doubt von T will probably be pleasantly arrested and fed on bacon and eggs for a month or two in order to improve his position.

"In fact there has never been any doubt in my own mind that Himmler and his outfit, who have very nearly gained all they wanted, were well informed about the movement which they had allowed to come to a nice little head. The result will probably be that he and his gang will preserve their own skins as long as possible by making the German Army fight until it is completely destroyed. From a long term point of view this is probably a good thing but from a more short term and human point of view, it naturally has a distressing side."

While this commentary goes far to explain why SOE took no active part in the military plot, the events in Germany precipitated a reorganization of SOE's German section: "I have as you know pulled Thornley directly under me," wrote Gubbins to Wilkinson on 3 September. However, German operations above all required meticulous case-handling and personal attention which Gubbins was in no position to provide. He was just about to leave on a visit to North America and Thornley, to his relief, found himself once again left largely to his own devices. But not for long.

At the beginning of November Gubbins appointed as head of the newly formed German directorate his old friend Gerald Templer, temporarily invalided home from Italy. Gubbins had high hopes of this appointment, but, apart from upsetting the Foreign Office with proposals for a general call to arms in Austria, Templer's forceful personality made little impact on SOE's penetration of the Third Reich. "The so-called German directorate expands daily," wrote Wilkinson from London early in the New Year, "but as usual in our business the volume of work is not proportionate to the multiplication of staff." Thornley's knowledge of Germany was unrivalled and he was not the man to be hectored by Templer or to be rattled by self-appointed experts who criticized Baker Street for its failure to exploit what they erroneously termed the 'revolutionary situation' which they claimed now existed in Germany. He was supported by the Foreign Office in his view that there was not the slightest chance of resurrecting an organized resistance movement from the ashes of the 20 July plot. In any case it was almost inconceivable that an alternative group would emerge with aims and aspirations remotely acceptable to the Foreign Office, which was now more determined than ever to avoid any involvement in German affairs which might damage Anglo-Soviet relations. Now that Himmler had succeeded in destroying his chief enemy, the traditional officer caste, no other national institution existed in Germany sufficiently powerful to overthrow the Nazi Party.

Templer, however, considered Thornley's attitude too negative. Supposedly 'embittered' German servicemen were now surrendering to the allies in their thousands, and it was a popular fallacy that among these prisoners-of-war many would be found willing to risk their lives to partake in the struggle to overthrow Hitler. It was not an illusion which Thornley shared. Nevertheless, SOE succeeded in recruiting some twenty-eight former members of the *Reichswehr* who were duly despatched to Germany with sabotage missions in the concluding months of the war. There is no record of their achievements but most of them appear to have survived.

The effect of the 20 July plot inside Germany should not be underrated. "It is not every day that a German field marshal is arraigned for high treason," conceded the ever-sceptical Thornley. Nevertheless, seen from

London, the lack of elementary security virtually ensured the failure of this conspiracy and was in stark contrast to the grim professionalism of the extreme left wing resistance groups which Thornley saw as the last remaining hope. Since the early years of the war, mainly through its representative in Switzerland, SOE's German section had maintained tenuous and most secret contact with representatives of the *Internationaler Sozialistische Kampfbund* (ISK), and ISK railway workers employed by the *Reichsbahn* had carried out a number of administrative and physical sabotage operations against German rolling-stock, mainly in the Basle marshalling yards. Although Thornley's plans for extending these operations to cover the South German railway network never came to much, ISK's virtually undetectable sabotage caused consternation – to put it no higher – among the German Movements Staff.* Moreover, it may be assumed that ISK's activities lent verisimilitude to Operation PERIWIG – Gubbins' ultimate intervention in German affairs.

Gubbins' brief exposure to the realities and limitations of clandestine work in Germany during the summer of 1944 had at least convinced him that there was no hope of organizing genuine resistance inside Germany on any significant scale. He had therefore welcomed a joint SOE/PWE project for creating an entirely fictitious anti-Nazi resistance movement inside the Reich, using black radio transmissions and other deception techniques which had been perfected as part of the deception plan which had covered the Normandy landings. By now Germany was the last theatre of special operations for which the Baker Street headquarters was directly responsible, and before delegating this executive responsibility to Gerald Templer Gubbins had set up a joint PWE/SOE planning section to control PERIWIG. The idea of creating a totally fictitious resistance movement appealed strongly to some members of Baker Street as a suitable culmination of SOE's endeavours. Yet it had every promise of being a success; many Germans were in a state bordering on hysteria as the Red Army approached the frontiers of Prussia and Silesia, and while the *Reichswehr* continued to fight dogged rearguard actions, opportunities for creating confusion and even panic on the home front were multiplying. The Foreign Office did not share Baker Street's enthusiasm, foreseeing that it would be almost impossible to explain a venture of this sort to the Soviet authorities for whom 'German Resistance' had an altogether different connotation.

Thus it was not until January, 1945, that the joint SOE/PWE section was permitted to function, then only on condition that there was no suggestion in the PERIWIG plan that German resistance was being backed by the

---

* The effectiveness of ISK operations was to some extent verifiable through top secret sources, Bletchley Park having succeeded in breaking the German railway ENIGMA code as early as 1941.

Western allies. Once again the delay imposed on Baker Street by the Foreign Office resulted in a potentially good idea being overtaken by events. Five agents were actually despatched to Germany in April, 1945, to carry out liaison duties with this imaginary underground movement, and all survived the war. But by now Gubbins had other and more pressing interests.

Not the least important consequence of Gubbins' decision to reorganize the German section in July, 1944, was that this reorganization gave Donovan the excuse he had been waiting for to withdraw the OSS liaison officer from SOE's German section. Henceforward OSS conducted its own operations into Germany without informing any British authority. This gesture of independence marked the beginning of the end of the policy of 'integration' which had been in force since Donovan and Hambro had signed the so-called London Agreement on 26 June, 1942.* 'Integration' had served British interests well enough, but had become increasingly irksome to Donovan, who was engaged in seeking Congressional approval for the establishment of a United States strategic intelligence service which would continue to operate after the war.

The original justification for the 'integration' of OSS officers in the country sections of Baker Street had been to prevent OSS operating independently in North-West Europe where, according to the London Agreement, the UK had primacy, and thereby crossing wires and endangering British secret agents already in the field. With the success of the Normandy landings, and the subsequent liberation of a substantial part of North-West Europe, the prime reason for integration had disappeared so far as SOE was concerned, and in July even the SIS had reluctantly conceded that OSS might pass its own intelligence agents through the German lines in the US sector of the bridgehead. OSS's post-war plans were obviously less of a threat to SOE than to the SIS, and Gubbins showed considerable sympathy for Donovan's wish to escape from British tutelage.

"The great Bill Donovan shows sense now in wishing to disintegrate," he wrote to Wilkinson on 3 September, "and of course he is absolutely right, as it is the post-war that we must now think of and our show must be British and not integrated. Needless to say I am encouraging him on these lines but the stumbling block of course is the 'Combined' [CCS] who can only really think of military operations and not beyond the armistice. I have as you know,

* In September, 1943, AFHQ had agreed that OSS should operate separately from SOE in Italy.

however, pulled X under me directly and his US integrated member now works separately in Grosvenor Street, so at least we have made a start .... I propose to go to Washington about 13 September for the briefest period I can manage; I must go there before the war ends and have already been delayed a month."

Looking back it seems remarkable that no head of SOE had found time to visit the United States until the autumn of 1944.* However, it is easy to forget the hazards and delays, not to mention the extreme discomfort and fatigue, encountered in crossing the Atlantic under wartime conditions. Gubbins travelled direct to Washington by stratocruiser, arriving on 24 October having greatly enjoyed his first trans-Atlantic flight. He had set himself four tasks:

"(a) To make contact with the Joint Staff Mission and the Combined Chiefs of Staff and find out whether SOE representation with them was adequate.

(b) To visit the Canadian Military and Civil authorities who had helped us so much in our work.

(c) To see Stephenson in New York, and the SOE office there and discuss outstanding problems.

(d) To see General Donovan and OSS headquarters."**

On arrival in Washington he had half an hour with the Ambassador, Lord Halifax, who showed particular interest in SOE's relations with OSS. Gubbins explained that up till now relations had been excellent but he had the impression that OSS would like to take the lead in the Far East and keep SOE in a subordinate role. He took a similar line with Sir Ronald Campbell, the Minister, and also with Sir Alexander Cadogan, who was staying at the Embassy awaiting passage home after the Dumbarton Oaks conference. There is no record of the Ambassador's response, but Gubbins seems to have had a more positive reaction from Field-Marshal Sir John Dill, the British representative on the CCS, with whom he discussed SOE's relationship with OSS regarding China and South-East Asia at greater length. Dill said that he was fully in sympathy with SOE's point of view that the Free French should be allowed to have representatives at SACSEA's HQ but the question of French Indo-China had not been settled at the Quebec Conference and further action would have to be initiated in London rather than through the JSM in Washington. As regards China, Dill advised that

---

* Even more remarkable that the head of the SIS never visited the US at all during the war years.

** Gubbins' report to Selborne dated 18 October.

attempts to squeeze Britain out, which he also had encountered, should be met with the argument that the United Kingdom had in fact greater commercial interests and more at stake generally in China than had the United States, and therefore must insist on being given an equal hand.

Gubbins then went to see Lieutenant-General Macready, the head of the British JSM. Macready confirmed that the JSM was kept adequately informed about SOE's activities and problems. Asked about the availability of supplies financed by Lease-Lend, Macready replied that the Americans had tightened up their procedures considerably and that requests for stores for SOE, which had previously been met without question, must in future be covered by a statement of operational necessity if they were to have any chance of success.

Gubbins was both slightly envious of the lavish scale of OSS HQ and impressed by the facilities and infrastructure which Donovan could count on in support of his secret operations. The research and analysis sections, staffed chiefly by academics, dealt with every sort of hypothetical situation with a teutonic thoroughness which caused Gubbins some amusement, but he reported favourably on the mapping section, equipped to produce up to five hundred specially drawn maps for various government departments. He noted that the OSS Planning committee included representatives from other departments. "By this and other means OSS is establishing itself fairly rapidly as a serious institution which can make some contribution to the war effort of the United States. It has a good deal of leeway still to make up, but the early animosities which afflicted it appear to have largely vanished." Nevertheless, some influential members of Congress remained suspicious of OSS's activities and long-term aims and even more so of the personal ambition of General Donovan to establish a powerful post-war undercover agency.

So far as the immediate future was concerned, Gubbins was given no clear indication of OSS's organization for Western Europe but Germany was obviously one of its principal targets and here Donovan was determined to go it alone, intending that OSS should take an active part both in forming and in executing US policy. Although Donovan was generous in acknowledging the help he had received from British secret services during the formative years of OSS, and in conceding that OSS had had neither the training nor the experience to have participated in any considerable extent in special operations in North-West Europe and Scandinavia, Donovan admitted that since the Normandy landing he was growing increasingly restive under the constraints which both the SIS and SOE had imposed on OSS for reasons of operational security.

In the Balkans, too, Donovan clearly intended that OSS should play a more active part than at present. He had always had a special interest in

South-East Europe dating from the confidential visits he had paid to these countries as an unofficial emissary in 1940 and 1941; and it will be recalled that, taking advantage of SOE's little local difficulty in the autumn of 1943, he had gone so far as to enlist President Roosevelt's support in an unsuccessful bid to take over the direction of Balkan guerrilla resistance. Moreover, at the various meetings which he and Gubbins had attended in the spring of 1944 to discuss the future shape of special operations in the Mediterranean theatre, he had scarcely concealed his resentment that the British had stolen a march in the Balkans and his determination to make this up. In his subsequent report to Selborne, Gubbins ascribed the reasons for OSS adopting "a very forward policy in the Balkans" to the fact that it is a theatre with wide scope for SO and SI work, and therefore promised quick results, which OSS badly needed to support their cause in Washington, and that "it is a territory which offers considerable scope for commercial development after the war". Gubbins found it particularly galling that Donovan had been permitted to include members of OSS in American post-war missions to Bulgaria and Roumania, a facility which the Foreign Office had denied Gubbins on the ground that the presence of SOE agents in the British missions would upset the Russians since Bulgaria and Roumania were in their sphere of influence. "I do things first and then I report to the President," Donovan boasted to Gubbins, who noted with some alarm the chaos that would result if the three wartime allies pursued separate policies in the Balkans, let alone in Germany.

It was no secret that SOE and OSS were already pursuing separate policies in South-East Asia. General MacArthur had so far not given OSS permission to work in the South-West Pacific area and for the time being its activities were limited to North Burma, Siam and Indo-China, territories in which SOE had already succeeded in establishing tenuous links with indigenous resistance groups, and the risk of crossing wires was very great. Nevertheless, Donovan made it clear to Gubbins that he considered South-East Asia as well as China to be a US operational theatre in which SOE should play second fiddle to OSS, and since MacArthur was proving uncooperative, Donovan hoped to be able to send his operational parties into Siam and French Indo-China from an OSS base in Australia. This news was unwelcome to Gubbins, particularly as the situation in Indo-China was already complicated by the US attitude towards de Gaulle and towards the resurgence of French colonialism.

During his visit to Washington Gubbins saw enough of OSS HQ to convince him of Donovan's determination to build up resources of both men and material, on a scale which SOE could not hope to match, for the purpose of furthering US policy in the post-war world.

He left Washington for Ottawa on the second leg of his North American tour, his intention being to pay a short courtesy visit to thank the Canadian authorities for the help they had given SOE over the years. However, on arrival he found that a very full programme had been arranged for him. His first engagement was to lecture to the senior students at the Canadian Staff College on European Resistance and the functions of special forces officers in the field. He found that many of his audience had recently returned from Europe where they had had first-hand experience of fighting alongside French resistance, and he described being "bombarded with very pertinent questions" at the conclusion of his lecture.

Back in Ottawa he gave a dinner party for the Chief of Staff, Lieutenant-General Murchie, and senior officials from the Department of External Affairs who had been specially helpful to SOE over the recruitment of Yugoslavs and Chinese and other foreigners residing in Canada. He found all of them extremely well informed on European affairs, "even down to personalities" and described them as being "intensely alive and overflowing with energy and enthusiasm ... mostly graduates of Oxford or Cambridge universities".

The following morning he lectured to senior officers at the National Defence Headquarters and subsequently paid a formal visit to the Department of External Affairs. In the afternoon he was received by the Prime Minister, Mr Mackenzie King, who, he remarked, "did most of the talking". His final visit was to the Canadian Chiefs of Staff whom he addressed on the subject of special operations in France and elsewhere. The same evening he flew to New York declaring himself greatly impressed by "the alert youthfulness of the Canadian authorities as a whole and their intense awareness and interest in events". Altogether it had been a pleasant change from the staleness and fatigue of Whitehall. SOE's organization in New York was unique. In 1940, when Stephenson had first set up his liaison section in the International Building in Rockefeller Center, the United States was still neutral. Although the nature of his activities and his special relationship with Colonel Donovan were known to President Roosevelt, his position as a foreign agency operating on US soil was delicate to say the least. He had been obliged to proceed with the greatest discretion since any public disclosure might have resulted in the 'America first' lobby demanding his expulsion.

Security being of overriding importance, it had been agreed in London that Stephenson should be responsible for all British clandestine activities in the Americas, which placed him in a uniquely powerful position. Gubbins described this arrangement as "almost the ideal set-up" comprising, as it did, an SIS section, an SOE section, a security section and a communications section – and, prior to America's entry into the war, a political warfare section as well.

But by the autumn of 1944 the responsibilities of the so-called Director of British Security Coordination were rapidly diminishing; relations with US covert agencies were now mainly confined to liaison; operations in South America had been suspended; and the special training school – Camp X – set up in 1941 not far from Oshawa on the shore of Lake Ontario, which had long been one of Stephenson's most popular show-pieces, had already been shut down. The New York office, too, had been greatly reduced in size; nevertheless Gubbins expected to encounter determined opposition from Stephenson to the transfer to Washington of the SOE section of his organization. Instead, Stephenson and most of his civilian staff proved more than keen, now that victory was in sight, to return to their civilian occupations, and Gubbins found himself having to persuade Stephenson to stay on at least until the defeat of Germany. In his subsequent report to Selborne, he recommended strongly that Stephenson should be persuaded to stay on "even after Germany has been defeated in view of his unique relationship with the Americans and in particular with General Donovan". "I am quite convinced that [Stephenson] has done a very big job in aligning American sympathy towards us without the American public having any idea that this was being done, and this has been expressed in many practical benefits of great value to this country; he has contacts with many really influential Americans in various walks of life."

Despite early misgivings he had found his North American tour far more rewarding than he had expected and he returned to London early in October resolved to press on with post-war plans for SOE, if possible matching those for OSS which Donovan had revealed to him. "It would be foolish to ignore the strength of OSS. It embraces so many facets of secret work that it can be likened to the NKVD, which it has probably taken as its model. Provided it survives into the peace, it will undoubtedly be used by the American government as an instrument of policy. Of the Big Three, is Great Britain going to be the only one without such an instrument? The additional strength that OSS gains from having so many services 'under one hat' should, before it is too late, be a lesson to this country."

"Very interesting and significant," Selborne minuted on 18 October. But by this time he had privately come to the conclusion that there was no post-war role for SOE as an independent organization and was himself contemplating resigning from the government and withdrawing from the scene when the Ministry of Economic Warfare came to be liquidated early in the New Year.

16

DISSOLUTION

The devolution of operational control of special operations to theatre commanders, once the paramilitary phase had been reached, was a development which Gubbins had always envisaged. It says much for his integrity that he never sought to evade the consequences of this doctrine, although, from the summer of 1944 onwards, the Baker Street headquarters had progressively fewer operational responsibilities and became virtually a supply and reinforcement agency. This subordinate role was carried out with an unprecedented efficiency, thanks to an infusion of eager young Staff College graduates, but it left many former country section officers bored and unsatisfied. Inevitably the thoughts of those who had pre-war jobs to return to were directed towards securing their early release.

However, there were many for whom SOE had become a way of life and who were convinced that the Baker Street headquarters or something like it would have an important role to play in the uncertain post-war world. Lord Selborne, to begin with, shared their views, and on 27 April, 1944, with Gubbins absent in India, he was moved to write to the Prime Minister requesting that SOE should be represented on the newly-formed Armistice and Post-War committee. This approach – the first of many – was firmly rejected. "My dear Top," wrote Churchill in reply on 1 May, "the part which your naughty deeds in war play, in peace cannot at all be considered at the present time."

On the other hand, Gubbins, stopping off at Algiers on his return flight from India, had had a far more sympathetic reception from Harold Macmillan. As Minister-Resident, Macmillan had met numerous BLOs recently returned from enemy-occupied territory. These young men had impressed him with their first-hand accounts, sometimes at variance with the reports he was receiving from the Foreign Office, which, he suspected, were too often coloured by the prejudice of reactionary emigré circles in London and Cairo. Encouraged by Dodds-Parker, Macmillan had already persuaded General Wilson, though never an admirer of SOE, to recommend that future allied control commissions to newly liberated countries should include a small element consisting of SOE officers with special knowledge of the country and personalities concerned. Much to Gubbins' satisfaction and, it must be admitted, somewhat to his surprise, this recommendation of SACMED was accepted by the War Office, and the establishments being prepared for the future military missions to Roumania, Hungary and Bulgaria made provision for representatives of SOE.

Shortly after his return to London, at an SOE Council meeting on 31 May, Gubbins, encouraged by this development in the Mediterranean theatre, raised the general question of SOE's future role. This prompted Robin Brook to write a policy paper entitled 'Post-Hostilities Role of SOE' which he submitted to Gubbins on 15 July. Brook's paper was read with particular interest by Selborne, who, judging its time-scale to be too indefinite to obtain Ministerial approval, used it as the basis of a memorandum of his own entitled 'The Role of SOE in the Immediate Post-Armistice Period.' This new draft was considered by a special meeting of the SOE Council on 31 July at which Selborne himself took the chair and, on 1 August, Selborne wrote to the Secretary of the War Cabinet submitting the final version of his memorandum for discussion by the War Cabinet and Defence committee. In his covering note he observed that no comments had been received from Macmillan "who is thinking much about this problem in the Mediterranean". Sir Edward Bridges replied that before Selborne's paper was circulated to colleagues he thought it advisable to seek the views of the Foreign Office. Accordingly, on 9 August, Selborne sent a copy of his memorandum to Eden as well as to Macmillan. As expected, Macmillan's reactions were favourable though his reply included a note of caution: "Between you and me the Foreign Office seem latterly rather jealous of my activities". Nevertheless, he wrote separately to Eden supporting Selborne's memorandum: "In view of the impending collapse and the need for such work not only in countries such as Italy, Yugoslavia and Greece, but with whatever part we may have to play in the control of countries such as Roumania, Hungary and Bulgaria, I think a decision is urgent". This sense of urgency was reflected in the Foreign Office to the extent that without informing Baker Street it took immediate steps with the War Office to veto the inclusion of members of SOE in the missions to Roumania and Bulgaria. Meanwhile, on Bridge's advice, the circulation of Selborne's Cabinet paper was deferred because of a new directive, approved by the Foreign Office, which the Combined Chiefs of Staff were about to issue to SHAEF and SACMED. This, in Sporborg's opinion, "really gives us all we require for interim purposes".

Though unaware of the Foreign Office's action in vetoing SOE's participation in the Bulgarian and Roumanian Control Commissions, Gubbins was far from happy about delaying, apparently indefinitely, a decision on SOE's post-war role. On 2 September he minuted Selborne: "It is urgent that we should get some decision on the post-war SOE set-up. We are losing a great many of our best people to Civil Affairs, Control Commissions etc....It is difficult to know how to hold them back....I agree with Sporborg that your present draft Cabinet paper has almost been overtaken by events of the last ten days. The missions that are being prepared for Roumania and Bulgaria in the War Office include an SOE section, and we are also selecting personnel ... so we are already in the armistice and post-armistice stage. I will discuss with you on Monday."

However, before this discussion could take place Gubbins learned of the Foreign Office veto which was confirmed in Eden's reply, dated 9 September, to Selborne's letter of 9 August about SOE's post-armistice plans.

"In cases where chaos or civil war may break out, [the only activities still open to SOE would be] to assist the party which is being supported by His Majesty's Government. This might possibly arise in Hungary or Bulgaria and also in Germany. Till such a situation of chaos does arise, I am strongly of the opinion that it would be better for SOE not to operate in armistice countries where there are no military operations in force under British command. Roumania, as you know, presents special problems and for reasons which you will appreciate, I do not think that SOE should operate any further in that country. It is now to all intents and purposes no longer an enemy country (the signature of the armistice will only regularize a *de facto* situation...) and military operations in the country are being conducted by the Russians and not by ourselves."

Selborne immediately returned to the charge. However, a meeting which he arranged with the Foreign Secretary on 13 September "when this matter can be finally resolved" ended without agreement. The following day Selborne addressed a somewhat discursive minute to Mr Attlee, the Deputy Prime Minister, in his capacity as Chairman of the Armistice and Post-War Committee. He pointed out that the British Chiefs of Staff, after consulting and having obtained the approval of the Foreign Office, had requested the Combined Chiefs of Staff to issue a directive defining the role of SOE/OSS (SO missions) in allied liberated territories and ex-Axis satellite countries. Selborne continued:

"In accordance with this policy there is to be an SOE mission in Paris in collaboration with their French opposite numbers working for the penetration of Germany. There is a similar SOE mission in

Brussels....So long as Germany is fighting it is necessary for SOE to operate in all European countries from which operations to Germany can be undertaken. Moreover, in countries like Roumania and Bulgaria, which have hitherto cooperated more or less willingly with the enemy, it is evident that such lines and links will be numerous and direct. The Germans will certainly not have failed to leave many undercover contacts and subversive organizations in these countries. Not only will these provide for suitably experienced people with the necessary previous contacts, such as SOE can claim to have, additional and valuable means for penetrating into Germany, it is more than possible that the allied authorities will require to have these German influences and activities combatted by subversive and unacknowledgable means."

This ill-argued minute played right into the Foreign Office's hands and, commenting to the Deputy Prime Minister, Eden recited at some length the objections he had already raised to SOE operating in Roumania. Noting that it was the intention of SOE to operate from Roumania into Germany, he observed, "It is doubtful whether the Soviet authorities will believe this, nor is it clear how in effect SOE will be able to operate into Germany across the Russian battle front without the cooperation of the Soviet military authorities." Eden continued to argue, very reasonably, "In any case we feel it is absolutely essential that no decision should be taken as regards embodying SOE representatives in the British section of the Inter-Allied Commission until the military and political heads of the British section have established themselves in Roumania, made contact with the Russians, and generally seen how the land lies. When they have been in Roumania for a short time, they will be able to judge whether there is any work which SOE can properly carry out in that country in conditions for which up till now there has been no precedent."

Despite SOE's renewed demands for equal treatment with SIS and allegations which no one disputed that the Soviet element of the Inter-Allied Commission in Rome was undoubtedly providing cover for members of the NKVD, the Foreign Office case for postponing a decision was unanswerable. Although Selborne and Attlee met and discussed the matter, in the event no members of SOE were included in the British elements of the Bulgarian, Roumanian or Hungarian Control Commissions.

In these circumstances it was extremely galling for Gubbins to learn from General Donovan that President Roosevelt had given him *carte blanche* for the inclusion of members of OSS in the US elements of the future Control Commissions in Sofia and Bucharest. Worse was to follow. While Gubbins was in the United States, Selborne, undeterred by this rebuff and encouraged by a paper which he had received from HQ Mediterranean Air Force — which despite subsequent disclaimers purported to contain the informal views of Air Marshal Slessor — had decided to redraft his memorandum on the future of SOE in the form of a minute to the Prime Minister. On 26 December, he wrote to Sporborg: "I have been impressed by a talk with Mr Attlee on the future of SOE in which he resolutely set his face against the establishment of anything in the nature of a 'British Comintern'. I have therefore redrafted the minute to the Prime Minister and would like to discuss it with some of my colleagues." After a lengthy description of the past achievements of SOE, designed to show that these were as often of economic and of political as of military value, Selborne dismissed any suggestion that a post-war SOE might in time become a 'British Comintern'. On the contrary, its functions would be purely defensive of British interests.

> "In the disturbed post-war years the government that neglected such machinery would be like an admiral who said he did not require submarines. The Americans are going to continue OSS as a permanent organization, and other countries are likely to make similar provision. I therefore recommend that in addition to maintaining that part of the organization which must in any event carry on their work against the Japanese, a nucleus organization should be retained to provide continuity and for post-war duties....I suggest that such an organization should be placed under the same control as the SIS though not amalgamated with it because the methods and technique are very different. In my view this should be the Minister of Defence or failing him, the Foreign Office."

Selborne's covering minute of 23 October enclosed two papers ("the first is mine, the second deals with the matter from the military standpoint and represents the personal views of Air Marshal Slessor. I think it very sound and able") which broached the question of his own future as well as that of SOE. "I would very much like the opportunity of explaining my views on this subject to you personally if you would let me come and see you.... My recommendation to you...is that on the conclusion of hostilities with Germany I should leave the Government and that SOE be placed under the Ministry of Defence. The day-to-day Ministerial work could be well performed by one of the Service under-secretaries ... reporting to you via Desmond Morton, as I do at present." A copy of these communications was sent to Ismay and to Bridges for their personal information.

From now on discussion of the future of SOE became intertwined with discussion of the future of the Ministry of Economic Warfare and of Lord Selborne personally. On 31 October Selborne minuted the Prime Minister about the future of MEW and his own desire "to leave the Government quietly due to disagreement over domestic policy and medical advice to take a rest." He continued, "Forgive me for summarizing what I tried to say to you on Thursday at lunch.... I hope you will agree to MEW closing down on 1 January... there would not be whole-time work for a Cabinet Minister in charge of SOE because SOE's war work has finished in France, Belgium and most of the Balkans. At the same time I am sure SOE has most important post-war work to do. I think therefore this is an opportune moment to integrate it more closely in the machinery of government under the Ministry of Defence for the rest of the war.... I think it would be very unfortunate if this were not decided before you went abroad for the conference with Roosevelt and Stalin, as it is impossible to keep first-class men from drifting away if there is not work for them to do."

Selborne having apparently eliminated himself from the running at his own request, Eden lost little time in staking his claim to assume Ministerial control of SOE after the closure of MEW. In a minute to the Prime Minister of 23 November, which he copied to Ismay for the Chiefs of Staff and to Selborne, Eden recommended that in the immediate future he should assume Ministerial responsibility for SOE until the end of the war with Japan. While not wishing to prejudge the post-war arrangements, he was sure that "the only sound plan in the ultimate future will be to place SO[sic] and SIS under the same controlling head". Selborne replied the following day: "I find myself in very cordial agreement with your recommendations.... I also am strongly in agreement with your view that SOE and SIS should report to the same controlling head. I would always keep them as separate organizations because their functions and techniques are essentially different, but there should be intimate coordination at the top. One point I should emphasize. I find it necessary to see Gubbins daily (generally for over an hour). I do not suppose it would be possible for you to give so much time to this work but whoever CD reports to should, in my view, be able to afford this time. As you are aware the most delicate questions are continually arising with potential repercussions on higher policy." On 25 November the Prime Minister replied to Eden: "This seems an excellent arrangement. But who is the personality you propose to put at the head of SOE? Why don't you take over Foot from MEW?"

This was the situation which confronted Gubbins on his return from a ten-day visit to Paris in the first half of November during which he been invested with the Legion d'Honneur with full military honours at a ceremony at Les Invalides.

This acknowledgement of his unique contribution to the liberation of France had given him great pleasure. Nevertheless, it must be observed that his absences in North America and Paris at such a crucial time were, to say the least, unfortunate so far as the future of SOE was concerned. Gubbins pointed out to Selborne in no uncertain terms the dangers implicit in a Foreign Office takeover and Selborne, realizing that he had been neatly outmanoeuvred by Eden, did what he could to retrieve the situation. Meanwhile Gubbins tried to enlist Ismay's support for an alternative solution. His representations seem to have had some result for on 27 November, Hollis, the secretary of the Chiefs of Staff Committee, minuted that the Chiefs of Staff had that morning considered the Foreign Secretary's minute which they accepted subject to:

(a) The control of SOE by the Foreign Office being considered as a temporary measure since they would prefer to see, in due course, both SOE and SIS under the Ministry of Defence;

(b) SOE should continue under its own head and not be subordinated to the SIS; and

(c) the head of SIS should deal direct with and obtain directives from the Chiefs of Staff on all operational matters.

By now Selborne was, in the jargon of the day, 'release happy' and his next minute to the Prime Minister on 28 November was to seek permission to make farewell overseas visits before relinquishing his office. Two days later the Foreign Secretary sent the Prime Minister his comments on the Chiefs of Staff's reservations:

(a) He agreed that the Foreign Office control should only be seen as a temporary measure but reserved his position on the eventual future control;

(b) he was convinced that SIS and SOE must eventually be brought under a single head. But he agreed that for the time being SOE should continue to work under its own head and

(c) he entirely agreed that the head of SOE should deal directly and obtain directives from the Chiefs of Staff on all operational matters.

The final word came in a minute from Selborne to Eden of 7 December referring to their conversation earlier that day and saying, "It is agreed between us that you become responsible for SOE as from Monday, 11 January, 1945. I was so glad to learn that your proposal is that Gubbins should do his day-to-day work with Alec Cadogan and Loxley, as they have always got on extremely well together and it will, in fact, be a continuation of what has been going on in the past."

There the matter might have rested had the Prime Minister not overturned these arrangements and persuaded Selborne to stay on in charge of SOE until the end of hostilities with Germany. Selborne was unquestionably very keen to leave the Government and it is not known what arguments the Prime Minister used to make him change his mind. But Gubbins saw it at least as a reprieve.

One of the advantages of having Selborne's office in Berkeley Square was that, apart from the members of the SOE Council, only a few key personnel in Baker Street were aware of the Ministerial battle over SOE's future. For the vast majority it was business as usual. Moreover, the increasingly bureaucratic nature of the organization meant that, although operational responsibilities in North-West Europe had been reduced by early 1945 to the bare minimum, the pressure of staff work had decreased little if at all.

Meanwhile, redundant field officers, consisting for the most part of former Balkan BLOs and members of Jedburgh teams, were being hastily transferred to South-East Asia where paramilitary operations were about to commence and where some of these old hands, for example Major John Harington, were to prove as outstandingly successful in jungle warfare as they had been with the European Resistance. Gubbins felt a particular affinity with these field officers, some of whom had served under him since the early months of the war and many of whom had become close personal friends. Whenever possible he insisted on seeing them as they were passing through London; it was a duty to which he attached particular importance, and his engagement book for 1945 shows how much time he devoted to it. It was these personal relations and the loyalty he felt to his supporters, quite as much as his desire to see established a worthy post-war successor organization to SOE, which sustained him during this time. So resilient was his personality and so cheerful and confident his outward appearance that few even of his closest associates realized the enormous strain under which he was living during the closing months of the war.

Early in the New Year Selborne left on his farewell tour of inspection of overseas stations and there was consequently a lull in the battle over SOE's future. For the first time for many months Gubbins was able to give his full attention to current business at Baker Street. The report which he prepared for Selborne's return at the beginning of February provides a useful catalogue of Baker Street's continuing activities in what may be termed its closing phase. It begins with a revealing statement: "On the whole things have been fairly quiet since your departure and we have been able to get along with our work without undue interference from other departments." Gubbins saw himself as being concerned firstly with China, where there was a long-standing territorial dispute with OSS; secondly, in providing reinforcements for SOE's operations in South-East Asia; and thirdly, in liquidating SOE's responsibilities in the Mediterranean. He next drew Selborne's attention to two important covert financial deals which Venner, the Director of Finance, had carried out on behalf of the Bank of England, before returning to Baker Street's more conventional paramilitary activities.

Although no longer responsible for policy, Baker Street was still operating in Scandinavia under the direction of SHAEF and Gubbins reported continued attacks in Norway on German communications including the blowing up of an important bridge and the sinking of a 9000-ton German transport vessel. In Denmark activity had centred on German rockets: a factory making parts for V1s and V2s had been destroyed and valuable blueprints about V2 designs had been stolen from the German authorities in Copenhagen and were being forwarded to London for the consideration of the CROSSBOW committee.

Considering how much of the report is devoted to 'arm's length' operation in South-East Asia and elsewhere, it is noteworthy that there is no mention of SOE's extensive operations in Northern Italy. In the New Year the Foreign Office had become increasingly concerned about the situation which, because of growing communist influence in the resistance movements in the industrial centres, was thought to carry overtones of the situation which had developed in Greece. Gubbins did not fully share this pessimistic view but, since he no longer had any direct responsibility for special operations in Italy, he could not object when the Foreign Office's fears were conveyed by the Chiefs of Staff to General Alexander. All he could do was to try and prevent too drastic a curtailment of supplies to Northern Italy where there were now no less than forty SOE missions and over a hundred thousand Italian Partisans. Though in favour of decentralization, both Gubbins and Selborne found it galling and frustrating that they had so little say in SOE's Mediterranean activities and that Baker Street's role was now effectively confined to providing money, stores and personnel. In any case both Selborne and Gubbins considered that it was very much an SOE responsibility to prevent the outbreak of civil war as the Germans withdrew; it was one of SOE's self-appointed post-hostilities roles. In any case wide-ranging administrative responsibilities were already being carried out by SOE in Central Italy at the specific request of the military and political authorities, who agreed that SOE was the best qualified agency to perform these tasks. However, to the Foreign Office, bent on demolishing SOE's claims to a post-hostilities role in any circumstances, direct involvement of Baker Street in current Italian affairs was undesirable if not unacceptable. Nevertheless, so long as military operations were continuing and SOE's activities were under the operational control of AFHQ, the Foreign Office was in no position to dictate SOE's role, a fact of which both Selborne and Gubbins were well aware and quite ready to exploit.

The Foreign Office had found other grounds for complaint, this time about South-East Asia. While in Algiers in 1944 Gubbins, with the informal approval of Dening, Mountbatten's political adviser, had encouraged the Gaulliste authorities to despatch some six hundred members of the *Force d'Intervention* to French Indo-China where both he and Mountbatten considered that they might usefully be employed in special operations. The

225

Foreign Office now complained that the transfer of so large a contingent could not fail to aggravate relations with Americans opposed to the involvement of Gaulliste supporters in French Indo-China.* Otherwise, Gubbins reported that operations had increased throughout the South-East Asian theatre, where they were playing an important role in Mountbatten's advance.

Even where operational control had been delegated to the theatre commanders, no opportunity seems to have been missed to harass the Baker Street headquarters, and Gubbins and Sporborg bore the full brunt. These attacks often occupied more of their time than the affairs of the countries for which Baker Street still had direct operational responsibility: Poland, Czechoslovakia and Germany. Nevertheless, Gubbins was closely involved with all three.

It had always been one of his secret aims to send a British mission to Occupied Poland, if only as a gesture of solidarity with the Polish Home Army. With the inauguration of the 'pick-up' service from Southern Italy Gubbins' dream became a practical possibility and in August a British mission was assembled under Colonel D. T. Hudson, a veteran BLO who had previously been SOE Cairo's representative with General Mihailović. By this time the advancing Red Army was casting a long shadow over Eastern Europe and the Foreign Office insisted that Soviet approval must be obtained before any British mission was despatched to German-occupied Poland. Owing to Soviet procrastination, it was 26 December before Hudson's mission was despatched to Poland (without Soviet approval). A fortnight later, Hudson had signalled that he was proposing to make contact with forward Soviet troops; but since mid-January he had been off the air. It was therefore with relief that Gubbins was able to report to Selborne that the mission was safely in Soviet hands.

Less fortunate was Major Sehmer, the leader of the SOE mission to the abortive Slovak rising, who had not, as expected, been overrun by Soviet troops and was now reported to have been captured by the Germans and shot. The brief references to Poland and Czechoslovakia in Gubbins' minute of 9 February do not adequately reflect SOE's special relationship with the Poles and Czechs or the disproportionate amount of time which Gubbins continued to spend on Polish and Czech affairs – by no means always on SOE's business.

In February, 1945, Polish GHQ in London, after consulting Gubbins, had disbanded the Home Army since the approaches which its members had made to the advancing Red Army had almost invariably proved fatal. As it

---

* Sir Orme Sargent, conveying these views, rebuked Gubbins for SOE's failure to keep in step with the Foreign Office without referring directly to the part Gubbins had played in this affair.

was, almost every day news was received in London of leading members of the Polish Resistance being arrested and summarily dealt with by the Soviet authorities. Out of loyalty to the Poles Gubbins made regular representations to the Foreign Office about the fate of these people, some of whom were known personally to the Polish section of SOE. However, the Foreign Office, in the interests of future Anglo-Soviet relations, was generally reluctant to intervene, more particularly since Gubbins' information was usually derived solely from Polish emigré sources. The dignity with which the London Poles, and Mikolajczyk in particular, accepted their fall from British grace in no way lessened the bitterness which they expressed in private, and Gubbins found his frequent meetings with his Polish friends and colleagues both painful and emotionally exhausting.

Largely at Selborne's and Gubbins' insistence, the Foreign Office had eventually agreed that the Slovak rising in the autumn of 1944 should receive British support in the shape of a small SOE liaison party and a very modest quantity of airborne supplies sent in from Italy. After the collapse of this revolt, a small number of air sorties to Bohemia and Moravia had been made from the United Kingdom on behalf of the Czech General Staff in London but these had been more political than military in character. It was not until the approach of General Patton's US Army to the Czech borders that military interest in Czech resistance revived. An SOE liaison mission was rapidly assembled and for a brief period Perkins became *de facto* HM chargé d'affaires in Prague, reactivating the Legation's Rolls Royce, which had been mothballed since the German invasion in March, 1939. Although this activity was little more than a gesture, it was not in Gubbins' nature to abandon old friends and allies because they had now become politically inconvenient and militarily of little value.

In return, both Poles and Czechs, unlike the majority of governments-in-exile, had expressed keenness to give SOE all the help they could in penetrating Germany, for by now Germany was the only target for special operations in Europe in which the Chiefs of Staff were seriously interested. The near success of Hitler's assassination had raised hopes that opposition to the Nazi régime was more general, particularly among the officer corps, than had hitherto been suspected. Although SOE's German experts remained sceptical about the possibility of doing anything effective, Gubbins came under heavy pressure to increase his effort against Germany. On 30 July he had written to Wilkinson, "I am reorganizing the direction of German affairs in view of the urgency dictated by recent developments and will let you know shortly what I have done." On 2 August, he had set up a special committee with himself in the chair with the following directive: "Germany must now be the first priority target for SOE and all our energies and resources must be concentrated on the penetration of the Reich itself."

It was also decreed that the German section was to have first claim on SOE's resources and given the opportunity to operate freely from allied territory close to Germany. It seems unlikely that this directive carried much conviction with its author for Gubbins certainly knew that even if there were widespread disaffection inside Germany – a hypothesis which Thornley resolutely rejected – it was now too late to organize the sort of resistance which could be coordinated effectively to assist the allied advance. Moreover, since a German defeat was now certain sooner rather than later, a general uprising, or even a revolutionary situation, promised merely to complicate the situation and play into the hands of the communists. There seemed everything to be said for letting the German Army be defeated by conventional means and not 'stabbed in the back'; and for total defeat to be followed by an orderly occupation.

Thornley, concerned with the minute particulars of infiltrating individual agents, had found the profusion of resources now put at his disposal merely embarrassing and his task had been further complicated by the appointment of Gerald Templer as head of the German directorate. Nevertheless Templer's appointment eased the pressure on Gubbins who was able to hand over to him the business of developing contacts with 21 Army Group, which he now considered offered the best chance of providing SOE with a permanent role in Germany in the post-hostilities phase. However, he had first to overcome long-standing prejudices, and at times hostility, on the part not only of the military staffs of 21 Army Group but also of the British element of the Control Commission. Both were suspicious of SOE's intentions and feared encroachments on their own spheres of responsibility. Gubbins at last was becoming fed up with the salesman's role and was glad to hand over this time-consuming task to Templer. Besides, he had his hands full with the allied governments.

The Poles had needed no persuading to cooperate in penetrating the Third Reich; they had the largest number of foreign workers in Germany, but the channels of communication via Poland were too extended for the sort of subversive activities which SOE hoped that the foreign workers would undertake. The Belgians were prepared to be helpful, but Gubbins reported that attempts to infiltrate Belgian agents had so far been unsuccessful. The French had their own organization and were unwilling to cooperate, and Gubbins reported that he had recently flown over to Paris in a vain attempt to persuade the French to be more helpful over the use of French foreign workers in particular. He had had to accept that, with few exceptions, the allied governments were deterred by the risk of reprisals against their own nationals from encouraging any widespread subversive action by their foreign workers. None the less their presence seemed like an open invitation into the heart of German industry, and some other means had to be found of initiating action, other than that provided by the Overseas Service of the BBC whose broadcast appeals by their very nature were too general to be effective.

In desperation Gubbins turned once more to Operation BRADDOCK. BRADDOCK had a long history; it was a scheme to scatter over Germany large quantities of cheap sabotage material and it may be recalled that the idea had originated with Lord Cherwell as far back as November, 1941. SOE had never liked it and the Air Ministry had liked it even less, but in view of Churchill's interest in the project reluctant permission had been given for the large-scale manufacture of two varieties of BRADDOCK. It was said that the only wholehearted supporter of Operation BRADDOCK was Lord Selborne, who not only chivvied Gubbins but occasionally succeeded in invoking the support of the Prime Minister. Throughout 1943 and early 1944 the Chiefs of Staff had found excuses for deferring BRADDOCK's operational use and by the time of OVERLORD there were three and three-quarter million of these devices in store. With instructions for use printed in a wide variety of languages, it was proposed to scatter them in areas where there were known to be concentrations of foreign workers, and under SHAEF's auspices a limited operation was carried out by the US Air Force on 25 September, 1944, when two hundred and fifty thousand incendiary devices were dropped. The enemy had seemed puzzled and annoyed and had circulated warnings throughout Germany. As a result of this modest success Gubbins had, *faute de mieux*, given this project his support and in his minute to Selborne noted that the use of BRADDOCK on a large scale was still being considered by SHAEF.

The other project in which Gubbins remained personally interested was PERIWIG, the plan to create an entirely fictitious resistance movement in Germany using deception techniques perfected at the time of OVERLORD. It will be recalled that the Foreign Office had not shared SOE's enthusiasm for PERIWIG, fearing that it would be difficult to explain convincingly to the Soviet authorities the purely fictitious nature of this resistance movement. However, SOE had succeeded partially in overcoming this objection and in his minute to Selborne Gubbins reported that it was intended shortly to ask the Foreign Office to lift their injunction that there should be no suggestion that the make-believe organization was being controlled from the United Kingdom.

The remainder of Gubbins' report was devoted to the various devices, special weapons and wireless equipment which were now coming into mass production. It was now too late for their employment anywhere in Europe and it was questionable whether they could even be shipped to South-East Asia in time. Nevertheless, it was confidently expected that many of these technical achievements would be put to good use in the post-hostilities phase and that the very considerable sums of money invested in their manufacture would not be wasted. There was no suggestion in Gubbins' report that production should be halted or even slowed down.

Although Gubbins had reported briefly that there had been no news of Alfgar Hesketh-Pritchard, who was operating single-handed in Southern Austria under appalling conditions as a member of CLOWDER mission, his report to Selborne did not refer to an acrimonious row with the Foreign Office about CLOWDER's plans for 1945. As we have seen in other contexts, AFHQ, unlike SHAEF, was fully prepared, even anxious, to make full use of SOE's expertise in newly-liberated countries. Consequently Wilkinson, working on parallel lines to Gubbins' approach to 21 Army Group, had produced plans for members of CLOWDER to be attached to Eighth Army for special assignments in the British Zone of Austria in the immediate post-hostilities phase. This outline plan had been accepted by Baker Street and in principle by AFHQ. Moreover, while Wilkinson was in London in December he had discussed his proposals informally with Geoffrey Harrison, the head of the Central Department who, so far as Austria was concerned, saw no reason why the Foreign Office should object. Confident of general approval, Wilkinson sent a copy of his plan to Harold Mack, the Political Adviser-designate to the British element of the Austrian Commission, for his personal information. Early in the New Year, unknown to Wilkinson, Mack had written to Harrison: "Have you seen this paper and have you any comments upon it?" In submitting Mack's letter Harrison had commented, "I see nothing to cavil at in the proposed plans for 1945. The contentious part of the report is the suggestion that SOE should 'bend a larger proportion of their effort to preparing their role in the occupational and post-occupational phases'." Troutbeck, Harrison's superintending Under-Secretary, was also in general agreement: "I cannot at first sight see any objection to the C-in-C having a mission of the kind suggested working under him for use in the British Zone".

However, Cavendish-Bentinck, to whom the papers were marked in his capacity as chairman of the JIC, was far more critical: "I am certain that we must put in a caveat that we cannot concur that, as regards Austria, or any other territory, SOE should 'bend a large proportion of their effort to preparing to fulfil their role in the occupational and post-occupational phase'." Although it echoed the instructions which Wilkinson had received from Gubbins, it was an unfortunate phrase which caused Sir Orme Sargent to minute Troutbeck: "We must certainly not allow SOE under cover of proposals of this kind to continue operations in the post-hostilities period. They have already tried to do so in the case of Germany under cover of negotiating an agreement with the Russians and we have scotched it. We must do the same in this case."

In his reply to an acerbic letter of Cavendish-Bentinck's complaining of

CLOWDER's plans, Gubbins wrote: "The memorandum to which you refer has been carefully worked out at the direction of SACMED and AFHQ under whose direction we are required to operate. We have taken great care not to take independent action." The date was 12 April and by then CLOWDER was fully integrated into the Eighth Army as No 6 Special Force which, in the early days of the Occupation, carried out a number of special assignments of exactly the kind described in the disputed memorandum. Mack himself in conversation with Wilkinson was later to acknowledge the advantage of having had at his disposal the experience of the CLOWDER personnel and was himself responsible for sending a memorandum by No 6 Special Force on the political scene in Carinthia to the Foreign Office without comment.

If nothing else, the CLOWDER incident had forced the Foreign Office to show its hand.

Meanwhile Gubbins, fed up with bickering with the Foreign Office and exasperated by the delay in obtaining a final decision about SOE's future, had promised himself a lightning visit to Italy before the German surrender, which was now expected daily. On the eve of his departure he had received an accusatory minute from Tommy Davies: "Through lack of forward planning or a formal charter, every section of SOE is gradually stagnating." However, Gubbins' spirits revived with the Mediterranean sun and the acclaim he received for SOE's successes in North-West Italy which had greatly exceeded expectations.

From Siena, where HQ SO(M) was now located, and where he had arranged to watch the first post-war *palio** he wrote in triumphant mood to Wilkinson, now with General Freyberg in Trieste: "I dined with Macmillan and had lunch and an interview with the Field-Marshal on Monday. Both were really charming and appreciative and I enjoyed myself.... I had Henry Hopkinson and his wife to dinner in Rome last night. It was most enjoyable and Henry was positively effusive in his thanks for what we had done for the Embassy, more particularly as regards carrying their communications with North Italy.... I am off to Milan the day after tomorrow, then I hope direct home by air.... The Noble Lord may leave us at any moment so I must be at home." Looking back at Michael's death at Anzio and beyond, it must seem entirely appropriate that Gubbins should have spent VE Day in Italy where, up to the last moment, SOE had been actively engaged, and where so many of his wartime friends and colleagues were now gathered.

In Gubbins' absence, Selborne had commissioned a final version of the memorandum on the future of SOE. It was to be the definitive statement of SOE's aspirations in the post-war world, and in submitting the first draft

---

* the traditional horse race

Sporborg commented, "So many people are now considering the future of SOE that I am sure that your authoritative views should be in the hands of the Prime Minister and the interested authorities with the least possible delay."

However, Selborne decided that a detailed rehearsal of all the old arguments for SOE's perpetuation, coupled with a lengthy repetition of the usual catalogue of SOE's wartime successes, was unlikely to impress Mr Churchill, whose attention at this time was bound to be focused on reconstructing a Conservative administration. He therefore limited the distribution of the SOE memorandum to Eden, Hollis, Morton and Gubbins, and took it upon himself to write a note on the future of SOE and a draft directive. Selborne's paper was not an impressive document and was based on the premise: "There is clear evidence that Himmler is preparing a German *Maquis* and secret organization after the model of *Scharnhorst* to achieve a third world war. On the principle that ex-poachers make good gamekeepers, it would be madness to scrap SOE so long as this menace exists."

However, Selborne's recommendation was that the future of SOE, together with the other secret services, should be placed under a single executive and administrative control and that each branch should retain its separate identity within the new organization which he recommended should be under a single executive head responsible to the Minister of Defence. Of more interest is the personal letter, dated 22 May, 1945, covering his submission. It was Selborne's swan-song, written with all the zeal of an imperfectly instructed convert:

"I attach an official minute on the future of SOE which I hope you will be able to consider favourably. In view of the Russian menace, the situation in Italy, Central Europe and the Balkans, and the smouldering volcanoes in the Middle East, I think it would be madness to allow SOE to be stifled at this juncture. In handing it over to the Foreign Office I cannot help feeling that to ask Sir Orme Sargent to supervise SOE is like inviting an abbess to supervise a brothel! But SOE is no base instrument, it is a highly specialized weapon which will be required by HMG whenever we are threatened and whenever it is necessary to contact the common people of foreign lands.

"I suppose that by nature I am the last person in the world to likely to favour this sort of activity, yet what I have seen these three years has convinced me of its necessity. It is no doubt my fault that I have been unable to persuade Eden that underground activities would prove useful to the Foreign Office after the war but if you asked your ambassadors — Clark Kerr, Killearn, Victor Mallet, Reader Bullard, David Kelly, Duff Cooper, Templewood, Halifax — if they would feel happier with or without SOE in the immediate future I have no doubt of the answer, and I think Resident Ministers like Harold Macmillan and Ned Grigg would say the same.

"Frankly speaking what I am afraid of is that the little Princes in the Tower will be put to sleep from which they will not wake up. I therefore hope that you will agree to issue a directive which will keep them alive until it is possible after the Japanese war to consider the whole future of our secret services dispassionately and sanely. Yours ever, (Signed) SELBORNE."

Meanwhile, as agreed between the Foreign Secretary and the Chiefs of Staff, the former "as a purely temporary measure" assumed control of SOE on Selborne's departure; and Lord Lovat, a junior Foreign Office Minister in the new caretaker government, was made responsible for dealing with SOE's day-to-day requirements. Lord Lovat's appointment met with Gubbins' full approval. On 4 June he wrote to Wilkinson, now head of the political branch of the British element of the Austrian Commission, "We are going along here quite reasonably well, and the appointment of a Parliamentary Under-Secretary to preside over us in Top's place is a good sign. Sheemy [sic] Lovat has the job; his first words to me were, 'You're the chap who refused to employ me in 1941'. However, he doesn't resent it and agrees he would probably have been dead if I had taken him. I have just had such a nice note from Eisenhower about SOE with most generous acknowledge-ments of our work − rather satisfying."

There seems to have been general agreement that the present arrangements were only provisional, and on 5 June Selborne's memorandum was circulated as a Chiefs of Staff paper. This prompted Orme Sargent to write to the Chiefs of Staff suggesting that an *ad hoc* committee be set up under a Foreign Office representative to consider Selborne's memorandum and make recommendations. As regards the proposal that SOE, SIS, MI5 and PWE should be merged in a new organization under the direction of the Ministry of Defence, Sargent observed that "it was difficult to give an opinion on this subject in the absence of any precise knowledge as to what the precise duties or charter of the Minister of Defence would be and what staff he would have at his disposal".

An *ad hoc* committee seemed as practical a way as any for discussing the matter, but when Gubbins learned that the chairman was to be Cavendish-Bentinck and the other members were to consist of representatives of the three Service Ministries, the Treasury, 'C' and himself, he realized he was heavily outnumbered and out-gunned.

The first meeting took place on 18 June. It was soon apparent that Selborne's memorandum was altogether unsuitable as a basis for discussion and there was general agreement that Cavendish-Bentinck should redraft the functions of the future SOE in a form which "he thought would be more acceptable to the Foreign Office". This development was not at all to Gubbins' liking and in desperation he decided to play his German card. SOE, he claimed, could carry out an important clandestine role in Germany: the functions he suggested included unattributable propaganda, clandestine counter-intelligence activities, the pursuit of enemy assets and looted property, and the building up of a long-term SOE organization. These cloak-and-dagger suggestions received little support from Sir Ronald Weeks, representing the German Control Commission, who said bluntly that on first thoughts he was opposed to the continuation of SOE activities in Germany, and he would like SOE to leave Germany, but to hand over any personnel they could to Counter-Intelligence. However, he agreed that Gubbins should visit him at 21 Army Group to discuss these proposals in more detail.

The next meeting, on 19 June, to which Gubbins was accompanied by Sporborg, took Cavendish-Bentinck's draft which recommended that "from the end of the war with Japan the SOE should become a wing of the SIS, and that meanwhile every effort should be made in the interests of efficiency and economy to unify the activities of the SIS and SOE". The skeleton establishment which Baker Street had been asked to provide at the previous meeting was discussed and severely pruned and when Sporborg subsequently protested, Cavendish-Bentinck, on 22 June, replied, "I entirely agree with you as regards the value to this country of the weapon of clandestine and subversive activity, but we must cut our coat according to our cloth and if we produce a large establishment it will be turned down, and there will be no SO organization in peacetime." Gubbins took this reply as both a warning and a threat; nevertheless his discussions at 21 Army Group had been partially successful and he had secured agreement that a small SOE headquarters should be retained in Germany for the foreseeable future responsible to the Major-General (Intelligence).

At the third meeting of the *ad hoc* committee on 25 June Gubbins found himself having to protest that the latest Foreign Office draft implied that SOE should become a small section of the SIS. C thereupon retorted that in the interests of economy and efficiency a fusion of the two organizations would be necessary in peacetime, while Cavendish-Bentinck drove the point home, stating that the view of the Foreign Office was that SOE should be retained but should become a wing of the SIS which, before the war, had controlled both special operations and secret intelligence. Cornered, Gubbins put up the best defence he could, protesting somewhat disingenuously that he had been unaware until that moment that the intention was to place SOE under the control of C. However, he realized that the game was up. When the fourth and final meeting of the committee was held on 16 July, Gubbins accepted without demur the recommendation that, as soon as practicable after the end of the war against Japan, SOE and SIS should be placed under a common executive head and meanwhile SOE and SIS should effect such measures of coordination as were practicable.

With the fall of the Conservative government and the departure of Lord Lovat, there was a brief interregnum while the new Labour Ministers took stock. On 21 August Bevin, the new Foreign Secretary, without consulting Gubbins, wrote to the Prime Minister, Clement Attlee, suggesting that, at the end of the war against Japan, which was now imminent, SOE and SIS should be placed under a common executive head, and recommended that this should be C. Two days later, on 23 August, Attlee replied, "While I agree as to a single head − that head being C − I should like to discuss the general question of policy with the Foreign Secretary and the Lord President before coming to any decision."

SOE's fate was now sealed, and all that remained were the formalities. On 11 September Bevin wrote to Gubbins:

"As you may know it was agreed by the Defence Committee on 31 August that SOE and SIS be placed under a common head.... I have discussed this with the Prime Minister and agreed that the head should be 'C'....I assume that, with SOE reduced to its minimum peacetime proportions, you yourself would no longer wish to direct its activities. I take this opportunity of expressing to you, on behalf of HMG, their high appreciation of your distinguished services in connection with the executive.... The efficient discharge of their difficult task was, I am sure, due in large part to your own direction and leadership. It made a valuable contribution to the winning of the war, and I trust that you and all those who served under you are justifiably proud of the part which you and they were able to play."

Whatever his personal feelings on receiving this communication, Gubbins was resolved that the disbandment of the Baker Street headquarters and the handover to C should be as orderly and professional as he could make it. In this resolve he was supported by Sporborg, his Deputy, and Venner, the Director of Finance, both of whom remained with SOE to the end. In a minute of 14 September Gubbins records, "I want to see C for a first discussion regarding the future SIS under his executive headship, and the position of SOE within it.... C agreed to the principle that I would establish and hand over to him the SOE component on the lines of the *ad hoc* report. He agreed that when Sinclair arrived I could deal direct with him on the many questions which would arise between us." It was a civilized arrangement which did not inhibit Gubbins, before his final departure, from writing what he described as "a mind-clearing exercise" though it is nothing of the sort, which he may, consciously or unconsciously, have intended as a sort of will and testament for his successor.

Beginning, as ritual now seemed to demand, with a long list of SOE's wartime successes "not only examples of sabotage and anti-scorch but equally important operations of a political or general nature," Gubbins goes on to recommend, among other things, the establishment of a worldwide network of dormant SOE agents, ready to spring into action on the outbreak of the third world war, backed up by an extensive production of material of a sort designed for special operations. Although no attempt is made to estimate the cost of these recommendations, Gubbins must surely have realized, had he not been so exhausted, that such proposals were quite unrealistic, and that no British government, let alone a Labour administration, was likely to sanction such vast expenditure on the secret vote in peacetime to meet contingencies which might never arise – and indeed have never arisen.

A more realistic appraisal was made by the Joint Planning Staff in a preliminary draft directive to SOE (subsequently Special Ops Branch (SOB)). Although falling far short of Gubbins' vision, the JPS draft was nevertheless too much for Sir Alexander Cadogan who noted that "so far as Europe is concerned, we presume that this effectively reduces the field to Austria and Germany". He went on to point out that "in the view of the Foreign Office there is no political requirement for SOE activities in either of these countries insofar as their object is to deal with any German or Austrian Nazi or other political movements. Moreover, the Foreign Office would see considerable political objection to the creation of even a skeleton organization in which Germans or Austrians took part whose object was to anticipate a Russian invasion."

Cadogan concluded that the Foreign Office was fully aware that SOE should maintain an organization which was capable of quick and effective expansion in time of war, "but their understanding of this direction is not that SOE should here and now set up an organization abroad which would be able to function if war broke out without notice tomorrow. It is rather that when we pass from a green to an amber light period, SOE should then set up their organization in approved countries abroad to meet the threat which has taken shape. Meanwhile, in our view, their preparations for such expansion should be confined to this country."

SOE was not included in the distribution of this letter but Sporborg obtained a copy from the War Cabinet Office and wrote to Cadogan on 7 September pointing out that the current SOE directive, which the Foreign Office had approved and issued to Baker Street, contemplated two forms of special operational activity, namely covert support to British national interests where threatened, and (in SOE's view by far the more important) the maintenance of an organization capable of quick and effective expansion in time of war. "It is the considered opinion of SOE that if, during the next few years, the functions of the special operations branch are in fact confined to those of a 'study group' there will most certainly be no possibility of this country making use of special operations on the outbreak of a future war."

Gubbins had been absent in Italy during this exchange of letters. However, Sporborg had a meeting with Cadogan and had the impression that the latter was "not unimpressed with certain of his arguments" and had finally said that, if the Chiefs of Staff accepted the JPS paper, he would see that the matter received sympathetic consideration in the Foreign Office. Gubbins was not invited to attend the meeting of the Chiefs of Staff which took the JPS paper on the future of SOE, but he wrote to C enclosing "a note of some points which I think you would like to have before you when you attend the meeting of the Chiefs of Staff Committee". The paper was dated 31 December, 1945, but by the time C received this brief, Gubbins, whose appointment had terminated on 1 January, 1946, no longer had any formal responsibility for special operations, which for purposes of this narrative now vanish into the mists of 'official secrecy'.

17

AFTERMATH

On 16 October, 1945, the War Office informed Gubbins that when his present appointment ended he would not be given further employment. It can have come as no surprise. At this time major-generals were two a penny, many of them with distinguished careers as divisional commanders, an experience which, owing to his secondment to SOE, Gubbins had never had. In the same month Lord Selborne had written to the Secretary of State for War asking for Gubbins' temporary rank of major-general to be made substantive. Lawson had replied that under existing rules this was not possible. On 22 February, 1946, therefore, Gubbins received formal notification that there was no further appointment for him on the Active List but that he would remain a member of the Army Reserve of Officers until 2 July, 1954, when he would reach the age limit for recall.

Gubbins retired with an array of foreign orders and decorations. Besides an advancement to KCMG in the New Year's Honours, 1946, he already held the Order of St Stanislas, III Class, from his tour of duty in Archangel in 1918, and the Polish Cross of Valour which he had been awarded for his work in Poland in 1941. The rule restricting to four acceptances of foreign Honours for services during the 1939/45 war was waived in Gubbins' case. In reply to a letter of enquiry from Lord Selborne, Mr Attlee, the Prime Minister, wrote on 21 June that "he would be permitted to accept for service in the war not only Polish, French and Belgian Honours, but also Czechoslovak, United States and Norwegian decorations ... also ... Netherlands, Danish and Greek awards .... He may then have, as a minimum, for service in both wars some twenty awards in all, British and foreign."

With only a substantive colonel's retired pay, Gubbins urgently needed a civilian job. His first offer as director of a rubber company came to him from one of his former officers, Colonel Ides Floor, but it proved uncongenial. In 1947 his old friend Edward Beddington-Behrens invited him to join the Board of Ocean Trust, a Finance House where expanding business included the reorganization and re-capitalization of W. Gray & Co, a large textile and carpet firm, of which Beddington-Behrens became Chairman and Colin in due course Managing Director. He was responsible for premises in London and for eleven factories in Yorkshire, Scotland and Northern Ireland making carpets, woollens, worsteds, linens and blankets. Each unit had its different products and its different problems and Colin, with his customary zeal, set about acquiring a considerable knowledge of textile techniques. He established good relationships with his fellow directors and with the factory workers. One of the former, Patrick Fleming, describes him when he visited the factories as seeming to know each employee and to be familiar with each personal life; and "if the character or competence of even quite a junior executive came to be considered, his judgement never seemed to be wrong.... his colleagues had the confident feeling that they were being kept informed and fully consulted. The result was that everyone in the outfit, from top to bottom, felt that he or she was in on the act. The shares were apt to drop from time to time but never the morale."

Though he played no official part in international affairs, Gubbins travelled extensively both as a businessman and to attend as an honoured guest the many celebrations and anniversaries of resistance groups throughout Europe. Particularly in the immediate post-war years his advice was often sought by leading personalities in the countries he had helped to liberate. It was perhaps natural that his wartime achievements should have received more recognition abroad than in his own country, which had not experienced the servitude of foreign occupation. However, his heart was still with SOE and much of his spare time was spent in setting up a Special Forces Club, of which the primary object was to perpetuate the comradeship which had been such a marked feature of the Resistance and as a means of dispensing financial support to its victims. Apart from the social and benevolent functions of the Club, a secondary objective was never far from his mind. This was the need to maintain a worldwide network which could be activated in the event of a future war and provide the nucleus of national resistance which experience had taught him would otherwise take years to develop. Having failed to obtain authority to keep an independent SOE in being in the post-war years, he hoped that the Special Forces Club might provide an alternative framework. In these plans he was ably assisted by founder members of SOE such as Douglas Dodds-Parker and Gerry Holdsworth.

But he also became deeply involved in the promotion of European unity. This interest had developed strongly as a result of his experiences in SOE and a fresh impetus was provided by an approach which he received from his old friend, Josef Retinger, who had been a pioneer in working for unity among the allied governments-in-exile in London during the war. In 1946 Retinger had given an important lecture at Chatham House on the European

Continent, after which, with the help of Paul van Zeeland, Paul-Henri Spaak and other pro-Europeans, he had established in Brussels the Independent League for Economic Cooperation*. Funds were forthcoming from, among others, David Astor, and an approach to Gubbins yielded a generous contribution from Edward Beddington-Behrens, for many years a committed pro-European. The League of Economic Cooperation was only one of many similar organizations devoted to European unity in the immediate post-war years, and in late 1947 these merged into an International Committee of the Movement for European Unity of which Duncan Sandys became the Chairman and Retinger the Honorary Secretary. The first so-called Congress of Europe was held at The Hague in 1948.

However, in the early 1950s British interest in European unity began to wane, and in particular Winston Churchill abandoned his support; the new Conservative administration refused to have anything to do with the European Army or with the European Coal and Steel Community. An even more serious rift was developing between Europe and the United States, and Retinger, like many others, was disturbed that Western cooperation, so painfully built up since the war, was about to disintegrate. Early in 1952, he discussed the problem with Paul van Zeeland and Paul Rykens, the Chairman of Unilever. They agreed that the problem was widely recognized by many people in many countries but that any initiative to overcome it might be suspect if identified with one of the major powers or with any particular political party. They therefore proposed that Paul Rykens should approach Prince Bernhard of the Netherlands.

After some hesitation, Prince Bernhard agreed to form a small discussion group of selected personalities. In addition to Rykens and van Zeeland, its members comprised de Gasperi and Pietro Quaroni for Italy, Hugh Gaitskell and Colin Gubbins for Great Britain, Antoine Pinay and Guy Mollet for France, Max Brauer and Rudolf Mueller for Germany, Panagotis Pipinellis for Greece and Ole Bjorn Kraft for Denmark. The preliminary meeting was held in Paris in September, 1952. It was from these small beginnings that what became known as the *Bilderberg Group* emerged, and its first conference took place in May, 1954. It is no part of this narrative to describe the *Bilderberg Group*, which came to include politicians, industrialists, bankers, writers, trades unionists, scholars and other leading personalities. However, as a forum for informal exchanges of views its influence can hardly be exaggerated and Gubbins considered it perhaps the greatest honour of his life to have been chosen as a founder member.

Any sense of anti-climax which Colin Gubbins may have felt after leaving

---

* Retinger had been a close and controversial friend of General Sikorski. At the age of fifty-seven he had volunteered to parachute into Occupied Poland, from which he had subsequently been evacuated in a semi-paralysed condition.

SOE was sweetened by a new happiness in his private life. His divorce from Nonie had been made absolute in 1944; in 1946, in Copenhagen at the home of her sister, Nancy Hostrup, whose husband had been active in the Danish Resistance, he met Anna Elise (Tulla), a blue-eyed Norwegian, daughter of Hans Didrik Jensen, a business man, of Tromsö. In June, 1940, Tulla had married Rolf Torbjorn Tradin, a Lieutenant in the Royal Norwegian Air Force, and in October had escaped with him from Norway by train across Russia and by boat from Japan to Canada. On Lake Ontario at 'Little Norway', a Norwegian Air Force camp, from March, 1941, until October, 1942, Rolf was an instructor in advanced training. Determined to get into the fighting war, he applied for transfer to England where he was attached to 612 Squadron RAF at Biggin Hill. Tulla was in the early stages of pregnancy when they left Canada in October. Her baby was born in April, 1943, but only lived for a few days and on 30 May her husband was reported Missing Believed Killed while flying over Caen in Northern France. She remained in London, working for the Royal Norwegian Air Force, until the end of the war when she returned to Norway.

Colin pursued Tulla until 1950, when she and Nancy came to stay at Obbe, a house he had bought at Leverburgh in the Isle of Harris. Here she accepted his proposal of marriage and the wedding took place on 25 September. Tulla was the right wife for Colin: she was calm, had an excellent sense of humour and a down-to-earth view of people and events. She did not, for instance, disguise the fact that she did not care for Edward Beddington-Behrens. Her antipathy coincided with Colin's growing disillusion with his work, which had been stimulating and challenging in the immediate aftermath of the war but which had now begun to bore him. He had little liking for salesmanship nor for the means by which sales were sought. In fact, except for its access to money, the business world was not for him. This disillusion increasingly soured his relationship with Beddington-Behrens. In 1955 matters came to a head; there was a row about the salary Gubbins was being paid, which he considered to be less than he had been led to expect it would be when he joined Ocean Trust. Although in due course the arguments were sorted out and Colin remained with Grays until he retired in 1969, the friendship was never the same.

At first Tulla and Colin lived in a flat in Duchess of Bedford Walk, Kensington, but they decided to find something in the country and only keep in London a basement flat in Campden Hill Court which Colin had had for some time. Tulla searched, and found White House Farm at Lacey Green in the Chilterns, a delightful house with a garden and an orchard, easily accessible from London. Colin was an enthusiastic and "very good gardener", said Tulla, "and planted everything in straight lines, like a regiment." He was in fact an enthusiast in all that he did, not least in his self-education. It is possible that his classical leanings developed when his parents returned from Japan and lived in Oxford and he had won a Classical scholarship to Cheltenham College. But there is little doubt that he had always felt a sense of deprivation that he did not go to university, and that now that he had the leisure to do so he would make up for it by educating himself in all the ways he liked best. He visited art galleries, he bought pictures, he read novels, and he went as often as possible to the ballet, which he loved. He was certain that a happy life was

> To know everything about something,
> To know something about everything,
> And to play a musical instrument.

He was sixty-five years old when he started learning to play the concertina which, he said, he found "a most effective aid to tranquillity", though he doubted whether his wife felt the same.

Lacey Green was their base in England for twenty-three years; Obbe, the house in Leverburgh, was their true love, where they went as often as they could between their social and business commitments and their travels for SOE reunions and functions. Each of them had spent their youth in similar surroundings and were accustomed to having access to first class fishing and shooting. In the Island, they had all this, and they had as well an easy relationship with the Islanders with whom they felt completely at home; Colin was proud of his position as Colonel in command of the local Home Guard, which he held from 1952 until 1956.

Despite this ideal life, Colin could not entirely escape from his public responsibilities. Besides attending celebrations and assemblies in countries which had been under Occupation, he was frequently consulted about aspects of SOE and asked to speak at schools and at functions of all kinds, military and civil. There were two particular seminars he was glad to attend: one in December, 1962, on *Britain and European Resistance* at St Anthony's College, Oxford, where the Warden was his old friend and colleague Bill Deakin, who had led the first British Military Mission to Tito in 1943; and the other at Manchester University in November, 1967, which comprised a series of public lectures on *Subversion, Intelligence and Resistance* organized by Michael Foot, the Professor of Modern History. Gubbin's contribution was entitled *SOE and the Co-ordination of Regular and Irregular War*.

Colin never fully recovered from Michael's death, but he had a genuine affection for his son Rory and Rory's wife Janette; and a close concern and pride in the welfare of their three children, Claire, Michael and Lucy. At the same time he never lost touch with his first wife Nonie; in fact, since the divorce they were on better terms with one another than they had been when married. Nonie asked him to bring Tulla to Harrold for lunch. "Mother and Tulla got on very well, I think," he wrote to Rory. Nonie was pleased because she had always said that she hoped he would marry again; that she had failed because she did not understand his 'blythe spirit'. She died of cancer in 1975.

With Tulla, in 1970, Colin attended celebrations in Copenhagen, Oslo, Amsterdam and Amiens. "I always knew," he wrote to Rory, "that this year, twenty-fifth anniversary of the liberation of Norway, Denmark and Holland, and of the end of the European War, would be hell − but I think this is the 'finale' for all time. I am sure it will be − anyway until the fiftieth and I shall not be here then. Am still waiting for details of programmes of happenings at these various places, and how to get there, and how many of the trips will be 'tickets paid' and so on − not many I fear − but I just have to do it all this last time, if only for our country's sake."

During 1970 the Gubbinses were also supervising the reconstruction of Obbe as their future home because they had decided in due course to sell Lacey Green and move permanently to Harris. In 1972, however, two operations for a detached retina in Colin's right eye − which left him, as he said, 'cock-eyed' −and, a year later, a blood clot in his leg, which among other things forced him to give up a lifetime's smoking, hastened their decision. By the end of the summer of 1975 Lacey Green was sold, the final packing had been done and the vans were at the door, "every inch of the garden and approach space covered with furniture with the chests packed with china (21 in all), 15 suitcases, 25 large parcels of tinned fruit, jam for deep freeze ... 3 old fashioned trunks, 3 divan beds plus chairs, bedding, garden tools etc." By Christmas they were settled in and looking forward to their life in the Highlands.

At a luncheon party in Stornoway on 23 January, 1976, Gubbins received his Commission as a Deputy Lieutenant of the Islands Area, Western Isles, an honour which he prized. Seventy-three years had passed since the boy Colin had been left with his grandparents in Mull to gain that "very special attachment and faith in all things Scottish".

Happiness was short lived, however; two weeks later, on 6 February, Colin had a heart attack. He died in hospital in Stornoway on 11 February, 1976, and is buried in Scarista Cemetery not far from the sea.

A Memorial Service was held at St Martin-in-the-Fields on Thursday, 20 May, 1976. The Prince of Wales, the King of Norway and the President of the United States sent their representatives; Prince Georg of Denmark came with the Danish Ambassador; Colin Mackenzie represented Admiral of the Fleet Earl Mountbatten of Burma, alongside others from Far Eastern countries. Belgium, Denmark, France, Norway, the Netherlands, wartime Polish GHQ and Polish Forces were all represented, with contingents of resistance fighters and leaders, Lord Selborne and many SOE colleagues and friends from all over the world. Douglas Dodds-Parker read the Lesson and Peter Wilkinson gave the Address, which he ended by saying:

"....of the decisive importance of Colin Gubbins' personal contribution to the allied victory, there can be no question. His name is honoured officially in many lands. For in the dark hours it was *his* duty to fan the spark and keep alive the flame of freedom. It was *his* exertions that gave hope to thousands of patriots in occupied countries all over the world. These men and women are unlikely to forget him. Nor will he ever be forgotten by his countless personal friends. They will always remember him with great respect, with the warmest affection and, above all, with gratitude. For whatever Colin Gubbins was called on to do in his long life, he not only did it extremely well, but he contrived in the process to make life extraordinarily rewarding and agreeable for anyone who had the good fortune to be with him."

SOURCE NOTES

1. *The Family 1649-1902.*
    1. *New Brunswick in 1811*; Journal of Colonel Joseph Gubbins (ed. Howard Temperley).
    2. J.S. Morrison: *Lawrence of Lucknow* (Bell and Sons 1934).
    3. Fraser: *Diplomat's Wife in Japan*; (Hutchinson, 1899)

2. *The Schools 1902-1913.*
    1. Gubbins private papers.

3. *The Shop and the Great War 1913-1918.*
    1. XXIX Bde. War Diary: PRO WO95.
    2. Ibid.
    3. Letter 21.6.16, Captain Sir Richard Sutton.
    4. Supplement to *London Gazette* 22.9.16.
    5. Brigadier E.E. Mockler-Ferryman private papers.
    6. *Thaw*, Edward Thomas.
    7. Diary, Edward Thomas (reprint from *Anglo-Welsh Review* 1971).
    8. Carton de Wiart: *Happy Odyssey* (Jonthan Cape).
    9. E.E. Mockley-Ferryman private papers.
    10. Letter to J.B. Astley.

4. *The Service Overseas — Archangel, Ireland, India 1918-1930.*
    1. Letter to J.B. Astley from Major-General Douglas Wimberley, 8 July, 1977.
    2. Gubbins private papers.
    3. Letter to J.B. Astley from Lieutenant-Colonel A.S. Colley, 1976.
    4. Gubbins private papers.
    5. Ibid.

5. *The Nineteen-Thirties.*
    P.A. Wilkinson (based on personal experience as regimental officer and in MI3 (a) War Office).

6. *The Polish Mission.*

   P.A. Wilkinson (based on personal experiences with No. 4 Military Mission).

7. *The MI (R) Mission in Paris.*

   P.A. Wilkinson (based on personal experience as GS03, and later as acting head, of No 4 Military Mission to the Polish and Czech Armies in France).

8. *The Norwegian Campaign.*
   1. PRO, WO168/103 142039.
   2. Connell, *Auchinleck*, p.113, (Cassell).
   3. Ibid. p. 115.
   4. Ibid. p. 122.
   5. PRO, WO168/103 142039.
   6. Connell, *Auchinleck*, p 123, (Cassell).
   7. Ibid. p. 125.
   8. Ibid. p. 119.
   9. PRO, WO168/103 142039.
   10. Ibid.
   11. Fraser diary, Liddell-Hart Centre, King's College, London.
   12. Connell, *Auchinleck*, p. 129 (Cassell).
   13. PRO, WO168/156 42048.
   14. Fitzgerald, D.J.L. *History of the Irish Guards in the Second World War* (Gale and Polden, 1949).
   15. Gubbins private papers; Andrew Croft; Major Baily.
   16. Alanbrooke papers, Liddell-Hart Centre, King's College, London.
   17. Ibid.

9. *The Auxiliary Units 1940.*

   Gubbins private papers. P.A. Wilkinson's experiences as GS02 (Ops and Plans).
   1. Churchill, *Their Finest Hour (Second World War)* p.231 (Cassell).
   2. Ibid., p. 584.

10. *SOE: 1940/1941.*
    1. PRO, CAB 121.
    2. Ibid.
    3. Dilks, *The Diaries of Sir Alexander Cadogan.* p. 31. (Cassell)
    4. Dalton, *The Fateful Years*, p. 370 (Muller).
    5. PRO, CAB 80/56
    6. Pimlott, *Diary of Hugh Dalton*, p.210 (Cape).

7. Garlinski, *Poland, SOE and the Allies*, p.39 (Allen and Unwin).

8. Foot *SOE in France*. p. 153 (HMSO).

9. Ibid., p. 159.

10. PRO, CAB 79/12.

11. Ibid.

12. CAB 69/2.

13. Pimlott, *Diary of Hugh Dalton*, p. 215.

11. *SOE: 1942*,

1. Pimlott, *Diary of Hugh Dalton*.

2. Bryant, *The Turn of The Tide*, p. 331 (Collins).

3. Pimlott, *Diary of Hugh Dalton*, p. 346.

4. Dilks, *The Diaries of Sir Alexander Cadogan*, p. 436.

5. Ibid. p. 435.

6. Ibid. p. 437.

7. Ibid. p. 445.

8. Foot, *SOE in France*, p. 231.

9. Ibid. pp. 204-207.

10. Sweet-Escott, *Baker Street Irregular*, p. 111 (Methuen).

11. PRO, CAB 80/62,

12. Pimlott, *Diary of Hugh Dalton*, p. 428.

13. PRO, CAB 80/62,

14. PRO, CAB 79/20,21,

12-16.

For the next five chapters there are no specific references, major use having been made of Professor David Stafford's *Britain and European Resistance 1940-1945* (Macmillan, 1980) and valuable contributions having come from the Foreign Office SOE Adviser.

17. *AFTERMATH.*

Gubbins private papers.

Background to the Bilderberg Group from *Joseph Retinger: Memoirs of an Eminence Gris.* ed. John Pomian (Sussex University Press, 1972).

The Fourth Dimension of Warfare (Manchester University Press, 1970).

INDEX

Pearson, Lieutenant-Colonel J. S. A., 137
Peddie, Major J., 51
PERIWIG, Operation, 210, 229
Perkins, Colonel H. B., 77, 81, 131, 227
Pétain, Marshal Philippe, 84, 93
Peter of Yugoslavia, King, 89, 149, 155, 163
Pile, General Sir Frederick, 208
PIMENTO circuit, 193
Pinay, Antoine (French Prime Minister), 240
Pipinellis, Panagottis, 240
Playfair, Sir Edward, 101
Pollock, Sir George, 181
Portal, Air Chief Marshal Sir Charles (later Viscount Portal of Hungerford), 84, 126, 127, 158, 178
POSTMASTER, Operation, 97
Pownall, Lieutenant-General Sir Henry, 184, 186
Prendergast, Captain J. H. (Indian Army), 52
PROSPER circuit, 123, 127

Quaroni, Pietro, 240

Raczkiewicz, Wlavyslav (President of Poland), 206
Raczynski, Count Edward, 205, 206
Rea, Lord (Philip), 143, 152, 169
Redding, Wing-Commander J. E., 143, 150
RELATOR, Operation, 90
Retinger, Joseph, 111, 240
Ribar, Ivo, 155
Ribbentrop, Joachim von, 37, 38
Richards, Sir Brooks, 145
Riley, Lieutenant-Commander Quintin, 51, 67
Ritchie, Air Vice-Marshal A. P., 169
Roberts, Sir Frank, 99
Romer, Tadeusz, 205
Rooks, Major-General Lowell W. (US), 165
Roosevelt, President Franklin D., 72, 95, 108, 120, 121, 143, 153, 157, 161, 190, 206, 214, 215, 220, 222
Roosevelt, Major Kermit, 51
Roosevelt, President Theodore, 51
Roseberry, Colonel C. L., 152
ROUND-UP, Operation, 173
Rowecki, General Stefan, 81, 128, 130
Rowlandson, Lieutenant-Colonel M., 116, 196
RUBBLE, Operation, 89, 90
Rykens, Paul, 240

Saltzman, Colonel Charles (US), 144
Salvadori, Massimo, 168
Sandys, Duncan (later Lord Duncan Sandys), 208, 240
Sargent, Sir Orme, 170, 172, 175, 191, 197, 226fn, 230, 232, 233
Satow, Sir Ernest, 5, 18, 20, 23
Saunders, Lieutenant-Colonel Hugh, 173
SAVANNA, Operation, 85, 94
Schonfeld, Pastor, 108
Sehmer, Major John, 225
Selborne, Earl of, Intro., 100, 101, 107, 110, 112, 116, 118, 120, 124, 126, 127, 131, 133, 135-7, 140-3, 153, 158-160, 164, 166, 170, 175, 176, 180, 185, 190, 194, 197, 198, 200, 201, 204, 214, 216-33, 238
SHINGLE, Operation, 163
Sikorski, General Vladyslav, Intro., 47, 80, 81, 110-2, 116, 128, 129, 176
Sinclair, Major-General John A., 235
Skinnarland, Torstein, 106
SLEDGEHAMMER, Operation, 121
Slessor, Marshal of the RAF Sir John, 165, 166, 180, 191, 192, 199, 206, 221.
Smigly-Rydz, Marshal Edward, 42
Smiley, Colonel David, 148
Smith, General Arthur, 91
Smolenski, General Jozef, 43
Somerville, Captain 'Bill' (Indian Army), 52
Sosnkowski, General Kazimierz, 43, 44, 81, 129-31, 180, 205, 207
Soustelle, Jacques, 157
Spaak, Paul-Henri (Belgian Prime Minister), 240
Sporborg, Harry N, 175, 178, 197, 218, 219, 221, 226, 232, 234-7
Stachiewicz, General Vaclaw, 42-44
Stafford, Professor David, 195
Stalin, Marshal Joseph, 94, 129, 153, 179, 204, 207, 222
Starr, George R., 193
Stauffenberg, Colonel Count Schenk von, 108, 208
Stawell, Major-General W.A.M., 146, 151, 153, 154, 161-5, 167, 180, 182, 191, 199, 200
Steel, Sir Christopher, 165
Steinbeck, John, 117
Stephenson, Sir William, 95, 212, 215, 216
Stevens, Colonel John M., 148
Stockwell, Major Hugh C., (later General Sir Hugh), 57, 65